THE BIG SANDY VALLEY

A History of the People and Country from the Earliest Settlement to the Present Time

William Ely

HERITAGE BOOKS
2007

HERITAGE BOOKS
AN IMPRINT OF HERITAGE BOOKS, INC.

Books, CDs, and more—Worldwide

For our listing of thousands of titles see our website
at
www.HeritageBooks.com

A Facsimile Reprint
Published 2007 by
HERITAGE BOOKS, INC.
Publishing Division
65 East Main Street
Westminster, Maryland 21157-5026

Originally published
Catlettsburg, Kentucky
Central Methodist
1887

— Publisher's Notice —
In reprints such as this, it is often not possible to remove blemishes from the original. We feel the contents of this book warrant its reissue despite these blemishes and hope you will agree and read it with pleasure.

International Standard Book Number: 978-1-55613-052-6

PREFACE.

ALMOST all writers of history dwell on the actions of men in their collective capacity. They describe the political and other machines set up by nations, states, or counties. The author ignores that method in his book, and chooses to follow families and single individuals from their entrance into the Sandy Valley to the end of their career, and tell what they have added to the history of the country.

The annals of almost every family noticed in this book have been furnished to us by a member of the family whose deeds we chronicle. We have guessed at nothing; and where necessary to give dates, have freely done so. We trust our book will be a valuable addition to the many books and periodicals treating on East Kentucky affairs, and that the people will appreciate our efforts to keep green in the memory of the rising generation the great deprivations which their ancestry were compelled to undergo in order to rescue the Valley from the clutches of wild men and ferocious animals, and make it the abode of peace and plenty.

THE AUTHOR.

CATLETTSBURG, KY.

INTRODUCTION.

I HAVE written the history of the Big Sandy Valley and its people with a view of being useful in my day and generation, by rescuing from oblivion many incidents of great moment, which, unless gathered up in book form, would be forgotten in this now fast, feverish age.

The history of a people is to tell who they are, from whence they came, and their characteristics, public acts and tendencies. The land wearing out in the old Colonial States, the people there began to look

WM. ELY, Author of this Book.

about for better land and cheaper livings. Kentucky, once a county of Virginia, was the nearest territory of unoccupied land to move to from Virginia, part of Pennsylvania, Maryland, and the

Carolinas. As early as 1789 the emigrants began to come to Sandy, and settle in the valley from those States. They knew that mountains and hills and streams would impede their progress; it dismayed them not, for most of them had, from near or far, looked upon the craggy peaks of the Alleghany, Blue Ridge, or Cumberland Mountains. On the point of land where the Sandy and Tug form a junction was the first settlement attempted, in 1789. Soon after, near the mouth of Pigeon, was the next; next at Pond Creek, on the Tug. All the inhabitants from these places were driven away by the Indians. Not until 1790 was it safe to stir up the redskins. Block-houses were built by the Damrons, and others, near Pikeville; by others near Prater Creek. The Aucstiers, or Auxiers, as now written, had built two, near the mouth of John's Creek. Over at Licking Station, now Salyersville, was a large fortification. At other places on the waters of the Sandy, similar forts had been erected to protect the early settlers from the tomahawk of the Indians. Our old pioneer ancestors were so well skilled in the use of the rifle, and were so brave, as to make it very hot for any red man to show himself in the valley. The Indians ceased troubling our forefathers and mothers in 1790, while they were murdering the whites, and stealing horses in the Scioto Valley as late as 1802. Yet game was much more abundant in the Big Sandy Valley than in the Scioto. It failed, however, to tempt them over. By 1806 many of the old families, whose descendants are now our foremost people, had taken up their abode in the valley.

As the reader progresses along in this volume, the doings of those pioneers will be chronicled. The majority of the early settlers belonged to the best families of the older States. They, it is true, brought their household goods on the backs of horses, for no roads had been opened up. Many families brought with them their slaves, and for many years after the settlement of the country more slaves in proportion to the population were found on Sandy than in the Blue Grass region. They soon had pay-schools established in every neighborhood, to teach the young.

Churches they did not have, nor did they need them; for on large occasions they used the shady dells to worship God in, according to the sentiment of one of America's great poets, that the woods were "God's first temples." They did not forget to honor the great Creator, however, in neglecting to build churches, for every householder saw to it that one room in his great log mansion was dedicated to the worship of God. And not only did they open their houses to the preaching of the Word, but one family would often support a big meeting of a week's duration, sleeping and feeding all who came to worship. This primitive custom has not died out yet. Especially does it still prevail among the primitive Baptists in the Tug

Valley, where churches are few. The early pioneers ground their corn on hand-mills, or beat the grains to meal in a mortar. They used bear's-oil in place of lard to shorten their johnnycakes. It was many years before they had much hog-meat or beef; but bear, deer, turkeys, and other game and fowls were abundant, which more than supplied them with meat. Honey was almost as plentiful as sorghum is to-day; and every Spring they made of maple-sugar and treacle enough to run them through the season. In a word, they lived at the fountain-head. The skins of the bear, the deer, buffalo, and other fur-bearing animals, afforded a revenue of wonderful proportions, and when the reader takes into account the vast sum added by the countless wolf-scalps at five dollars apiece, and the ginseng crop, he feels that his ancestors were engaged in a more lucrative business than saw-logging. As to clothes, the thrifty housewife worked up the flax and cotton raised by the men, and prepared it for clothing for the family, and coverings for the beds, as well as table-cloths and towels. Even handkerchiefs were woven from the flax, and served on many occasions as wedding-gear. Many of the men could sport breeches made of dressed deer-skins, and shoes made of the same material were found on the feet of both sexes. When the wolves became less troublesome, sheep were raised, and supplied the people with another article of clothing, both for man and woman. Every house had a spinning-wheel, a reel, and a loom, and the wholesome damsels of that day knew well how to use them; while the mother spun the flax and wool into thread, the old grandmother knitting the hosiery for the family, and the little girls filling the quills. Those were busy days. No idlers then.

The amusements of the people were adequate to their wants. House-raisings, log-rollings, corn-huskings, were engaged in by the men; wool-pickings quiltings, and flax-pullings by the women; the latter participated in by the beaus and lasses. Many of those gatherings wound up at night with a play, and sometimes with a big dance.

The morals of the people were good. The men were brave, and the women virtuous. That handy little imp, the modern pistol, was almost unknown then. When men fell out, they generally very coolly fought it out with their fists, and ended the matter by shaking hands all round. No feuds then. Of course many drinkers to excess were found in that day, for men everywhere partook of the fiery beverage. But intoxication did not prevail as alarmingly as it has since the apple has become so large a factor in potent drinks on Sandy. We should say, however, that a great reformation has been going on for twenty years, and the sale of liquor is, in the Kentucky counties, outlawed by the people.

Christian progress and esthetic taste bid fair to raise the people of the valley to a higher plane than is attained in any other part of the State. The somewhat isolated location has kept the valley exempt from the grosser vices of the age.

It is a good place to move to.

THE BIG SANDY VALLEY.

FIRST SETTLEMENT ON SANDY.

THE following certificate so kindly put into the author's hands by Mr. Richard F. Vinson and Dr. Milton Burns, would at first thought seem to leave no doubt that the neck of land lying between the Levisa Fork and Tug, in sight of where Louisa now stands, was the first place where a permanent settlement in the Sandy Valley was attempted to be made. The very same year, 1789, the Leslies attempted to make a settlement at the mouth of Pond Creek, on the Tug River. They, like Vancoover and others at the Forks, were driven back by the Indians, who were at the time prowling around in the valley.

The Leslies returned in 1791, but instead of stopping at Pond, they went on to John's Creek, and formed what to this day is known as the Leslie Settlement. The Leslies must have been the earliest permanent settlers in the Sandy Valley, yet immediately after their coming, the Damrons, the Auxiers, the Browns, of Johnson; the Marcums, on Mill Creek; the Hammonds, the Weddingtons, the Pinsons, Justices, Walkers, Morgans, Grahams,

Williamsons, Marrs, Mayos, Lackeys, Hagers, Laynes, Borders, Prestons, and others, followed closely on their trail.

AFFIDAVIT OF JOHN HANKS.

I was employed by Charles Vancoover in the month of February, 1789, along with several other men, to go to the forks of Big Sandy River, for the purpose of settling, clearing, and improving the Vancoover tract, situated on the point formed by the junction of the Tug and Levisa Forks, and near where the town of Louisa now stands. In March, 1789, shortly after Vancoover and his men had settled on the said point, the Indians stole all their horses but one, which they killed. We all, about ten in number, except three or four of Vancoover's men, remained there during that year, and left the next March, except three or four men left to hold possession. But they were driven off in April, 1790, by the Indians. Vancoover went East in May, 1789, for a stock of goods, and returned in the Fall of the same year. We had to go to the mouth of the Kanawha River, a distance of eighty-seven miles for corn, and no one was settled near us; probably the nearest was a fort about thirty or forty miles away, and this was built may be early in 1790. The fort we built consisted of three cabins and some pens made of logs, like corn-cribs, and reaching from one cabin to the other.

We raised some vegetables and deadened several acres of ground, say about eighteen, on the point, but the horses being stolen, we were unable to raise a crop.

[Signed,]   JOHN HANKS.

This deposition was taken in 1838, the deponent being in the seventy-fifth year of his age.

PIONEER CLOTHING.

What did they wear eighty years ago in the valley? The men wore buckskin breeches and hunting-shirts of same material, home-made linen or cotton shirts made by their wives and daughters. They generally wore moccasins made of buffalo hide. Their hats were either made by a local hatter out of the abundance of fur at hand, or made at home out of fur skins.

The ladies of the valley dressed well and comfortably in those good old days. They spun and wove the cotton and flax into cloth for the family wear, out of which they made handsome dresses and other female wear. They bleached the cloth at the spring branch until it was spotless white. Another part they would color with barks, and make the most handsome stripes. And when made up in the latest style of that day, and worn by the belles, the beaux were as much struck with the beautiful decoration of their sweethearts, as the beaux of to-day are when their girls appear in silk. Sometimes they wore deer-skin slippers, which were very nice. The old men who linger behind say that the women not only dressed comfortably, but looked handsome in their home-made wear.

WHAT DID THE PEOPLE EAT?

THIS question is sometimes asked at the present time. Their bill of fare was a very good one. A more tempting one could hardly, to-day, be furnished by the best livers on Sandy. Bear-meat boiled, or roasted before the fire, or on wooden bars over a furnace made for the purpose. Venison broiled on the coals, or boiled and eaten cold. Pheasants hung up before the fire and roasted to a fine brown. Johnnycake made of corn-meal beaten in mortars or ground on hand-mills, shortened with bear-fat, with some stewed dried pumpkin put in the dough. Wild honey in the comb, or strained; maple molasses in abundance in its season, and plenty of maple-sugar to sweeten their spice or other domestic tea. Huckleberries, services, and other wild fruit as relishes. The epicure of to-day would delight in such a meal.

Hog-meat and beef soon followed along, with a little flour, and after 1820 coffee was used quite often. The old pioneer did not lack for plenty to eat, and that of the best.

THE STORE DRESS.

AN elderly lady living on Peter Creek, in Pike County, related to us an incident in which her grandmother, when a young lady, was one of the actors. She and a young lady friend were the first in the settlement, seventy-five years ago, to own a store dress each, and a pair of store shoes. The goods was of the brightest colors, and made in handsome style, ready for the approaching Sunday religious service in the neighborhood.

The young ladies all rigged out in their showy gowns, with shoes and stockings in hand, when Sunday morning came, started on foot to meeting. On their journey they came across a herd of cattle browsing on the pea-vine. One of the beasts, catching a glimpse of the girls' new gowns, became frantic with fright, which was communicated to the whole drove, and they scampered away with the velocity of a train on a railroad. The cattle had never seen any calico before.

THRILLING ADVENTURE.

ABOUT the time the Leslies came to the valley, say 1790, Charles and Emla Millard, the former the grandfather and the latter the grand-uncle of A. J. Millard, of Big Creek, came down on Tug from Clinch River to hunt bear and deer for their pelts. They encountered a roving band of Indians, who showed fight. Emla getting behind a tree, with the river between him and the redskins, placed his hat on a bush so concealed by the undergrowth of pea-vine that the Indians fired several shots into the hat, thinking it was on a man's head. Millard halloed over to them to come out from behind the timber, as he had done. While one of the savages was on his all-fours, peering out, Millard fired, striking him on the hips, and with a yell he fell dead; the other Indians scampered off. Millard went over and found a horn full of powder and pouch full of balls; retracing his steps, he and his brother made off up the river. When they came to John's Creek they found it overflowing its banks, but plunged in, and being laden down with deer and bear skins, Charles was drowned. His body was never found. A creek which empties into John's Creek at the place where Charles Millard was drowned, is to this day called Miller's Creek, the *d* being left out.

BIG SANDY VALLEY.

This valley is one hundred and fifty miles from north to south, and about eighty miles wide, on an average, from east to west; in area as large as some of the prosperous Northern States. It is drained by the Big Sandy River, or as is now sometimes called the Chatterawha, with its Levisa and Tug Forks, and their numerous tributaries. Both these rivers rise in south-west Virginia, twenty miles or less apart, both flowing almost directly north on parallel lines of from twenty-five to forty miles apart, until near their junction, twenty-five miles from the Ohio, where they unite and flow on to the Ohio in one stream. The Sandy and Tug Rivers are fed by numerous tributaries, some of which are in size and volume of water carried off, sufficient to be known as rivers, rather than creeks. Among the principal tributaries of the Sandy may be mentioned the Blaine, which heads in Elliott and Morgan Counties, Kentucky, and flows in a north-easterly direction, and enters the Sandy eighteen miles from its mouth. Its length is seventy-five miles.

Paint Creek heads in Morgan County, Kentucky, runs thirty miles east, and empties its turbid waters into the Sandy at Paintsville, sixty miles from the Ohio. Paint is a short but a broad, deep stream, affording water enough to float out great rafts of logs from very near its head.

John's Creek is a stream more than a hundred miles long; heads up near the sources of the Big Sandy and Tug, between the two, and runs nearly equal distance, parallel with them, and empties into the Sandy eight miles above the mouth of Paint Creek.

Beaver is a long straight stream, indeed quite a river, heading in Knott and Letcher Counties, Kentucky, running north-east on a very straight line into the Sandy, twenty miles above John's Creek. Shelby rises in Letcher and Pike, and is a stream like all previously named, capable of floating large rafts. It flows into the Sandy River above Pikeville.

Rock Castle and Wolf Creeks empty their waters into the Tug River from the western side, both rising in the same section, but flowing apart. The Rock Castle joins the Tug eight miles above its mouth, while Wolf makes a short cut and plunges into the same stream forty miles above. Pond is a short but powerful water-way, heading in Pike County, and emptying into the Tug fifteen or so miles above Wolf. Peter Creek, above on the same side, is quite a stream. From the east side of Tug River is Pigeon, Sycamore, and others, to say nothing of the almost countless smaller creeks and creeklets which help to swell the tide of the Sandy and Tug Rivers from south-east and west.

This system of water-ways drains a part or all of the counties of Boyd, Lawrence, Elliott, Morgan, Magoffin, Martin, Floyd, Johnson, Pike, Perry, and Knox, in Kentucky; and Wise, Dickinson, Tazewell, and Russell, in Virginia; and McDowell, Wyoming, Logan, and Wayne, in West Virginia. The bottom or level lands on the two large rivers widen out in some places more than a half mile. The soil is a rich sandy loam, as productive as are the Ohio bottom-lands. Most of the tributaries are equally rich in soil, while, if possible, the cove lands, which are always abundant in a hilly country, interspersed with so many streams like the Sandy Valley, are still more productive.

The bottom and cove lands produce heavy crops of grain, tobacco, and meadow-grasses, while the hillside lands serve well in grass, grain, and fruit, of nearly every species peculiar to a north-temperate latitude. In early day this valley was the great center of the ginseng industry, and while not so abundant as formerly, it is yet found in considerable quantities. Other medical roots abound. Wild and domesticated bees find a congenial home here, making honey and beeswax, articles amounting to great value. Fur skins add much to the wealth of the people. Poplar, oak, cherry, walnut, sugar, beach, hickory, linden, sycamore, and other timber, abound in every valley, cove, and mountain-side.

NAVIGATION.

THE Big Sandy River is navigable for steamboats to Pikeville, one hundred and five miles, the Tug River for ninety miles, making nearly two hundred miles of navigable waters; whilst, in addition to this, the tributaries named in this chapter, and some short ones not mentioned, are navigable for rafts of logs and other timber and lumber for at least nine hundred miles more, making a total of more than a thousand miles of navigation, centering at the mouth of the Sandy, or Catlettsburg. This valley has a peculiar topographical formation. Could one stand on some commanding height and look down upon the valley, it would appear in shape like a great oval basin, the southern end resting at the base of the Cumberland Mountains, the northern dipping into the Ohio River at Catlettsburg, while on the east the mountains of Virginia and West Virginia raise their tall peaks as a wall of adamant, while the hills of east Kentucky, covered in living green, form its western boundary, thus compelling an outlet, and an only outlet, at the mouth of the Sandy River, and head of the valley.

On the main streams and tributaries of the Sandy Valley, especially in the upper part of it, quite a considerable population had gone in from North Carolina, Virginia, and Maryland, long before Shortridge, David White, or the Hamptons had settled at or near the Mouth. They had brought their domestic stock with them, and some also their negro slaves, and commenced opening up the county to civilization before scarcely any thing had been done lower down the valley. The Auxiers, Meads, Staffords, Borders, Williamsons, Strattons, Leslies, Ratcliffs, Lackeys, Osburns, Prestons, Cecils, Porters, Hatchers, Laynes, Weddingtons, Friends, Hatfields, Marcums, Runyons, Justices, Prestons, Porters, Brewers, Fulkersons, McDowells, Clarks, Goffs, Garrards, Browns, Dixons, Maguires, Grahams, Morgans, Robinsons, Belchers, Bevins, Walkers, Mayos, Hagers, Millards, Stumps, and others, were, some of them, much earlier than David White, at the Mouth in 1798.

With such a vast country, and with a growing population with productions to sell and wants to supply, it is reasonable to suppose that the people of the valley in that early day were put to great inconveniences in exchanging their products for the necessaries and comforts of life. They of course had to go to the Mouth to make the exchange. But even there they found no store at which to trade, but with their crude push-boat or canoe laden with the fruits of their toil, had to continue on three miles further to Burlington, or down to Limestone; or they could sometimes get an entire outfit of Joseph Ewing, who commenced store-keeping in 1815 or 1816, one-fourth of a mile above the Mouth of Sandy, in Virginia. These drawbacks existed to annoy and embarrass the old-time settlers of the valley, until Williams and Catlett opened out a large store just in front of where G. W. Andrews & Sons' large brick now stands. From this time onward, embryo Catlettsburg increased in trade and commercial importance, until it is now, 1886, reckoned in commercial circles as the most thriving emporium of East Kentucky.

From 1815 to 1834, the greatest competitor, with merchants at Burlington and Limestone, and at or near the Mouth of Sandy, was Frederick Moore, who stopped much of the up Sandy trade at the Forks by buying produce, and furnishing supplies from his large store.

Now, in 1886, Catlettsburg has a population of three thousand souls, with large wholesale stores and growing industries, while Burlington contains a population of less than two hundred, living principally off the product of their gardens and fruit-trees. Frederick Moore got quite wealthy, but much of it was made by dealing in Catlettsburg real estate.

In 1830 the vast forests of timber in the valley had no real value attached to it. This year, 1887, more than a million dollars' worth has been sold to dealers at Catlettsburg, or passed on to cities below. In 1830 the existence of stone-coal was almost unknown. Now long trains of cars pass out on the Chatterawha road daily, laden with the best of coal from the Peach Orchard mines, fifty miles up the valley.

Salt springs abound in every county in the valley, and salt has been made from the water of these springs from the earliest settlement of the country until the present time.

COAL–OIL.

PETROLEUM has been known to exist in the valley for fifty years. Since 1865 many wells have been bored to bring up from the caverns below the oleaginous fluid. In many places oil of the best quality has been "struck," but so far not in paying quantities. Scientists say, however, that when the proper level is struck, oil will be found in vast quantities. In boring for oil at Warfield, in Martin County, some fifty-seven miles from Catlettsburg, on the Tug River, a trunk of gas shot up with the sound of thunder, and throwing out a light in all directions for many miles around, which at night enables people to read without the aid of any other light.

The gas here, if utilized, would run all the machinery of the manufactories from Catlettsburg to Louisville, including Cincinnati. Salt in great abundance was made at Warfield previous to the war by Governor Floyd, of Virginia, and since then by Colonel Barrett, the present proprietor there. The gas would furnish fuel so cheap that salt could be made here as cheaply as at any point in the Ohio Valley.

POTTER'S CLAY.

POTTER'S CLAY of the finest quality is found in several places in the valley, especially in Boyd

County. In 1847 an English company bought several thousand acres of land on the bank of the Sandy, two miles above the mouth, for the purpose of erecting potteries to turn out the finer grades of cupboard ware. Some of the clay found here was sent to England and made into cups and saucers, and several sets of them, sent to the vicinity of Catlettsburg soon after, in quality compared favorably with the best of China ware. Those named, with other valuable minerals found in the valley, added to those already noted, together with the vast timber supply, to say nothing of the fine lands and genial climate, with few changes, are destined to make the Big Sandy Valley one of the most prosperous countries in the Central West.

PIONEER PREACHERS.

OF the early preachers of the Sandy Valley, Rev. Marcus Lindsay made a more lasting impression than any other who went before or followed after him. He was a Methodist divine of great talent and culture. For four years he, as presiding elder, went up and down the valley proclaiming the Gospel, with an eloquence of irresistible power. Many gray-haired men now living wear his honored name. Mr. Lindsay traveled the Sandy district about the time of the War of 1812. After Mr. Lindsay, Rev. William B. Landrum was the most noted. He commenced his ministerial career on Sandy much later; not, indeed, until 1834. He was no great preacher, but a very useful, popular one. He married more people than any man of his time in the Sandy Valley. Bishop Kavanaugh preached much in his younger days in the lower part of the valley, and the great Bascom has held spell-bound Sandy audiences.

Of lay, or local preachers—

Rev. R. D. Callihan, now an octogenarian, of Ashland, Ky., has been longer in the service than any other, being sixty years an active preacher of the Word.

Rev. James Pelphrey, of Johnson County, and Rev. Wallace Bailey, of Magoffin County, Baptist preachers, have each been preaching near sixty years. The latter died in 1885.

Revs. John Borders, Benjamin P. Porter, Andrew Johnson, George W. Price, and Goodwin Lycans, of the same Church, served long and faithfully in the ministry; but those of them now living are too far advanced in years to be very active in the ministry.

But we must not fail to give a brief notice of two of the most prominent and useful men of that early age—the brothers Spurlock, Burwell and Stephen. While not living immediately in the valley, yet they were only a short distance away, on the Twelve Pole, and they made frequent visits up and down the valley, preaching as they went. They were men highly gifted, of great power in the pulpit, and were loved by all. Burwell Spurlock was one of the greatest reasoners of his time, and was authority upon Bible exegesis. Stephen, while not so clear as a reasoner, was, perhaps, more powerful in his appeals to the people. They were true yoke-fellows in the Gospel, and were enshrined in the hearts of the people; they were connected with the Methodist Church.

A man of wonderful power in the pulpit was Rev. Philip Strother, who preached in the valley for many years. He had a most captivating voice, was a man of true eloquence, and had superior descriptive powers. He was greatly loved by the people, and his name is worthily perpetuated in his gifted son, Hon. Joseph Strother, at this time judge of the county court of Carter County. He was an old-time Methodist, and did much to make that Church the power for good it has been and is in all that section.

A man of the most marked peculiarities in the ministry was Rev. Henry Dixon, of the Baptist Church. He was a fine fiddler, and in his old days always took his fiddle with him to Church, carrying his Bible under one arm and his fiddle under the other. He would introduce the service by playing several tunes, and then close in the same way. The novelty of such service always attracted the people, and the old man always gave them wholesome advice.

TEACHERS OF EARLY DAYS.

JOSEPH WEST taught school from Prestonburg down to the mouth of Tug. He has been a teacher for fifty-five years, and now, 1887, is still handling the rod. He lives in Martin County, and is greatly respected.

Lewis Mayo, Esq., was a teacher of great learning and ability. He commenced teaching in 1837, and kept schools of high grade for twenty-five years. He was a noble Christian gentleman. He died near the close of the Civil War.

James McSorley taught county schools for forty years in the Lower Sandy Valley.

M. T. Burriss, now of Rockville, is one of the old-time teachers of the valley. He was raised on John's Creek, in the Leslie settlement.

Prof. Wm. N. Randolph, of Paintsville, reaches back to the days of bear and wolves, when he first took up the ferule to teach young ideas to shoot. He is still at it.

William Murphy, of near Catlettsburg, taught county schools twenty-five years. He died in 1877.

Charles Grim, of Johnson County, was an old-time teacher for many years, and being a very small man, always had to surrender to the boys on Christmas, according to the custom of those pioneer days. The rule then was, "Treat or be ducked," the treat consisting of not less than one bushel of apples.

SALT SPRINGS AND WELLS.

THAT salt water abounds in every section of the Sandy Valley is a fact well known from the earliest times until now. Henry Clay, the great orator, in partnership with John Breckinridge, the grandfather of General John C. Breckinridge, owned a large boundary of land on Middle Creek, Floyd County, Kentucky, ten miles from Prestonburg, where the earliest salt-works in the valley existed. Salt was made here in 1795, and almost continuously until some time after the great war closed. The original owners disposed of their title to the land for a mere trifle, and the Harrises, the Hamiltons, and others, worked the wells, sometimes on a small and sometimes on a large scale. During the war, the salt made at the Middle Creek wells sold on the ground for two and three dollars a bushel. The wells are now in repose, awaiting enterprise to work them again.

At Warfield, on Tug River, some sixty miles above Catlettsburg, great quantities of salt have been made, both before and since the termination of the war. The works were first started by Governor John B. Floyd & Brothers, of Tazewell County, Virginia. They built up quite a little town there, and made great calculations to enlarge the works; but the war coming on, Governor Floyd, the prime mover in the industry, went away, leaving in charge agents to look after the welfare of the property until his return. But going into the Southern army as a general, he went down amid the clash of arms, and never returned to Warfield. Salt could be made there now at a small cost; for a company, on boring for oil, at about a thousand feet, struck an inexhaustible supply of gas, which is still burning, although several years have passed since it was developed. It lights the country for miles around with a more dazzling light than could be done with millions of jets of artificial gas. We say that it is inexhaustible, because General George Washington, when making his wonderful survey up the Tug River, says, in his Field Notes, when at the point opposite where Warfield now stands, that he found a burning spring bubbling up out of the water. This was in 1766. Salt can be made from the salt water in every county in the valley, which has been done in seasons of extreme low water in the river, preventing merchants from keeping a full supply on hand.

Near the mouth of Blaine, on the Virginia side of the river, salt in considerable quantities was made as far back as 1813. Judge Robert B. McCall's father was engaged at that place in boiling salt, as were his grandfather on the maternal side. McSorley, the father of John McSorley, was the clerk and store-keeper at the same time. He afterwards went to teaching, which he followed the remainder of his life, which terminated some years ago.

THE MOORE FAMILY.

FREDERICK MOORE, the founder of the house of that name in the Sandy Valley, was of Teutonic origin, his ancestors coming to Philadelphia or its vicinity before the Revolution. When quite a young man he married a Miss Van Horn, sister of John Van Horn, so well and favorably known among the old settlers of the Lower Sandy Valley. Soon after, or perhaps before, his marriage with Miss Van Horn, he established a nail factory in the city of Philadelphia, working twenty-five operatives. This was before cut-nails were made. This plant of Mr. Moore's was equal to one now working four hundred men. The War of 1812 coming on, played sad havoc with the young man's business; it broke it entirely up. But young Moore, true to the instincts of his race, did not sit down and lament his lot, but saved the remnant left of his hard earnings, and with the money bought a stock of goods, hired the late John Van Horn, whose sister he had several years previously married, to clerk for him, left his wife and

FRED. MOORE.

their two children (Sarah, afterwards Mrs. Poage, and later Mrs. Savage, a little girl of two years; and Frances, afterwards Mrs. William T. Nichols, then a young infant) with relatives in the East, and started with the goods for the "Forks" of the Sandy, then six years before Louisa was a town, which place he reached in 1815. He bought a large tract of land, including the plat on which the beautiful town of Louisa now stands, but added to his possessions a much larger boundary on the opposite side of the river, taking in the land on which now stands the town of Cassville, West Virginia, but then Virginia.

Mr. Moore, soon after his arrival, found himself at the head of a most extensive and prosperous mercantile business, the principal articles of traffic being in that root so highly prized by the Celestials, ginseng, and fur skins.

In 1818, after an absence of three years, he sent on to Philadelphia for his wife and two little daughters, to come on and occupy the comfortable home he had provided for them, one-half mile below the "Forks," on the Virginia side. The wife and children found no palace cars, as now, to journey in to reach their future home, but endured many discomforts and tedious delays in making the long journey. At length the mouth of the Sandy River was reached, and the tired mother, with her two little daughters, was safely resting at the Catlett House, the *Alger* of that day, at the "Mouth."

When tea was spread, and the guests all seated round the festal board, a laugh rang out from all at the innocent remark of little Sarah, who told the servant, who passed her the bread made of Indian meal, that she did not eat "chicken-feed." This was the first corn-bread the little girl had ever seen, and she insisted on being supplied with bread.

After resting a night, the mother and children went on board of a packet bound for the noted "Forks," twenty-five miles above. The packet was nothing more nor less than a push-boat, like one sees to-day. The boat was manned by several stalwart Sandy giants, all under the control of the now venerable William Biggs, but at that far back time not yet out of his teens. The refined, gentlemanly bearing of Captain William Biggs at once made Mrs. Moore his friend, which was shared by all the Moore and Biggs family in after life. Mrs. Moore was the only lady passenger aboard the boat. When time came on to prepare for dinner, the captain blushingly asked his lady passenger if she would lend a helping hand in getting up the noonday meal. The scene at the hotel, the evening before, had convinced the young navigator that nothing but wheaten bread would be permissible to set before such a lady as he, by his own native instinct of gentility, knew his passenger to be. He had more than one man aboard who prided himself on getting up the best of "corn-dodgers" or "johnny-cakes," but flour to them was as unknown as was

Indian meal to Mrs. Moore and children. They had the bliss of eating flour-bread at weddings, and once or twice at a "hoe-down;" but how it was made was beyond their culinary knowledge.

Mrs. Moore at once proceeded to take her first lesson in bread-making. In her country men baked the bread in large clay ovens; the higher class of ladies, to which Mrs. Moore, neé Van Horn, belonged, never. When the viscous dough stuck with pertinacity to her tapering fingers, she lost all patience, and asked the bewildered young captain to help her out of the sad predicament her effort to be useful had brought on. Captain Biggs hastily dipped a gourd of water from the river, and poured the liquid upon her outstretched hands, and soon her spirits revived as she saw no permanent harm was done.

The little craft soon reached the "Forks," and the Moores were settled in their home, which in after years was to be visited by as many (if not more) distinguished people as that of any homestead in the valley. Mr. Moore prospered as merchant, tanner, saddler, shoemaker, and farmer, and for a short time distiller, but abandoned the latter as soon as he saw the evil effects the poisonous liquid had upon the community.

In 1821 Louisa was made the capital of the new county of Lawrence, and the people of to-day owe Mr. Moore a debt of gratitude for the large-sized lots, the broad avenues and streets, which make Louisa the beautiful little city it is. He built a number of large brick edifices, that even shame some of the buildings erected long since. Mr. Moore was not only a close, compact business man, but was equally a public-spirited citizen.

One great reason of the financial success that fell to Mr. Moore's lot may be attributed to the fact that while a strict party man, a Whig, he let office-seeking severely alone. Yet several offices were forced upon him—colonel of the militia, magistrate of his district, delegate in the Legislature—trusts that he filled with great acceptability to his constitutents in Virginia. He not only had every one of his numerous children well educated, sending them from home, at great expense, to seminaries or colleges, to take on the finishing touch, but he did much to promote education for the poor of his section.

The old red mansion of the Moore's was the stopping-place of all Methodist preachers as long as it was occupied by the family; besides great statesmen and lawyers were frequent guests. Mr. and Mrs. Moore never failed to liberally supply the wants of the sick poor for miles around with dainties from their well-supplied larder. Three sons and six daughters made happy the Moore household. The mother and daughters were zealous Church members and Christians. The sons inclined the same way. The father never subscribed to any religious formula, but he acted like a Christian, in visiting the sick and administering to their needs, helping the widow and orphan, assisting in their support, and visiting the prisoner in jail. This great and good man died, aged ninety-two years, in 1874. His noble wife followed him in 1881, at the age of eighty-six. They not only left to their children a large material inheritance, but their noble example for good during a long, well-spent life.

Mr. Moore was at heart opposed to slavery; but as he grew rich, slaves fell to his ownership. They were treated with great humanity. The chief man-servant, James Brown, or Uncle Jim, never left the family, but clung to the younger generation of Moores until the day of his death, which occurred in 1885, aged near one hundred years. When Mr. Moore and wife grew too frail longer to continue at the head of the household, the sons and daughters agreed that the good old servant should never want for any comfort as long as he lived. They kept the vow, and when he died they gave his remains a Christian burial, and wept at his departure. "Uncle Jim" was a sincere Christian.

Ben Burk, a great admirer of Frederick Moore, told the author that once a great scarcity of food prevailed in the latter's neighborhood, and that he could not bear to hear of the cries of distress coming up from the poor people around him, and handed out meat with such a lavish hand, to appease their hunger, and that without price, that his wife had to lock the meat-house door to keep her benevolent husband from giving away the last joint of bacon on the place.

He had a great respect for preachers, and would notify his hands and servants, when one came to the house, that, he being a minister, they must use no improper language in his hearing. While one of these gentlemen of the cloth was visiting at the Moore mansion one day, a hand on the place used profane language, which so offended Mr. Moore that he rebuked the man in similar language, and called the preacher aside and begged not to blame him or any of his family for the man's rudeness.

Mr. and Mrs. Moore gave to the world nine children, three sons and six daughters. They have all borne aloft, unsullied, the Moore-Van Horn escutcheon, and, like their parents before them, are first-class citizens, and respected for their many virtues. W. F. Moore, the oldest son, is a man of extensive reading, and is one of the most scientific farmers of Boyd County. The youngest son and child, Frederick Moore, Jr., is, like his oldest brother, a farmer also, but lives in Lawrence County. His only marriageable daughter is the wife of a noted physician of West Virginia.

COLONEL L. T. MOORE,

WHILE not the oldest of the family, is, in consequence of his great ability as a leading lawyer, not only in the valley but in the State, and being a public man of high repute, nominally, at least, the leader of the family of Moores in the valley. He was educated at Marietta College, and became a lawyer, opening an office at Louisa when admitted to the bar, soon after he had reached his majority. About this time he married a daughter of Colonel John Everett, of Guyandotte, Va., a lady of rare beauty of person and accomplishments of mind. He took high rank as a lawyer from the start, and gained in popularity with the people, owing to his fervid eloquence and warm friendships.

His friends at Louisa urged him to make a race for the Legislature on the Whig ticket. He consented, on condition that his chief issue should be, if elected, to urge the passage of an act establishing normal schools in the State to train young men and women for teachers. One St. Clair Roberts, a man of great popularity at the time, possessing an implacable will, yet destitute of the common rudiments of an education, was nominated by his party to run against Moore. Fortified by his own ignorance, he appealed to the people not to squander their taxes on such nonsense, and defeated the man who was the people's real friend.

In 1859 Mr. Moore was nominated by the Whig party of the Old Ninth District for a seat in Congress. He made a brilliant and successful race against William Moore, or *Billy*, as his friends called him, who was the nominee of the Democracy. Billy Moore was not only a man of talent, but was a wily politician, while Laban T. Moore was unknown to most of the people of the district except in his own county; yet before he had gotten half over the district, in a joint debate with his able competitor, he had convinced all who heard him that he was not only a young man of brilliant endowments, but was an orator of great ability. He was elected by two hundred and forty-six majority, and, soon after the result was known, his friends in Mason County donated the largest steer in their county to be barbacued in honor of the young mountaineer's election. The gathering took place at Catlettsburg, where people from all parts of the district attended. The great ox was roasted by John F. Faulkner, an old barbacuist, still living, as lively as ever. The dell where the monster meeting was held is still known as the Moore Barbacue-ground.

The Congress in which he served was a stormy one, just on the eve of the Civil War; but he bore himself with manly fortitude against the shafts of hate from both sections, and, while a Southern man by instinct and in feeling, when the final hour came to break up the Union of the Fathers, he spoke out in thunder-tones against it, and declared himself a Union man. In the Spring of 1861 he came home and made speeches in advocacy of the old Government; and in the Fall of the same year, with William Vinson, L. J. Hampton, and others, was instrumental in getting into service the 14th

Kentucky Regiment. He was its first colonel, but soon resigned, to make place for one he thought better qualified to lead the troops to victory. He was a Union man during the war, but freely criticised the methods of carrying on the war. He voted for McClellan in 1864.

In 1863 he moved to Catlettsburg, where he now lives. He was elected to, and served one session in, the State Senate from his district, commencing in 1881. He was made chairman of a special committee to improve the school laws of the State. He did the work well, and ever since the free schools of the State have grown in favor with the people. He was pushed by his friends for a seat on the Appellate Bench. He was defeated for the nomination, yet his successful rival was defeated by a stiff majority in a district largely in his favor, politically.

Colonel Moore has a large and profitable law practice, and does not care to turn aside to fill offices. He is one of Catlettsburg's most honored citizens. His family consists of himself, wife, and four daughters. His oldest daughter, a graduate of Vassar College, a young lady of superior talent, and entering upon literary pursuits, with the prospect of a long life of usefulness before her, was stricken down before her plans were fully carried out to use the talents and accomplishments she possessed to better the race of man. Her mantle has fallen on her sisters, who are doing much, by deeds of charity and kindness, to assist the young to get a moral and intellectual training to fit them for lives of virtue and usefulness. The young ladies are Christian workers, are members of the Methodist Episcopal Church, South, but stop not within Church lines in their noble deeds of doing good to others.

Colonel Moore, like his father before him and his brothers, is an ardent Mason, and foremost in many good works.

The oldest daughter, Sarah, married John Poage, an iron manufacturer, by whom she had one child, a daughter. She became the wife of H. C. Gartrell, who, dying, left her with several children. Mrs. Gartrell lives on her fine farm, called "Cliff Side," half-way between Ashland and Catlettsburg. Mrs. Poage married, for her second husband, Pleasant Savage, by whom she had four children, three sons and a daughter.

HON. S. S. SAVAGE,

THE eldest son, is a lawyer and prominent citizen of Ashland. After the death of his father, which occurred at Louisa in 1862, where the family then lived, the widow, with her children, moved to Catlettsburg, where Samuel studied law, and practiced for several years. He filled the office of town police judge with acceptability to all classes of people. He afterwards moved to Ashland, and was soon after elected county judge, and filled the office with firmness and ability. He is regarded as one of

Boyd County's most talented men. He is a Democrat in politics, and a leader of his party. He is married, and has a wife and several children. He has the most imposing presence of, perhaps, any man in his county.

Frank, his brother, was first a banker, but has for years been engaged in mercantile pursuits in Cincinnati. Alfred, the youngest, is a contractor on public works. The daughter is engaged in literary pursuits in Ashland. The mother died many years ago.

Frances married W. T. Nichols, who was prominent in business circles, first at Louisa, then at Catlettsburg, and finally at Ashland. They had one daughter, who married a gentleman living in Brooklyn, New York; and as they had no other children, they moved to that city to enjoy her society. Mr. Nichols died there several years ago; but Mrs. Nichols, though bowing beneath the weight of years, was able to visit her Sandy friends in 1886, and make them happy by her presence.

Another daughter married Talton Everett, of Guayandotte. They reared a large family of children, who fill high positions in life.

Mrs. Wallace, of Louisa, is also a daughter. Her husband, Thomas Wallace, came from Ohio, and became one of the foremost business men on Sandy. He was assassinated by a rival in business many years ago, yet, notwithstanding his sudden taking off, left his large business in good shape, and his family well off. A son of his, Hon. Frank Wallace, of Louisa, is the State senator of his district. G. W. Castle, his son-in-law, has filled several positions of trust, among them county attorney. Another son-in-law, Mr. McClure, is county superintendent of schools. The youngest son of Thomas Wallace has been police judge of his town. Another daughter of Fred. Moore is the gifted Mrs. Sullivan, postmistress of Louisa. Her husband, Rev. C. M. Sullivan, a distinguished preacher of the Methodist Episcopal Church, South, died soon after the Civil War, leaving her three sons to cheer her pathway in life.

COLONEL GEORGE W. GALLUP,

WHO married Rebecca, the youngest daughter of Frederick Moore and wife, came from New York State about 1850, quite a young man, and engaged in school-teaching at South Point, Ohio, where he gave great satisfaction to his employers. He subsequently went to Louisa, studied law, and was admitted to the bar at that place. He went into partnership with Colonel L. T. Moore, his brother-in-law, which continued to 1861. When the 14th Kentucky was organized, in the Fall of 1861, Mr. Gallup went into the regiment as quartermaster. In less than a year, owing to the resignation of Colonel Moore, and, still later on, the resignation of Colonel Cochran, who succeeded Colonel Moore, Lieutenant Gallup was promoted to the colonelcy of the regiment. Some dissatisfaction was occasioned by Gallup's promotion, but the new colonel soon showed his officers and men that he was "the right man in the right place."

The 14th was in many a fiery skirmish and hard-fought battle. Especially was it exposed to the enemy's lines in its march on Atlanta from Nashville, under Sherman. Colonel Gallup was not only popular with the other officers of the regiment, but was idolized by the men for his kindness and humanity to them. His daring and bravery was equal to his humanity. In a hotly contested battle, on the line from Nashville to Atlanta, an orderly from the commander of the brigade rode up to Colonel Gallup, saying that the general wanted the 14th to capture a redoubt which was vexing the entire brigade. Colonel Gallup was in a position to know that it would take five thousand men to capture the enemy's works, and told the orderly to so report to his chief.

GEN. G. W. GALLUP.

The orderly soon returned, and mildly intimated to the colonel that it was a lack of courage that prevented his moving with his command on the enemy. Stung with indignation, Colonel Gallup, with drawn sword, telling his men to stand still, marched up within a hundred feet of the redoubt, the bullets raining all about him. The orderly scampered away, soon returning with an apology from his chief.

Colonel Gallup, no doubt, would have attained to a general's place, had not red-tape and jealousy intervened to prevent it. After three years of heroic discharge of duty on the tented field in battling for the old flag and the old Government, he returned to the peaceful walks of life, settling down in his old home at Louisa, never again taking up the practice of the law, but engaged in the milling and lumbering business.

Moving to Catlettsburg, he became a contractor on the C. and O. Railroad, and then took the contract to build the Key's Creek Mining Railroad, in which he lost heavily. On the retirement of Ben Burk, whose health failed, Colonel Gallup was appointed, by President Hayes, to succeed Mr. Burk as postmaster at Catlettsburg. He held the office till the day of his death, in 1881, discharging the duties required with singular faithfulness.

George W. Gallup was no ordinary man. Had he continued in the lines of literary pursuits which he had marked out in his youth, he would have risen to literary fame. While he was a good lawyer, he never liked its practice. After coming in contact with large bodies of men in the war, he was ever after inclined to engage in works that required great numbers of operatives to perform the work. And as colonel in the army, so was he as the employer and manager of large forces of workmen—liberal, considerate, and just. He wanted his employés to fare well, although himself might fail to get *his* money.

He was an impressive speaker, and sometimes could be called eloquent. He was brought out by the Democracy, soon after the war, as a candidate for State senator. The district was Republican, and Colonel Gallup was beaten, although he made a gallant fight. He never after acted with the party, but declared himself a Republican, and remained one until death.

He was an adherent to the Methodist Episcopal Church, South, and belonged to several benevolent orders. He left a widow and one grown son. The son, George Frederick Gallup, succeeded his father as postmaster at Catlettsburg, and, like him, made friends by the impartial and business-like manner in which he discharged his official duties. He was dismissed to make room for one who, although he made a good postmaster, failed to have the claims that Fred. Gallup had to recommend him to the office.

For meritorious conduct Colonel Gallup was brevetted brigadier-general.

COLONEL JOHN DILS, JR.

IN getting up the material for the history of the people of the Big Sandy Valley, the author invited Mr. Dils to furnish for its pages all of the more important events coming under his notice. During his nearly half-century residence in the Upper Sandy country, constantly mixing with the people in their social, business and political affairs well qualified him for furnishing historical matter impossible to get from any other source.

The graphic and scholarly way in which he has discharged the task is sufficient reason for giving his manuscript, as it came from his own hands, a place in the book, without any alteration whatever.

COLONEL JOHN DILS, JR.

Colonel John Dils was born, 1819, in Parkersburg, Wood County, now West Virginia. His father was John Dils, Sen., and his grandfather bore the same name, who, together with his brother Henry, emigrated from Pennsylvania, on the Monongahela River, near Brownsville, and came to West Virginia, and settled in Wood County, near Parkersburg, about the year 1789. They had both served in the War of 1776, and were active participants, with the Ohio colonies of Belpre and Marietta, in the Indian troubles on the frontier, in the early settlements of that day. His father was with the Wood County militia under Colonel Phelps, who went to arrest Colonel Burr and his men on Blennerhassett Island, under the proclamation of President Jefferson in 1806. But failing to find him on the island, Colonel Phelps, with a part of his men, hastened to the mouth of the Big Kanawha River to intercept Colonel Burr's retreat; but Colonel Phelps was again foiled by the wily foe.

Residence of Colonel John Dils, Jr., Piketon, Ky.

I have often heard my father express words of sympathy and kindness toward the unfortunate Blennerhassett and his beautiful and accomplished wife, who were the owners of the historic island that bears their name. To be reared amongst the living actors of those stirring events of our country's history, has made an impression and left a charm that no romance or fiction has ever been enabled to supplant the real, as imbibed in my early boyhood. The very air was rife with the tales of the wonderful deeds of early frontiersmen. Ransom, a swarthy, dwarfish negro, who became the property of my cousin, James Stephenson, was the servant and waiter of his royal queen, Mrs. Blennerhassett. He was a good fiddler, and a favorite with the youngsters in his nocturnal visits, and many were the joyful reels I participated in under his teaching and inimitable music; and when tired with "tripping the toe," we would gather around our sable friend to listen to some wonderful stories he was so fond of relating of the prairie queen whom he had so proudly served, but now "far away from her own dear island of sorrow."

But it was meet for me the spell should be broken, by leaving dream-land and the magic of the hour. In 1836 Mr. Callihan, who had married my sister the year previous, stopped at Parkersburg on his return from an Eastern trip of purchasing goods, to get me to accompany him to his home at Pikeville, Ky., which I accepted, as I was anxious to be with my sister. And thus it was Big Sandy became my future home, where I now live, and have resided ever since, save a short time during the late war, when it became expedient to remove my family to a safer and more congenial place. The impression, as I traveled alone up the Big Sandy

Valley for the first time, would be difficult to recall, save its wild but rich presentation of both land and forest, and its far excelling any thing of the kind in the majesty of the mountains that I had ever seen. The people I found to be plain and simple, with unbounded hospitality. Most of them were the early pioneers of the country; some had been soldiers of the Revolution, and many others of the War of 1812 and the Indian wars. The country abounded with game. Bear and deer were abundant, and hunters were numerous and happy. Hunting was the principal occupation of both young and old. In the season for killing game a man without a gun was out of occupation, unless he was a merchant or preacher. A good gun was worth a good farm or first-class horse, as I have often heard hunters say.

The peltry taken from the wild animals found a ready sale. Many a fat bear and deer's carcass, after being stripped of its hide, was left to be devoured by ravenous wolves, wild-cats, etc. It would be marvelous to the present generation should I relate some of the old hunters' yarns of experiences in their hunting expeditions. I am now thinking of some of the old Nimrods; such men as the Pinsons, Maynards, Colleys, Belchers, Owens, and a host of others, not forgetting Uncle Barney Johnson, of block-house and golden wedge fame. This golden wedge Barney plowed up on his farm from an Indian burying-ground, and gave it to a

COLONEL JOHN DILS, JR. 49

blacksmith neighbor to braze bells with, not knowing its worth. I heard the brazier say it was the best brazing metal he ever had in his shop.

In addition to the abundance of game to supply the roaming hunter, it was the land of honey and ginseng. It was no trouble for a little boy or girl to make from one to three dollars a day in digging the latter article. It was generally collected in the Fall of the year in its green state, and sold to the merchants, who had it clarified for the Eastern market before shipping. Ginseng was the principal commodity of exchange in all the Upper Sandy counties, and I can only say the amount collected and shipped down the Sandy River annually was really fabulous. But the bear, deer, and ginseng have long since mainly disappeared, and the fine timber of the forests is fast following in the same footsteps.

About the 1st of December, 1837, I was intrusted by Mr. Callihan with a considerable amount of money, which I belted around me, to overtake a large drove of hogs which belonged to Mr. Callihan's partner, H. B. Mayo, of Prestonburg, and which was in the care of his son, A. I. Mayo. The country I had to pass through was entirely strange to me, with only a settlement here and there, being almost an entire wilderness. As I had to pass through the Pound Gap of the Cumberland, but little better than a bridle-path, and as I had heard that was the main passage of the Goings and Murry gangs of horse-thieves, to East Tennessee, I had many misgivings whether I would be able safely to deliver the money. But, nothing daunted, having procured a weapon, I had determined to deliver the charge or die in the effort.

About twenty miles from Pikeville, where the Shelby Creek forks, instead of going to the left, I took the right-hand path, and, after traveling near fifteen miles from the direct road to the Pound Gap, I learned my mistake, but was told if I would cross the mountain, which was very high and rough, to the left, I could again fall into the right road, some six or eight miles distant. It was then snowing heavily. I was directed to follow a dog-trail which had just passed over the mountain, returning home from a bear-chase; but while I could climb the rugged mountain with little difficulty myself, I found it quite different with the horse I was leading. Indeed, I found the progress so slow and the dog-trail becoming so dim and difficult to follow from the snow-storm, with also a good prospect of a night's lodging in the snow, my better judgment was to right about face and retrace steps, which I hastened to do, as night would soon be on me. It was near ten o'clock when I drew up at the house of my kind friend, S. Hall, that night, for lodging, having traveled fifteen miles, with no other incident than having the pleasure of seeing a large bear cross my path not more than a mile from Mr. Hall's house. After partaking of a hearty supper of good fat bear-meat, sweet milk, corn-bread, etc., and relating the incidents of the day, not forgetting to mention I desired an early start in the morning, I soon found myself tucked away in good, warm feathers, with a light heart, happy in the thought that the belt with the money was all safe around me, and by the next day's travel, nothing happening, I would be relieved of all dread and care by safely delivering it over to Mr. Mayo; all of which it was my good fortune to accomplish after traveling more than fifty miles, not seeing over a half-dozen houses in the space.

In 1840 and 1841 I taught two subscription schools of five months each per session. In November, 1842, I was married to my present wife, Miss Ann Ratliff, third daughter of General Wm. Ratliff, of Pike County, Kentucky. The following year I went into the mercantile business with R. D. Callihan and Jno. N. Richardson, known as the firm of Jno. Dils, Jr., & Co. In two years following, it was changed to Richardson & Dils.

In 1846 the war with Mexico broke out. President Polk issued a proclamation, calling for volunteers, and a company of one hundred men was made up at a general muster, a few days after the announcement. I was elected captain, C. Cecil, Sen., first lieutenant, and Lewis Sowards second lieutenant; but the company was never called into service on account of being too remote for transportation.

In 1852, after twelve years of uninterrupted pleasant business relations with my friend and partner, J. N. Richardson, I bought him out, and continued the business in my own name until the War of the Rebellion in 1861. In October of the same year I was arrested at my own house, by the order of Colonel Jno. S. Williams, who commanded the Confederate forces, then camped around Pikeville. I was only a private citizen, but was treated as a felon, and sent as a prisoner of war to Richmond, Virginia, under a heavy guard, and placed in the notorious Libby Prison for safe-keeping. My wife came to Richmond as soon as she could get permission to pass through the lines, and I was liberated a few days before Christmas. As we were traveling through Buchanan County, Virginia, on the head of Sandy River, we stopped to feed our horses and take supper, in order to reach Grundy that night, so as to make the next day's ride lighter; for we were anxious to get home the day following, to see our little children, whom she had left in the care of a trusty servant and a brother-in-law.

But that night's ride came near being my last. About a mile from where we got supper, we were called to halt by a party concealed in the timber on the hill-side. My wife was just before me on a bridge. As she did not hear the summons, I called out to her to stop. I asked the concealed party what they wanted. They evaded my question.

I requested them to come down; I wanted to see who they were, so I could report them. They halloed out, "Go on." We started, but I was fired at three times before I got that many lengths of my horse, the shot just brushing the back of my head, and dashing the little twigs from the brush in my face. We moved up pretty lively after that for a few miles.

I visited Washington the February following, with a view of getting relieved from any military obligation I might be considered bound to observe to the Confederate States. I was neither sworn, nor did I sign any parole, but was simply discharged, as I understood. But still I did not feel just like a free man; not that I wanted to go into the service, but I knew my failing: I would speak out my sentiments—therefore I desired to be relieved from any trammels, however constructively viewed. After seeing my friend, Hon. Green Adams, I laid the matter before him to assist me in the difficulty. My friend introduced me to the President, Abraham Lincoln, who gave me a special invitation to visit him as often as I could, which marked favor I was pleased to accept, seldom missing a day, as each visit made it more interesting and charming as time fleeted away. I refer to this, as it was my good pleasure to have the opportunity to listen to what that good man had to say to each of the many who were hourly petitioning him for some favor, and wherein his inestimable worth could be seen both in the Executive and the great, swelling, loving heart for the people.

In August, 1862, some of the advance troops of General Kirby Smith arrived near Pikeville. I was robbed of a large stock of goods by a party under the command of Colonel Menifee, and some of Colonel Caudill's command. I had to flee the country for life. I arrived at Frankfort, after stopping a short time in Louisville, the fourth day after leaving home, giving the news of what was going on. I wanted guns, as no peace could be had at home on any terms.

There were a great many people gathering in Frankfort, as the State was in a fever of excitement. Governor Magoffin resigned, and the Hon. James Robinson was inaugurated. I had the pleasure of seeing Senator J. J. Crittenden, with an introduction. He informed me that in the War of 1812 he formed the acquaintance of my father, both being soldiers under General Harrison. I was invited to his house to take tea with himself and his excellent wife, and was very kindly and cordially received. He had much to say to me about the war, and asked many questions about what I had seen while in Richmond, and also about friends who had left Kentucky, and were supposed to be in Richmond. He went with me to the arsenal the next day, to see that I got such guns as I desired, speaking many kind words in favor of myself and the people for whom I wanted the guns. I found him the "noblest Roman of them all," and shall ever venerate him for his kindness to me and for the interest he manifested in the mountain people.

A commission to recruit a regiment came to me at Catlettsburg about the first of September, without any solicitation or agency on my part; I learned that it was done through such friends as the Hon. J. J. Crittenden, Garrett Davis, and others. It was several days before I could get my own consent to accept; but, there being so many refugees from the Upper Sandy counties (Pike, Floyd, etc.) that wanted to go into the service of the United States army soliciting me, I finally acquiesced, and recruited the first day about two hundred men, and soon after raised, at a considerable personal sacrifice, what is known as the 39th Kentucky Regiment, Mounted Infantry. Its efficiency or inefficiency as an auxiliary in the service of the Government has gone into history, to stand the test of an impartial judgment of the loyal mind, where its friends rest in confidence of a just verdict.

THE RICE FAMILY

IS ONE of the most noted of all the old families which has given to the Big Sandy Valley its prestige in developing men of marked ability. Their ancestors were of the Celtic race, and lived in Wales. James M. Rice's grandfather came to America before the great Revolution. He took sides with the

Colonies, and fought for freedom. His son, the father of James M. Rice, came from his Virginia home, east of the Blue Ridge, in 1799, and settled near Guyandotte, Va. The next year he married, and in 1802 his most noted son, James M., was born.

It is not our purpose to go very far away for materials, although ever so abundant, or we would say more of the father of James M. Rice before he brought his young family from the neighborhood of Guyandotte, and settled on what is now known as the Toler farm, adjoining Coalton, in Boyd County.

James was then a small boy, on whose shoulders was placed a heavy load in helping his father on the farm to make a support for a growing family. This, it must be remembered, was in 1814. No iron furnaces, as now, had been established, giving employment, though the wages might be meager, to the men and boys of toil. The only place in reach of young Rice, where work could be had, was at the salt-wells on Little Sandy, where Grayson now stands. The youth had a hungering and thirsting after an education, and had seized on every opportunity to attain what he so ardently desired. The few and imperfect schools in his settlement were attended whenever he could be spared from work. Every book procurable by his scanty means was not only read, but studied. With his education barely commenced, before he was twenty years of age, he left his father's house, and went to the salt-wells, and cut wood and boiled salt. But while his labor was arduous and exacting, he still continued his studies by reading at night by the light of the salt furnace. By the time he came to man's age, he had so improved his time that he was known as one of the best scholars of his age in all the country round about.

At this period of his life and expectancy, the celebrated John M. McConnell, one of the most brilliant men and lawyers that ever lived on Sandy, was attracted to young Rice, whom he looked upon as a young man of great intellectual endowments, and as one, if having encouragement, who was destined to fill an exalted place among his countrymen. He invited Mr. Rice to come to his home and study law in his office. Mr. Rice informed Mr. McConnell that he had not sufficient means to defray the expense of such a course, but was answered that that matter could be attended to farther along. Mr. Rice entered upon his study at Greenup, where McConnell lived, and soon mastered Blackstone, Chitty, and other writers on fundamental law.

The time came when he must go out from under the friendly roof of Mr. McConnell and family, and commence the practice of his chosen profession. He desired his preceptor to make out his bill for board and instruction, for which he intended giving his note, assuring Mr. McConnell that the first money he should earn in his practice should go to the payment of the note. Mr. McConnell told him he would not accept his note, nor receive any consideration in money; that his stay had been a pleasure to him and his household; that he felt amply paid by the assiduity with which he had pursued his studies, and his gentlemanly bearing under his roof. "But," said the great McConnell, "if ever in the course of your future career, a bright young man, without money or influential friends, presents himself in your way, take him to your home and to your office, and do by him as I have done by you. This is all the pay I want, or will accept." The young lawyer bowed himself away, resolving that, whether prosperity or adversity should fall to his lot, the injunction should be kept.

Mr. Rice's great talents soon brought him a good practice at Prestonburg, where he settled soon after being admitted to the bar.

About this time, or before, he married Miss Jane H. Burns, daughter of Rev. Jerry Burns, a talented Methodist preacher, who was the grandfather of Hon. Harvey Burns, Judge John M. Burns, and Roland T. Burns. Miss Burns was a lady of strong mind and rare gifts, one well calculated to fill the position of the wife of a rising young public man. They first settled in Prestonburg, Mr. Rice at once taking high rank as a lawyer. After remaining six years at Prestonburg, Mr. Rice moved his family to Louisa, and by that time his law practice had grown to great magnitude. Most of his time was spent in attending the courts of his district, making the journey on horseback. Yet, notwithstanding the great draft made on his time in giving it to his chosen profession, he found opportunity to cultivate the amenities of life, making friends wherever he went, and to give much thought to the politics of the day.

In 1836 he was elected to the State Senate from the district, and took high rank in that august body, notwithstanding his party in the Senate was in the minority. While serving his constituents in the Senate, he had the misfortune to lose his wife by death, which greatly affected him. A man of less nerve would have been tempted to yield up his office and return to private life; but a man of strong mind and intellect, like Judge James M. Rice, pausing to weep for his dead, felt that the living had claims upon him which had to be met also.

In 1840 he married, for a second wife, Miss Matilda, daughter of Richard Brown, then living on his farm at the Levisa and Tug Point, and a sister of Hon. George N. Brown. The second marriage, like the first, was one every way suitable to a public man like Judge Rice. His first wife had left him five children, two sons and three daughters, whose mental and moral training, so well begun by their own mother, was now to be carried forward by the step-mother; and it would be hard to find a wife and step-mother who discharged every duty she owed to husband and step-children with more intelligence, discretion, and love than did Mrs. Matilda Rice. Her husband was all the world to her, and, taking his children in her charge, she instilled into their hearts and minds the principles best calculated to develop them into strong men and women. No mother ever displayed greater devotion to her children than did Mrs. Rice in rearing to manhood and womanhood her step-children, and few mothers have been more amply rewarded than Mrs. Rice in the success of her arduous labors.

Jacob—or Jake, as he wrote his name—at twenty-three, was the finest orator and most brilliant young man of his age that ever lived on Sandy. Like his father, he was a lawyer, and his friends predicted a bright career for him. From childhood he was troubled with obesity, which grew with his age, not only hindering his locomotion, but depressing his naturally bright intellect. Notwithstanding this great drawback, he was a good lawyer, a popular orator, and one of the most genial of men. He filled a seat in the Legislature from Lawrence and Boyd, and was one of the most noted Free Masons of Eastern Kentucky, filling the principal chair in the Grand Lodge of the State. He was a religious man, and often preached as a lay preacher of the Southern Methodist Church, of which he was a member. He had his defects; but they were the foibles of human nature, rather than great sins. He died from paralysis, commencing at Frankfort, while a member of the Lower House in the Legislature, and terminating in his death at his home near Louisa, in 1884. He left a large family.

The youngest son, John McConnell Rice, if not more brilliant than his gifted brother Jake, has proven himself to be a man of intellect, and a leader among men. Like his father and brother, he, too, is a lawyer. On being admitted to the bar in 1853, he removed to Pikeville, where he practiced until 1860, when he went back to Louisa, taking at the bar there the place of his father, who, the same year, moved to Catlettsburg. While at Pikeville he was elected once to the Legislature, and once from Lawrence and Boyd. In 1868 he was elected to Congress from the Ninth District, and re-elected in 1872, carrying on all the time a large law practice. In 1884 he was appointed judge of the Big Sandy Criminal Court, and was elected without opposition for a full term in 1885, which he is now filling.

He received the plaudits of his party in every official position he has occupied by their suffrage; but as criminal judge the entire body politic rise up and applaud him as a just and upright judge. No honor of an official nature has ever been sought by him without obtaining what he asked for.

The judge married Miss Poage, a daughter of William Poage, a prominent citizen of Greenup County. They have two sons and three daughters. One of the daughters married James H. McConnell, the postmaster at Catlettsburg. One married James

Q. Lackey, of Louisa; and another married Benjamin Thomas, a noted engineer, now in charge of the Big Sandy River public improvements. One of the sons married Miss Abbott, a worthy young lady of his native town; and the remaining son holds an important office in the revenue department of the Government.

Hon. James M. Rice, during the session of the Legislature in 1860, went to Frankfort, and labored with so much candor and ability as to impress upon the members the advisability of cutting off portions of Greenup, Lawrence, and Carter, and forming the county of Boyd. Many others did much to achieve the same end, but none did so much as Judge James M. Rice. The same year he moved to Catlettsburg, where he lived till his death. During his residence here he gave most of his time to the practice of his profession. Always taking a deep interest in the political affairs of his country, his devotion to his party was great, and it is likely that he sometimes felt that he should have received more benefits from it than fell to his lot. A man may be talented, no matter where he may live, but oftentimes his greatness "is wasted on the desert air." A Democrat, be he ever so brilliant, can make no headway in a Republican State; and *vice versa*. During Judge Rice's prime, the State of Kentucky was overwhelmingly Whig. Almost any Whig could have beaten the Democratic party. Had Kentucky been Democratic at that period, Judge Rice would, no doubt, have risen to the highest places of official honor known to the Commonwealth.

Less than a year after his removal to Catlettsburg, the great Civil War commenced. Judge Rice was strongly Southern in his feelings, but at the same time declared secession to be a heresy, contending that the Southern leaders were making a great mistake in breaking up the Government to obtain the rights they could only hope to get within the Union. While his sympathies were with the Southern people, he conducted himself during the entire conflict with that dignity and discretion so becoming in one of his exalted position. Only once during the war was any indignity cast upon the great man, and that, of no great moment, was caused by a green subaltern in the Union army, over-zealous in the discharge of duty.

The sons of Judge James M. Rice we have fully noticed. His three daughters must now receive our attention. Amanda is married to a worthy gentleman named Culter, and lives in Florida. Another daughter married Samuel Short, a prominent citizen of Lawrence. They are both dead, leaving no children save an adopted daughter, the wife of F. F. Freese, Esq., of Louisa. The other daughter married John Jones, a son of Daniel Jones, at one time a prominent citizen of Prestonburg. Mrs. Jones died many years ago, leaving several children.

Judge Rice was one of the most considerate of

parents, ever laboring for the advancement of his children. He provided not only his two sons, but the daughters as well, with the best education the schools and colleges could afford. While he was always a friend of morals and Christianity, and his house during his entire married life was the home of the preacher, he never publicly professed faith in Christ until two or three years previous to his death, when he united with the Methodist Episcopal Church, South. He was a man of strictly temperate habits, never indulging in the use of stimulants, and even gave up the use of tobacco many years before he died. His mind and all of his faculties were undimmed to the last, and his sudden death was a fitting termination of the life of one so majestic. On the 24th day of October, 1870, his heart ceased to beat, and the great man was gathered to his fathers. He left a widow, in addition to the sons and daughters named. The second wife never bore him any children, but she lives to-day, keeping green the memory of her departed husband, and taking the most lively interest in the welfare of his children and grandchildren.

We omitted to state under the proper head that Mr. Rice at one time filled the office of circuit judge by appointment with great ability.

Before finishing our paper on the Rice family, we must refer again to Judge James M. Rice's great friend, John M. McConnell. That the former never ceased to remember his preceptor with gratitude, is evinced by the fact that he named one of his two sons after him. The present judge of the Big Sandy Criminal Court, Hon. John M. Rice, bears the honored given name of his father's first great friend, McConnell. The naming of a child is only a sentiment, and while Judge Rice did not ignore a sentiment, he was ever on the alert to discover a young man answering the description pointed out by McConnell, whom he could take to his home and office, and do for him as Mr. McConnell had, unsolicited, done for himself. At last the opportunity came. John McDyer, a bright, talented young man, without means to defray his expenses, presented himself to Mr. Rice, and informed him that he wanted to enter his office as a law student, but he did not then have the means at command to pay for such a course. Mr. Rice bade the young man welcome, and told him that his board and tuition should be free. Mr. McDyer pursued his studies with alacrity and was soon admitted to the bar; and, had not his life been cut short by fatal disease almost at its threshold, it is believed that he would have made a great name as a lawyer. He married a daughter of George Hutchinson, of Lawrence, and sister of I. B. Hutchinson. He left a widow and a daughter and son. The widow soon followed her young husband to the grave; the daughter is married, and lives in Lawrence; and the son, John McDyer, is one of Boyd County's most prominent citizens.

But the sublime friendship formed between the houses of McConnell and Rice does not cease when James M. Rice, the real founder of the Rice dynasty, on Sandy, pays back in kind the benefits he had in early manhood received from John M. McConnell, the founder of the McConnell family in Kentucky. Near fifty years had come and gone since McConnell's dust had returned to earth, and Judge Rice had also been laid in his grave, when James H. McConnell, son of Charles L. McConnell, and grandson of John M. McConnell, wooed and won the heart and hand of Ida, daughter of Hon. John M. Rice, and granddaughter of Judge James M. Rice, thus cementing in love the friendship formed by their ancestors half a century before.

THE RICE FAMILY, OF JOHNSON,

Settled in the county in 1815. They came from Virginia. They are mostly farmers, and some of them wealthy ones. Martin Rice, of Jennie's Creek, is one of the richest men in Johnson. Two of his sons are leading merchants of Paintsville. One of them is clerk of the Circuit Court. Other members of the Rice family are professional men. The Rices of Johnson are mostly adherents of the Methodist Episcopal Church, and are Republicans in politics.

Another large branch of the family is found in Floyd, Pike, and Martin. They, too, are mostly tillers of the soil, and, as a family, maintain the reputation of good citizenship. The latter branch are mostly Baptists, though some Methodists are found in the family. In politics they are divided.

JOHN N. RICHARDSON

WAS raised in Philadelphia. He was educated in the academy owned and conducted by Thomas Smiley, the author of Smiley's Arithmetic. He came west in 1833, when quite a young man, and stopped at the Mouth of Sandy. "Dad" Owens fell in with him there, and insisted on the young Philadelphian's going home with him to Pike, to take charge of his mercantile books, as he discovered the young man to be an expert in book-keeping. Mr. Richardson yielded, and for near twenty years made Pikeville his home. He married a daughter of Thos. Ratliff, the sister of General Ratliff, of that place. He became a merchant, and did a great trade in ginseng, furs, etc. He became a very religious man while there, and did much to promote the cause of religion and sound morality. He moved, about 1852, to Greenup County, and took charge of the office of the Pennsylvania Furnace, then owned by W. M. Patton and others. Joseph Patton was assistant manager.

Quitting there in about 1854, he moved to Catlettsburg, and formed a partnership with his old partner, R. D. Callihan, and opened a store in Ashland, continuing to live in Catlettsburg. The firm built a flour-mill in Ashland, the nucleus of the large mill now owned by the Poages. In 1861 he opened a store in Catlettsburg, and by his trained business foresight made a good thing during the war. He for some time was cashier of the Bank of Ashland, and was regarded as a capital officer. But his health failing, he was compelled to withdraw from business in 1866, and died in 1867, lamented not only by his immediate family, but by the entire community. The business houses were all closed in respect to his memory, on the day of his funeral.

His son William is now, and has been for years, the cashier of the Ashland National Bank. Another son has filled for two terms the office of sheriff of Boyd County. Another son is a prominent business man in Ashland, and of literary ability. His eldest daughter, Meriba, was a lady of rare Christian graces and mental accomplishments. She was educated at the Female College, Wilmington, Delaware. She died ten years ago, greatly lamented by all who knew her. Another daughter is the wife of a prominent preacher in the West Virginia Conference, Methodist Episcopal Church. Another daughter is the wife of a prominent Ohio River steamboat man.

The widow still survives, blessed by her dutiful children, who often call at the old homestead where the mother resides, surrounded by the comforts and luxuries which follow a well-spent life.

We failed to say another son occupies a high business position in a commercial town in Ohio.

JOHN M. McCONNELL

WAS of Scotch-Irish descent, and born in Western Pennsylvania, about 1790. He received a good education before he was sixteen, at which time he was apprenticed to the tailor and draper business. While working faithfully at his trade, he by no means failed to snatch every moment of time not due his employer, to carry on a course of study previously laid out in his mind on quitting school; and living in Cannonsburg, then containing a college of learning, his opportunities were increased by the friendships he made with not only many of the students, but the professors as well. They assisted the bright apprentice in carrying on a collegiate course, by going to his room of evenings, and giving him the benefit of studying the text-books with them. While he did not have the opportunity of reciting to the professors in the hall, he mastered the lessons, and had them well grounded in his mind, so that when his apprenticeship expired, at twenty-one years of age, his education was as complete as many of the students who had given their days as well as their nights to study.

In 1813, when twenty-one, his employer gave him twenty-five dollars in money, a horse, saddle, and bridle, a large pair of saddle-bags, and a new suit of broadcloth; and he left his native State and struck out for Kentucky, which he reached opposite Portsmouth; he rode on to Greenup Courthouse, and made a halt. After tarrying a short time here, he went to Woodford County, but soon came back to Eastern Kentucky, and went to Prestonburg, where he taught school, and read law with Robert Walker, one of the early lawyers of that town, famous for great lawyers. About this time he married Lucy Lewis, a daughter of Charles Lewis, of what is now Carter County, and settled in Greenup, where he lived the remainder of his days.

From his entrance on the practice of his profession until the day of his death, Mr. McConnell stood at the front rank of the profession, and as one of the most eloquent men on the stump of his day found in the State. As money flowed into his hands from his great and extending practice, he made investments in the infant industries of his county, which yielded him large returns. Being a gentleman of taste and culture, he went to work to set up an establishment equal to almost any one found in the older settlements of that day. He purchased a large boundary of land fronting on the Ohio River, four miles above Greenupsburg, where he laid out a four-acre plat fronting on the bank of the beautiful river, and in the center erected a splendid two-story brick mansion, setting out shade-trees in regular order, with vegetable garden and negro-houses in the rear, shrubbery and flowers of the most delicious odors, arranged in plats, and lining the pebbled walks in front. After finishing the house in the best style known to mechanical art, and furnishing it with the most skillfully wrought furniture, and when ready to move in and occupy the splendid home, without any apparent sickness, in the year 1834, at forty-three years of age, he departed this life. He had burnt the candle of life at both ends, but accomplished as much as ordinary mortals achieve in double the time. Commencing life with comparatively nothing, he died leaving over fifty thousand dollars in money, lands, and negroes, to his widow and children.

His only son, Judge Charles Lewis McConnell, lives in Catlettsburg, and is highly respected. The daughters all married men who occupy prominent places in business and society. The widow followed her husband to the grave about twenty years after his departure.

Mr. McConnell was a State senator four years, and was regarded as one of the most eloquent of that then august body. He was not only an orator, but excelled as a conversationalist. We give an instance of his rare elocutionary power in common conversation, which was related to us by the author's father-in-law, Robert Walter, of Blaine. Mr. McConnell made many journeys from Greenup to Prestonburg, and back; and on these trips he invariably stopped with Neri Sweatnam, a fine liver, and a jolly good man to stay with all night. On all such occasions Mr. Sweatnam would send his colored servant "Bill" to tell Master Robert that the great man (meaning McConnell) had arrived, and to come over and hear him talk. He must have been a charming talker, as Mr. Walter often said that he surpassed all of the great men he ever heard speak or talk. He named Menifee, Cox, French, Rice, Moore, Andrews, as his models of greatness, but said that McConnell surpassed them all as a charming talker.

THE PRESTON FAMILY.

The early ancestor of this family in the Sandy Valley was Moses Preston, born and raised in Bedford County, Virginia, who, on coming to man's estate, found his country in the throes of the approaching Revolutionary struggle, and patriotically enlisted on the side of freedom. He fought through the war, and at its close returned to Bedford, and married a Miss Arthur, from which name are perpetuated many of the given names worn by the Prestons.

In 1800 Moses Preston moved into the valley, and settled on what is known as the Morgan farm in Floyd, thence to the forks of Beaver. He came down to near George's Creek, and settled on the farm, where he lived and died, which latter event occurred in the seventy-sixth year of his age. He was all his life a sterling Jeffersonian Democrat. He was the father of six sons and five daughters.

Isaac, the oldest son, married Polly Sloan, of Pike County, of an old-time house up there. They lived all their life on a farm in the vicinity of Peach Orchard. He, like his father Moses, died in the seventy-sixth year of his age, his wife Polly reaching the grand age of eighty-five before she was called to shuffle off the mortal coil. They left a large number of descendants, who are among the best citizens of the Sandy Valley. Milton T. Preston, the enterprising merchant of near Peach Orchard, is a grandson of theirs.

Stephen, the second son, married a Miss Miller, and, like his brothers, settled on a farm near where he lived in his boyhood. Here he lived, and here he died, at the age of seventy-four. Although he had traveled through Indiana in early manhood, he returned to his native soil, happy to keep his place among brothers and sisters. His wife, Pricie, was a devoted Methodist. She still lives, at the age of eighty-one, active in body and mind. They have many descendants to honor their name. Among them is Robert M. Preston, a bright, intelligent gentleman of Peach Orchard.

Moses was the third son, whose life we will pass over at present, as he was not only like his brothers and sisters, a good citizen, but was destined to become a historic figure in Big Sandy annals.

John, the fourth son, married Kizzie Fitzpatrick. She still survives. They raised a large family of sons, and one daughter. Henry, the fifth son, married Betty Kanes, and settled on a farm on Nat's Creek, where he resided until his death, which occurred at seventy-two years of age. His wife lived at the homestead the rest of her life. She died in the eighty-sixth year of her age. Both husband and wife were staunch Methodists. They left fifteen children, many grandchildren and great-grandchildren behind them. Among the former is McDonald Preston, the merchant and hotel-keeper at Richardson, Kentucky. Arthur Preston, a well-off merchant and timber-dealer of Graves' Shoal, who is a rising man in his section, is a member of this branch of the Preston family.

Arthur, the sixth son, married Nancy Miller, and first settled on Rock Castle, but soon after moved to the Tygart Valley, in Greenup County. After remaining a few years in Greenup County, he came back to the Sandy River, and settled on the farm, where he died, at the Graves' Shoal. He was known as a model farmer and stock-raiser, and prospered in business. His first wife died in 1852. He afterwards married Sarah Peery, daughter of David Peery, of Virginia. She lived until 1881, and then passed to the better land. He died in 1884, leaving a host of descendants, who are not unworthy of their ancestry. Susan, the eldest daughter, married Abraham Mead, and lived on a farm on Mead Branch. She died in 1847, and left numerous sons and daughters. She was a very pious lady, a member of the Methodist Church. Linda, the second daughter, married Jesse Price. They first lived near Graves' Shoal, but subsequently moved to near the mouth of Buffalo, and after a few years, about 1873, they settled in Paintsville, where they both died, at a good old age. They were Baptist people, and pious. Among their sons we mention Washington Price, an able Baptist preacher, and, although bowed down with the weight of years upon him, he is able to bear the burden of seven Churches upon his shoulders, as the pastor of each. A. J. Price, another son, was a prominent merchant and Baptist preacher in his life. A grandson is a prominent educator, now living in Ohio.

Polly, the third daughter of Moses Preston the first, married John Hawes, a Methodist preacher. They settled on George's Creek. From there they went to Indiana, but only to return to Flat Woods, Lawrence County, where they settled for life. Their farm was about a mile above Louisa. Wesley Hawes, a former prominent citizen of Lawrence County, holding the office of sheriff and other official honors, was their son. Judge Asbury Hawes, a merchant and farmer of Prosperity, is another son of theirs, and, like his ancestors is a Methodist. Allen P., another son, served as captain in the Union army. Jane married Archibald Borders;

Betty married Abraham Childers. They lived mostly on a farm on the bank of the Sandy, although they spent some time in the Rock Castle region, the husband dying many years ago, and she growing old (now seventy-eight years), lives with her children, near Richardson, and seems happy and contented.

The Prestons, from the beginning on Sandy, have, as a family, sustained an unblemished reputation for truth and honesty, and most of them are well-to-do people. In politics they are Democrats, with rare exceptions, inclining to the Methodists in religion, though some are Baptists. As a representative member of the Preston family, we give, in another place, the portrait of young Arthur Preston, the progressive merchant and trader of Graves' Shoal, a young man of mental vigor and a leader of the younger generation of the Prestons.

MOSES, OR "COBY" PRESTON,

THE third son of Moses Preston and his wife, *née* Miss Arthur, was one of the remarkable men whom the Sandy Valley has developed. He was born near the birth of the present century, and on coming to manhood married Elizabeth Haney, a woman of worth and great energy. She bore him a large family of children, who, following in the footsteps of their honored parents, are the foremost citizens in the Sandy Valley and in the homes they have hewn out in the far South-west.

Soon after Mr. Preston's marriage with Miss Haney, being of a restless disposition, he, with his young wife, moved to the Scioto Valley country; but, finding chills and fever as abundant as good land, they shook the dust, or mud, from the soles of their feet and hastened back to the Great Sandy country. While the move down to Scioto was attended with expense, the plain, economical ways of life which Mr. Preston adopted in early life, and kept up until the hour of his death, enabled him to return to the Sandy Valley with more material wealth than he had at starting. On his return he settled on the place known at the time as the Spencer farm, now the Kise farm, some miles below George's Creek. Here he lived many years, and prospered greatly.

MOSES PRESTON, SR.

Alone, and afterward with his brother-in-law, Archibald Borders, he was among the first to engage in peeling and running tan-bark to Cincinnati, floating it down in barges, constructed, often, out of lumber sawed by hand, called whip-sawing. He and his brother-in-law, Judge Borders, were as well and favorably known to the old-time tanners and other business men of the Queen City as are the great timber-dealers of the present time known to the mill-men and builders of Cincinnati. He established a reputation for honesty and fair-dealing unsurpassed by no one in the business; in some instances the bark went off without being subject to measurement, so much confidence had the buyers in Mr. Preston's honesty. While tan-bark was a specialty with him, he was almost as well known as a large timber-dealer. He also sent barge-loads of hoop-poles and staves to the Cincinnati market. Dealing in bark, cooper-stuff, and saw-logs combined seems to us to be sufficient for one man's busy attention; but to one with the business foresight of "Coby" Preston this alone was insignificant, and at the same time he carried on a large general store, and cultivated many farms. By applying business rules to every department of his extended pursuits, he made money at all, and was never accused of overreaching the hireling that wrought for him.

About the time Johnson County was formed into a separate jurisdiction, which was in 1843, Mr. Preston moved up to the mouth of Paint Creek, and ever after, as long as he lived, made that place the center of his business enterprises, although he alternated his residence between the mouth of Paint and Paintsville, one-half a mile above, having good residences at both places.

Like all dwellers on the highway with a good house, he entertained the wayfaring man in a sumptuous style at his home on the river.

The wife of his youth, after sharing with him his sorrows and joys, and assisting her husband by her good counsels and domestic skill, sickened and died, leaving behind a number of sons, who, by following the good and wholesome advice given them by their mother, and walking in the footsteps of their father, have, nearly all of them, come to the front as business men and upright citizens in the vicinity where they were brought up.

After the death of his first wife, Mr. Preston married Nancy, a daughter of David Peery, of Tazewell County, Virginia. They lived in great peace until his sudden death, in 1870. He and his wife being on a visit to his brother Arthur, at Graves' Shoal, after dinner he went to the barn to saddle the horses, to return with his wife to their home at Paintsville, when one of the animals kicked him so severely that he died almost instantly. His death was not only a sad blow to his family, but was profoundly regretted by the entire people of the valley; for in more respects than one a prince among the people had fallen when the life went out of the body of Moses, or Coby, Preston. While his death was sudden and unexpected to him and others, he had had the sagacity to make ample provision for his wife, and had, as his sons started out in business, aided them with a liberal hand; so that no family jar rent the bonds that bound the family together, after he had left the busy haunts of men. Mr. Preston was an honest man, the noblest work of God.

Coby, or Moses, Preston took a deep interest in political affairs, although he was never an office-seeker. He ignored, to some extent, Church formularies, but squared his life by the Golden Rule. His portrait will be recognized by the old-time Sandians as one of peculiar correctness.

The modern-built brick mansion, the Paintsville residence of his son, Captain Frank Preston, bears testimony to the progress of architecture in the Sandy Valley.

Residence of Frank Preston, Paintsville, Ky.

He is, in some respects, the representative of the family. He is a man of wealth, character, and enterprise, and has the confidence of the entire community in which he lives, as a merchant, a timber-dealer, a steamboatman, and general business man. He married into one of the most prominent families of the Sandy Valley, a daughter of General Daniel Hager. He sends his sons and daughters to the best colleges and schools, to receive their mental training. Himself and family are members and liberal supporters of the Methodist Episcopal Church, South. He, like his father, is a strong Democrat, but not an office-seeker.

James, another son, died many years ago. Greenville lives in Texas. Martin is, and has always been, a prominent business man of Paintsville, and has a son engaged in literary pursuits, besides being a lawyer and preacher. Moses rose to eminence as a merchant, but died many years ago. His wife, another daughter of General Hager, after her first husband's death, married Dr. Turner, a prominent citizen of Paintsville. William and Montraville are both prosperous farmers and saving business men, living near Paintsville.

THE MARR FAMILY,

OF the Sandy Valley, is one of French origin, descendants of the Huguenots. The family settled in Maryland before the American Revolution. They served the cause of freedom, and were good patriots.

The Marr family spread over the land, from the ancient seat in Maryland, to South Carolina, and numbers among its members many whose deeds have made them noted in business and literature. The grandfather of Thomas Marr, of Catlettsburg, came to Sandy before the commencement of the present century, and settled in the John's Creek country. One of his sons married a Miss May, a daughter of Thomas May, of Shelby, Pike County. Thomas Marr and his brothers are descended from that union, on their maternal side.

The Marrs have ever been held in esteem for their integrity and fair dealing, and by intermarriage are allied to many of the old houses of the valley. Hon. James Marr, a brother of Thomas, is the efficient prosecuting attorney of Letcher County. Another brother is a prominent business man of Pike.

The Marrs have ever been noted for the firmness with which they stood by that which they thought to be right. They favor all measures calculated to make men better citizens. They are patrons of religion, and in politics are firm Democrats.

Captain Thomas married the second daughter of Benjamin Williamson. He and his family are among Catlettsburg's most prominent people.

THE MAY FAMILY,

OF the Sandy Valley, were here by its representatives as early as 1796. The author has failed to gather any material on which to base a consecutive history of the doings of the May family.

Thomas May was the first, or, at least, amongst the first, of the family coming from Virginia and settling on Shelby Creek. He was a very jovial man, fond of fiddling and dancing, and popular with his neighbors. He owned more slaves than any man on Sandy, either in his day or since, footing up in number seventy-one.

Other branches of the family settled further down the river, more largely at Prestonburg. They have spread over a half-dozen counties in the Sandy Valley and adjacent section. The Mays have from the beginning been at the front in public life, one of them representing his district in Congress. Colonel A. J. May developed into greater renown as an officer in the Confederate army than any other native of Sandy. He is a middle-aged man, now living in Tazewell County, Virginia, where he has practiced law ever since the close of the Civil War.

Many of the Mays filled county and legislative offices. David, of Pike County, especially, has been foremost as a public man. Several of the Mays are local preachers in the Methodist Episcopal Church, South. The Mays of the immediate Sandy Valley are Democrats, but some of them in other and distant counties are Republicans.

THE MAYO FAMILY

Is ONE of the oldest, as well as one of great respectability, in the valley. Jacob came from Fluvanna County Virginia, and was appointed clerk of the Floyd Circuit Court in 1800. Harry B. and Wilson came later.

Lewis Mayo came to the valley in 1837. He

was a finely educated man, and devoted his life to teaching. He raised a family of sons and daughters, who well kept up the reputation of the Mayo house.

L. D. Walton married one of Lewis Mayo's daughters. The wife of Harry Davis, at the mouth of John's Creek, is another. William Borders, of Paintsville, married a third. Mrs. Allen P. Borders is a daughter of the same; and the wife of Hon. James E. Stewart is the youngest one of these fair daughters. A son, who bears his father's given name, is a merchant on Sandy.

The various branches of the Mayo tree have spread to all parts of the valley, carrying with them industry, morality, and intelligence.

NERI SWEATNUM

AND family came from near Washington City in Virginia, in 1818, and bought an immense boundary of land on Blaine, which is known to this day as the Sweatnum neighborhood. He was a man of wealth and fine manners, as was also his wife, who was a Cross. Their home was the resting-place of the Methodist preachers, for they were ardent Methodists. It was the stopping-place for most of the great lawyers and statesmen who so frequently, in an early day, passed by the Sweatnum neighborhood on the road from Louisa to West Liberty, and from the interior of the State to the Sandy country.

Mr. Sweatnum and wife, in their day, often entertained Judge French, Leander Cox, Richard Menifee, John M. McConnell, Watt Andrews, Judge James M. Rice, and other noted men. Although Mr. Sweatnum was a strong Henry Clay Whig, he always said that he liked Judge Rice, of his own county, better than any of the great men who stopped with him. Rice was much younger than he, and his jolly, ardent nature, as well as the great talents of the judge, won the love of his heart.

Mr. Sweatnum had a servant named "Bill," who used to attend the elections with gingerbread, to sell for his own profit, and was sharp enough to cry it off as *Rice-cakes*, if Rice was a candidate, knowing that *Master* Rice was very liberal to the blacks, if he was a slave-owner; and that while his own master was a Whig, and Rice a Democrat, his personal liking for the judge would cause him to wink at his selfish zeal in promoting the election of a Democrat.

Mr. Sweatnum died in 1861, his wife preceding him two years. He had six sons and two daughters. Dr. Sweatnum, of Louisa, is the youngest son. John Sweatnum, of Bath, another. Claiborne Sweatnum, Neri, and Elza Sweatnum, the three latter of Blaine, are the living sons, Zephaniah having long since died in Iowa. Mrs. Judge Dean is a granddaughter of Neri Sweatnum, Sen., and so is the wife of the author of this book. He has three or four grandsons, who are noted physicians, among them Dr. J. M. Sweatnum, of Omaha, Nebraska. Many of his descendants are in California; and his youngest daughter, with her husband, John Osburn, lives in Arizona. The oldest daughter was the wife of Robert Walter, both of whom have been dead for many years.

The great landed estate of Mr. Sweatnum is every foot held sacred by his descendants, who still keep alive the family traditions. Mr. Sweatnum was a good man and true, and his family came to honor.

"Bill," the old slave spoken of, lives in Catlettsburg, coming slyly from Ironton, at which place he had taken shelter from the Knights of Birchbark, a very brave band that, ten years ago, terrorized many poor people, both white and black, for having but one shirt to wear, and whose wives went barefooted. "Poor Old Bill" scampered away from Kentucky soil simply because the old man believed in witches. He is near ninety years old, yet does as good, honest work as men of fifty; and had he now the value for all the hard work he has done, he could pay for the Alger House, the Opera-house, and Carpenter's mammoth house thrown in.

JOHN FREW STEWART

WAS born in December, 1833, in Western Pennsylvania, and was educated at Westminster College, New Wilmington, Pennsylvania, continuing there for three years. He then followed teaching for six or seven years, when, in 1859, he began the study of law in the office of Moore & Gallup, at Louisa, procuring his license in 1860. In August, 1862, he was elected county attorney of Lawrence County, Ky. He entered the army as a private in September, 1862. At the organization of his company, in November of the same year, he was commissioned second lieutenant of the same, and at the organization of the regiment (Thirty-ninth Kentucky volunteers) February 16, 1863, he was promoted to first lieutenant and adjutant of the regiment, in which capacity he served to November, 1864, when he was promoted to major of his regiment.

J. FREW STEWART.

His first appearance in Kentucky was as principal of Big Sandy Academy, at Catlettsburg, in October, 1857. Many of the prominent young men of the Sandy Valley were students under him, notably the Moore boys, the Richardsons, Prichards,

Burgesses, Pattons; also, S. G. Kinner, our Commonwealth's attorney, and many others. In Johnson County, where he lives, he has been deputy collector internal revenue, United States commissioner, county school commissioner, and county judge. Judge Stewart is married, but has no children. He owns and occupies a beautiful homestead in Paintsville. In politics he is a Republican. In religion he is a member of the Methodist Episcopal Church.

ALBIN STEIN.

THE picture of Mr. Stein is produced to represent the German element of the Sandy Valley, and also to represent the manufacturing industries, and, furthermore, to represent an old-time house, some of the members of which came to the valley in an early day. The Steins have the blood of the Sovains, an old honored family of Alsace-Lorraine, coursing through their veins. The Sovains had representatives in America at Philadelphia in 1755. Their descendants came early to the Sandy Valley, and by marriage have become allied to some of the most prominent people in East Kentucky.

Charles Stein, the father of Albin, came to the Sandy Valley from Germany, and set up a tannery near Catlettsburg in 1852. After several years he returned to the father-land, and finally married there. But, once breathing the free air of America, he was not satisfied in a country overrun with kings, dukes, and petty princes, and resolved to make his permanent home in the land of the free. Having a son born to him, he was anxious to have him educated in the universities of Germany, and it was arranged that the mother should remain in Germany with the son until his education was completed. The father, returning to Catlettsburg, commenced at once to prepare the way for mother and son to join him so soon as the boy's education was finished. After many trips, on the part of the father, over the sea, young Albin's mental training was completed, and in 1877 the family were all together in Catlettsburg.

ALBIN STEIN.

Albin is the junior member of the firm of Charles Stein & Son, tanners, Catlettsburg, now the most important industry in the place. The Steins are an educated people. Albin speaks several languages with fluency. He is an official member in the Presbyterian Church, is an ardent Odd Fellow and Mason, and a young man of society.

BENJAMIN SPRADLING,

Of Paintsville, who is near ninety years old, came to the neighborhood, where he still lives, from Lee County, Virginia, in 1796. Wild beasts and Indians roamed the valleys and hills when he first came to the country. But his good genius and strong constitution have been sufficient to successfully withstand these, for he is as hale and hearty as some men are at sixty. His descendants are numerous, and include many of the best people in Johnson and adjacent counties. He is Paintsville's oldest citizen.

THE CASTLE FAMILY

Is a remarkable family in numbers. They are to be found in every county in the valley. They are mostly farmers, though a number are engaged in the trades, while some are merchants, and some are professional men. James Castle, a former citizen of Johnson County, moved to Missouri several years ago, where one of his daughters developed into great prominence as a vocalist. His son, George W. Castle, is a prominent citizen and lawyer of Louisa. John W. Castle, another son, is postmaster at Paintsville, and is an extensive manufacturer of burial-cases. He is a local preacher in the Methodist Church, South. The James Castle family are Democrats, while many other members of the Castle family in Johnson County are Republicans.

THE STEPPS, OF MARTIN,

CAME to the valley among the first settlers, and were brave pioneers. The older ones were noted hunters. The grandfather of Judge Stepp undertook to construct a plow by making the shovel out of a sugar-kettle. After breaking up the old boiler until he had gotten it in the shape of a shovel for a plow, he was perplexed how to make the hole in which to put the wooden bolt to fasten the iron to the upright. But an idea struck him, and he at once carried out the thought, by which the difficulty was overcome. He cut out a patch from his linen shirt, and stuck it on the old kettle where he wanted the hole made, and ordered his son to place a good load in the trusty rifle, and let her rip. The hole was made and the plow was soon finished, and plowing set in on the Stepp estate. What hardships did our ancestors have to endure in opening up the Sandy Valley to civilization! Old Grandfather Stepp should have had a patent issued to him for his invention.

Judge Stepp, one of his many descendants, was one of the best county judges Martin County has ever had.

THE SCOTT FAMILY,

OF Pike, while not among the oldest of the early-time families, is quite noted for its standing and respectability. William Scott was the oldest ancestor of the family. He came from Virginia, and settled on John's Creek, in Pike County. The Scotts have ranked as good farmers, traders, and merchants. John and Henderson Scott are among the best merchants of the John's Creek Valley. William Scott, their cousin, first husband of Mrs. Ferrell, of Pike, was a very successful merchant at that place, but died many years ago, greatly respected.

THE STAFFORDS,

CONSTITUTING the large and influential house of that name living principally in Johnson, came from Giles County, Va., in 1808, and settled in what is now Johnson County. They have ever been noted for their industry and thrift. Many of the Staffords are wealthy farmers and traders, and stand well in their community. They are Democrats, as a rule; are Methodists and Christians. John Stafford, of White House Shoals, was a man of wealth and great prominence in his day. He raised a large family of sprightly daughters, who became wives of a number of the first young men of the valley. He was a distinguished old-time Methodist, the Stafford mansion being a great stand for the early itinerant preachers, who preached in the house.

JOHN SMITH,

THE father of Lindsay Smith, of Round Bottom, West Virginia, and Edmund M. Smith, of Catalpa, Kentucky, Mrs. Powell, Mrs. Hatton, and Mrs. William Pollard (formerly Mrs. Maupin)—all three living on the waters of the Sandy, near their place of birth—came, when a boy, from North Carolina, about 1809, and took up his abode with his kinsmen, the father and uncles of Abraham and Ross Cyrus. From earliest boyhood he gave signs of the thrift and economy that marked his days of manhood; for John Smith, or Uncle Jack, as he was called by the younger people around him, while he was comparatively young himself (he died before he reached sixty years), was looked upon as the most intensely hard-working man on Sandy, and at the same time one of the best financial managers in his community. Of course, he succeeded in accumulating an ample fortune, owning that splendid farm now owned and occupied by his son, Lindsay Smith, known as the Round Bottom, in West Virginia, on Sandy River, besides much other property. He did a good part for his children, leaving them a handsome competency; and as those traits so essential to success in economic life were transmitted to each of them, even to the third generation, no family on Sandy holds a higher average in material prosperity than the John Smith family, of Round Bottom. Many of his descendants are occupying places of trust and honor in the communities where they live, and no family, taken as a whole, stands better and higher in the social and Church circles than does this noted family. The members of the entire family are either members of, or lean toward, the Methodist Church, South. In politics they are Democrats.

Mr. Smith died about 1856. His consort lingered on the shore of time till 1885, having passed nearly ninety yearly mile-stones before she was followed to the silent city of the dead, loved and honored by her children, grandchildren, and great-grandchildren, and esteemed by her neighbors for her many virtues and Christian graces. Her daughter, Mrs. Hatton, fell a victim to poison, administered by some fiend, who attempted to destroy her entire household, in December, 1886.

Rev. Joe H. Wright, of Wright's Station, married a granddaughter of John Smith and wife. Bascom Butler, the prominent railroad official of the Chatterawha, married another; Hon. Albert Fulkerson, of Kansas, still another; and the accomplished wife of John F. Hager, the noted attorney of Ashland, is also a granddaughter; besides other alliances equally notable. Charles H. Warren, the noted merchant of Rockville, married a great-granddaughter of this honored pair.

THE STEWART FAMILY.

THE Stewart family, of Boyd—or at least the family of which the Hon. James E. Stewart is the representative (for several families bearing the same name are unrelated to each other)—are of Irish descent. James Stewart, grandfather of James E. Stewart, and father of Colonel Ralph Stewart, came from Giles County, Virginia, in 1813, and settled on the Sandy in what was afterwards Lawrence County. Some years after James Stewart came with his family from Giles County, Virginia, his aged father came out to see him. He was born and raised in Ireland, and was the earliest ancestor of this branch of the Stewart family in America, although other branches of the prolific tree had gone from Ireland to Connecticut, from whence they spread west into Pennsylvania and Ohio. Colonel Ralph Stewart, the son of James Stewart, was a young man when he came with his father to the Sandy Valley, for he was born in 1792. In 1829 he married America, daughter of Reuben Canterbury, of Canterbury. His wife was many years younger than he.

Colonel Stewart owned and cultivated a large farm on Durbin Creek, near the Sandy River, where he resided until his death in 1876. He was a man of strict integrity, and was always regarded as one of the prominent men of his county. While not a seeker after place, he filled many positions of trust and honor. He raised a large family of children, who have reflected credit on their good training by him and their mother. Their eldest son,

HON. JAMES E. STEWART,

ON coming to age, studied law, and opened an office at Paintsville in 1855. He soon after married Miss Cynthia, daughter of Lewis Mayo, one of the leading men of the Middle Sandy Valley. The war coming on, 1861, found Mr. Stewart a sympathizer with the Southern side, and for words spoken in its favor he was sent to Camp Chase, where he remained a prisoner for a year or more. On being released by exchange, he returned home. Soon after this the oil fever struck the Sandy Valley, and Mr. Stewart's knowledge of law, and also of business, enabled him to make quite a snug thing out of the venture. After the war he bought a handsome property in Louisa, to which place he moved, and where he still resides. He filled the office of district prosecutor for six years, and also for the same length of time he was judge of the Criminal Court of his district. He filled both offices with great satisfaction to the people. He is now engaged in his law practice, and also in other business. One of his bright sons was called away by death when just entering on what seemed to be a career of usefulness. The Stewarts have ever been Democrats of the most pronounced type, and James E. Stewart is no exception to the rule. They are also Methodists in religion, Mr. Stewart being a prominent layman in the Methodist Episcopal Church, South, at Louisa. Colonel Ralph Stewart's widow died December 27, 1886, aged seventy-four years.

John Stewart, a brother of Colonel Ralph Stewart, married a Miss Burgess, a daughter of an old settler of that name, and one of the ancestors of the house of Burgess, of Boyd and Lawrence.

THE RATLIFF FAMILY

ARE among the oldest settlers on Sandy. James Ratliff was the founder of the house, coming to Pike near the commencement of the present century. He was a man of strong convictions, and always sided with the cause of virtue and morality. His son, General Ratliff, was also a man of great mental vigor and of strong will. For twenty years he was sheriff of his county, and filled other places of trust and honor. A daughter of his is the honored wife of Cob Cecil, Sen., of Catlettsburg, and a sister is the widow of the late John N. Richardson, of Catlettsburg. Mrs. Colonel John Dills, Jr., is a daughter of General Ratliff. W. O. B. Ratliff, a descendant of the general (a grandson), is a man of mark in the valley and a large timber-dealer.

The family has spread over the entire valley, and embraces a host of people, many occupying prominent places in the affairs of life. Firmness and decision of character, with great individuality, are characteristics of the family, which has done much to shape the destiny of the valley. The prominence of this family deserves more than this passing notice; but the author was unable to procure any of the family annals to draw from.

THE RUNYONS,

OF Pond, were North Carolinians. Aaron, the ancestor, came with his wife to what is now Pike County, in 1795. His son John, a little boy, came with them. John was the father of Mitchell, who died near Catlettsburg in 1880, aged fifty-six; his father dying in 1840. In addition to Mitchell were Asa H., who owns a nice farm on the Sandy River, three miles from the mouth, in Boyd County (he moved from Tug Valley in 1884), John C., Thomas, Wm. A., Aaron, and Moses, the youngest. Sarah married William McCoy, and Matilda, another daughter, died young.

The Runyons have ever been noted for industry, economy, and good morals. They are all good livers, and some of them might be called wealthy. They are a strict Baptist family, and keep the faith of their fathers. They are moderate Democrats in politics. They have always taken a decided interest in the cause of education.

RULE FAMILY.

ANDREW RULE, the ancestor of the Rules, was born March 16th, 1787, and died in 1883, aged ninety-six years. He came to Sandy in 1808, and settled on Paint Creek, two miles from Paintsville, in 1813, where he lived all of his life. He was a good farmer and good business man, whose family has ever been noted for thrift and energy. His descendants are numbered among the best in the valley.

JAMES RICHMOND,

IN about 1840, came to the Sandy Valley as an itinerant dry-goods merchant. By close attention to business he became a very successful merchant at the mouth of John's Creek, accumulating considerable wealth. He died suddenly in the early part of the Civil War, leaving a son and a daughter. The son, John Richmond, married a daughter of Samuel Auxier. He is a farmer and storekeeper near the mouth of John's Creek. The daughter is the wife of Elijah Auxier.

JOHN D. MIMS

CAME to the Sandy Valley about 1833, with a stock of goods, and opened a store in Pikeville, Ky. He prospered, and accumulated considerable wealth, having the great ginseng and fur trade as a foundation on which his business rested. In 1854 he moved to Catlettsburg, and continued in business as a merchant there until he was permanently disabled by a paralytic stroke in 1883. He died in 1886. Mr. Mims carried on a large tannery at Catlettsburg for fifteen years. It is now the property of C. Stein & Son. He was a native of Lynchburg, Virginia, and was a young man when he settled in Pikeville. He first married a Miss Atkins, who, dying, left two children—Colonel David A. Mims and Mrs. Martin Fulkerson. He then married a Miss Friend, of Prestonburg, a sister of Mrs. John Henry Ford and of Mrs. Captain A. C. Hailey. A number of sons and two daughters were born of the latter marriage. One of the daughters (the eldest) married a Mr. Kilgore, and lives in Minnesota. The youngest daughter married W. T. Young, and lives in Catlettsburg. Three of the sons—Robert, Theodore, and John—live in Minnesota. Colonel David A. Mims is a real-estate dealer in Garden City, Kansas. Lon Mims, another son, is a prosperous wholesale hardware merchant at Catlettsburg. Few men for fifty years filled a more prominent position in Sandy commerce than did John D. Mims.

CAPTAIN THOMAS D. MARCUM.

Josiah Marcum, the great-grandfather of Captain T. D. Marcum, settled in the Lower Sandy Valley almost as early as any other settler on the Sandy. His seat was near where Cassville, Virginia, now stands. He was a typical hunter, and encountered the roving Indians. Like most hunters, Josiah was an expert gunsmith, which art has descended to many of his offspring. The subject of this sketch when a small boy worked at the business with his father, who was, in addition, a blacksmith as well. The opportunities of Captain Marcum to obtain an education were few indeed. Being the oldest of a large family, he was kept busy in the shop and on the farm, assisting in making a support for his little brothers and sisters. But having a bright, active

CAPTAIN T. D. MARCUM.

mind, and an inherent determination to rise in the world, he applied himself to the study of every book on education which fell in his way, and obtained all the advantages possible while attending the few and imperfect schools possible for him to attend. With these disadvantages to contend against, it is greatly to his credit that, on reaching eighteen years of age, he was found teaching school at the Falls of Tug, and was held to be the best teacher in the country.

When the war against the Government at Washington came upon the country, young Marcum, at an early period, declared for the Union, and enlisted as a private in the 14th Kentucky Volunteer Infantry. He was made lieutenant, and at the battle of Middle Creek, in 1862, acted with great gallantry as aid to the commander on that occasion. He went with the regiment in its marches through Georgia, and by his dash and courage was often on the staff of his superior officer. In 1864 he was made captain of his company. After serving with bravery and courage for some time, he resigned, and came home, and immediately commenced the study of the law. He was admitted to the bar at Louisa, Ky., where he practiced until he was elected register of the land-office in 1875, running ahead of his ticket. It is conceded by his political friends and opponents that he made the best register ever filling the office.

In 1878 he came with his family to Catlettsburg, and started the *Kentucky Democrat*, which he still edits and publishes. Quotations from the columns of the *Democrat* are more numerous than from most papers of the State. The circulation is greater than any country political paper in the State.

Captain Marcum aided his five younger brothers in obtaining an education, and helped them to a better way in life. Of the six brothers, four are lawyers—one the attorney of Lawrence County; one the county attorney of Wayne County, W. Va.; and another a bright lawyer at Cassville; while another brother holds an important office in the legislative department of West Virginia. Still another is a prominent business man and marshal of the town of Catlettsburg.

Captain Marcum has a wife and two grown daughters, and a son. The family are refined, and grace the best circles of social life. The entire household are working members of the Baptist Church.

As an editor Captain Marcum uses a free lance, and cuts keen; but after an affray he is as calm as any knight of the quill dare be, and holds himself ready for the next fray.

THE AUXIERS.

THE following family annals of the Auxiers were furnished the author by Major John B. Auxier, of John's Creek. The major is now seventy years old, and has a vivid recollection of many things that occurred sixty years ago; but most of the information he gives was obtained from his father and his father's three oldest brothers, from his great uncle, Simon Auxier, and from old Mother Hager, the mother of General Daniel Hager, who is himself now an octogenarian.

The great-great-grandfather of Major Auxier, brothers and sister, came to Pennsylvania from the Rhine, in Germany, in 1755. His wife was a Hollander. They lived in Pennsylvania until after the Revolutionary War. They had five sons. Simon, the oldest, served seven years, or during the Revolutionary War. He was under Washington at the battle of Trenton; was with the troops sent from Virginia to aid General Greene in the South; was at the battle of Guilford Court-house, and was at Yorktown when Cornwallis surrendered. Samuel, the grandfather of Major John B., volunteered when fifteen years old, and served the last three years of the war; the other boys were too young to make soldiers.

After that war the major's great-grandfather, whose given name was Michael, settled in Russell County, Virginia. His son Samuel, the grandfather of the major, came with his wife, Sally Brown, to the Block-house Bottom in 1791. The Hammons and some other families came with them, and built two block-houses one-half a mile below the mouth of John's Creek. On the 7th of August, in the same year, Samuel Auxier, father of the major, was born.

In 1795 the grandfather of the major moved down into the Bottom.

In 1798 or '99 the few men in the neighborhood agreed to meet at the mouth of Middle Creek and go on a buffalo-hunt. When the horn sounded to move, the grandfather of the major, then in his prime, fell back from the main body of huntsmen, and to overtake them spurred on his horse, which shied against a tree, and so wounded him that he died in eight or nine days. He was buried in the Block-house Bottom. His death was felt to be a great loss to the early settlers.

In 1813 the major's father, the late Samuel Auxier, married Rebecca Phillips, by whom he had eleven children, seven sons and four daughters. Nat., the father of A. J. Auxier, of Pike, whose picture adorns this book, was the oldest. The wife of Samuel Auxier died in 1835, after which he married Agnes Wells. By her he had five children, three sons and two daughters. Margaret was the oldest and Ann the youngest. Sixteen children in all composed the Samuel Auxier family. This numerous host of children grew to honorable manhood and womanhood, and, without an exception, formed matrimonial alliances with families of high social and moral standing in the valley. The Auxiers are related to most of the better people of the valley.

The grandmother of Major Auxier, wife of the Auxier who was killed while on the buffalo-hunt, and great-grand-aunt of W. W. Brown, of Paintsville, died in about 1862, aged ninety-nine years. Simon Auxier, the grand-uncle of the major, died near the Mouth in 1825. Michael, one of his brothers, died at ninety-nine years of age, in Adams County, Ohio, where he lived with his son-in-law. This was in sight of Vanceburg, Ky.

In 1801 or 1802 Samuel Auxier, the father of the major, had a little son named Elijah. He was some three years old. He followed his brother Daniel into the woods, where he was chopping timber. There was a thick cane-brake from the house to the woods; but a swath had been cut out, leading from the house to the timber. Soon the little fellow grew tired of being away from his mother, and asked permission to go home. Daniel, thinking of no danger to the child, placed him on the track and started him homeward. All the afternoon Daniel thought the boy safe at home with his mother; the mother, meanwhile as confident he was with his brother. When night came on, and Daniel returned to the house, he was horror-stricken not to see the child. The mother, of course, was frantic at the absence of her little pet. Couriers were sent out in great haste to Damron's Fort, near Pike, and the little settlement near Prater, and over to the Station on Licking, notifying the men that little 'Lige Auxier was lost in Block-house Bottom. The men were not invited to go in search of the lost child; but, true to the native instinct of humanity so conspicuous in the early settlers, they took up their rifles and a wallet of wild meat, and started on the run to the scene of distress. Some of the brave, noble men sprang from their leafy beds, and sallied forth on their mission of mercy. Who does not feel like offering up a petition to the Father of all good to send blessings down on the heads of their descendants? The men divided in sections, and scoured the country for miles around, never giving up the search until a week had passed.

Some wild beast had dragged the little boy to its lonely den, and devoured him.

Daniel Boone was certainly on Sandy. In 1795 or '96 he came to the Block-house, and joined Nat. Auxier, the uncle of the major, in a bear, deer, and wolf hunt on Greesy Creek, in what is now Johnson County. They built a camp on that stream, still known as Boone's Camp. A post-office, bearing the name, is located at the camp; M. L. K. Wells, a brother-in-law of Dr. Z. Meek, is the postmaster. Nat's Creek, below, was named after Nat. Auxier, who killed many bears, deer, and wolves on the serpentine stream.

The author has used the name of Major John B. Auxier to save space, and as the major is now the oldest living representative of the sturdy house of Auxier, so famous in the valley, the other members of the family can not but justify us in this course. The Auxiers were always respected, and were qualified to fill any public trust; but their modesty has always been equal to their bravery, and seldom has any of them stood for office. John B. has been surveyor of his county, and was a major in the Union army. Nathaniel, the father of A. J. Auxier, now of Pike, was by many regarded as the most brainy man of his day. He died in 1867. His son, A. J., is a lawyer and filled for one term the office of District Attorney with great vigor. He has also been United States Marshal for the District of Kentucky. Other members of the house have filled official stations. Of the sixteen children of Samuel Auxier, thirteen still survive. In politics the Auxiers are divided. In religion they are Methodists, and mostly belong to the Southern branch.

NATHANIEL AUXIER.

When Major Auxier was born, not a church was found in the valley; coffee was unheard of; a calico dress was a curiosity. Mortars to pound the corn into meal, and the slow grinding hand-mill, were generally in use, with only here and there a horse-mill. Bear's-grease was used for shortening, and deer-skins to make breeches for the men and moccasins for the women. School-houses were mere shanties, and school-teachers generally took their grog to school. Yet faithful preachers went up and down the valley, preaching a better life for the people. Many heard them gladly, and opened their houses for the preaching of the Word. On the Lavisa Fork the people were mostly Methodists; on Tug, they were generally Baptists.

Slaves were numerous, Tom May, of Shelby, owning seventy-one; yet no one was "stuck up" that held them. The people were all on an equality.

The living was just splendid. Plenty of bear-meat, venison, pheasant, and wild turkey, accompanied with maple molasses, wild honey in the comb, and spice-wood or other native teas, formed a home-fare good enough to tempt the appetite of an epicurean, especially when the brown johnnycake was taken into account. Now the people on Sandy have all the luxuries of life. They live in painted houses, and sleep on downy beds; the ladies are clothed in satin, and the men look with contempt on homespun wear. But are they as happy as their noble ancestors? The people of the present generation are more knowing than their fathers, and therefore their responsibilities are greater. Let the descendants of the old-time people do as well in proportion to their opportunities, as did their fathers, and the valley will blossom as the rose in material, intellectual, social, and religious prosperity.

REV. Z. MEEK, D. D.
(See frontispiece for portrait.)

THE REV. ZEPHANIAH MEEK, editor and founder of the *Central Methodist*, for a short time called the *Christian Observer*, may be properly styled a man of destiny. He is now (1887) about fifty-four years of age, but when in his usual good health looks much younger. He is a Big Sandian by birth and education; Johnson is his native county. His father was a man of sprightly mind, lacking only aspiration to have brought him to the front as a foremost citizen in any community. His mother was a woman of strong mind and great force of character, rounded up by a sweet Christian spirit. She was a model of industry, economy, and thrift, more than supplementing her husband's efforts in rearing to manhood and womanhood a large family of sons and daughters, many of them now occupying advanced and honorable places in the community where they live.

Zephaniah, the second son, like most Big Sandy boys, as well as girls, married young. He chose for his wife Miss Mary Jane Davis, a member of an honorable, old-time Sandy Valley family. She, by her solid sense, wise counsel, and fervent piety, has proven herself a worthy helpmate all along the road of married life. He, with his young wife, after a few years in business in the country, settled in Paintsville, the capital of Johnson County. Having in his boyhood days but few opportunities to procure an education, he used these the best he could, and supplemented the lack of high-schools and academies by reading and studying the best books obtainable by loan or purchase. By systematic study, consecutively pursued, he was at thirty superior in knowledge and mental culture to almost any of his age in his native county. His religious independence in his early youth was so marked as to cause him to pass by the door of the church of his own people to enter the communion of one more liberal and broad in doctrine and discipline. He at once entered upon a career which, under the circumstances, is almost marvelous.

In early life he taught school, like most men who have come to prominence. Then he acted as county and Circuit Court clerk, and for some years mercantile pursuits engaged his time, all the while adding to his fund of knowledge by every means within his grasp.

On coming to manhood he was licensed to preach as a local or lay preacher in the Methodist Episcopal Church, South, the only organization of Methodism above Louisa, from the separation in 1844 to the time of the war in 1864. He was regarded as a strong man in his Church, as well as an enterprising citizen in his community.

Soon after the close of the war in 1865, having made considerable money in oil speculations, he moved to Catlettsburg, and made investments there. In the Spring of 1867 he started the *Christian Observer*, now called *Central Methodist*, as an organ of his Church, employing Rev. Shadrach Hargiss, a man of culture and ability, but broken in health and destitute of means, to assist him in its management. It soon took high rank, and every week showed improvements on the paper. At first the printing was done by contract at the *Herald* office; but the young editor chafed under the restraints and drawbacks incident to that mode of getting out the paper, and at once settled the question by purchasing an interest in the *Herald* office, adding a power-press and many other needed appendages. This was in 1868. The name of the paper was changed to that of *Central Methodist,* and it was made a sixteen-page paper, rivaling in workmanship, artistic beauty, and general appearance any Church paper of the denomination in whose interest it is published, and superior to the majority, not only in mechanical make-up, but in the ability of its editorials and correspondence.

By the editor's wise management, the paper has attained an unprecedentedly large circulation, which is constantly increasing. He displays as much ability in selecting matter for the columns of the paper, and by culling over the correspondence, as he does in the vigor of his prolific editorials. The

Central Methodist has been a power in lengthening the cords and strengthening the stakes of Southern Methodism in more conferences than one where it circulates. While the editor has his whole mind on the welfare of his paper, and, of course, has chosen the high and exalted plane of theology in which to display his talents, it is well known by many persons conversant with the fact, that it is not only in the field of religious journalism that he excels, but he is equally at home when his trenchant pen is inditing matter for a political paper. It has been an open secret for more than a decade of years that he was the author of the vigorous and scathing articles which appeared in the *Herald*, a Democratic weekly, in 1874, which attracted such wide attention at the time, but were attributed to another.

Mr. Meek has given to all of his numerous children, who have arrived at suitable age, a classical education, and to one a university course; while another son and all his daughters were trained in the halls of a college. The Rev. Lafayette Meek, his first-born, after being trained in the East Kentucky Normal School, spent a year in Millersburg College, but transferred to Vanderbilt University, taking a varied course, and finishing up in the School of Theology. Leaving there, he went out into the itinerant field in the Tennessee Conference, but, almost at the threshold of what seemed to be the commencement of a successful ministry, was stricken down with that fell disease, typhoid fever.

He was brought from the malaria-smitten region of West Tennessee, his young wife with her infant accompanying him, to his father's house, where he was nursed with loving care, and attended by the most scientific physicians, hoping also that a change from the polluted air that smote him down, to the uncontaminated breath of his native mountains, would restore him to health and usefulness. But God ruled otherwise. He died on the 2d day of October, 1885, in the thirty-first year of his age, mourned by all his relatives, and lamented by all others who had formed his acquaintance.

Mr. Meek has two other grown sons, both well trained in the "art preservative of all arts," upon whom chiefly falls the duty of performing the mechanical work of printing and mailing the paper, while a bright daughter, Miss Hessie, greatly aids her overworked father in performing the literary and clerical labor in the office.

Technically, Mr. Meek is a traveling elder in his conference, but only takes such pastoral charges as are within his reach, selecting entirely new territory in which to perform his ministerial work, his ardent labors on his paper being too pressing to allow of constant labor in the pastorate. He received the degree of D. D. from the Kentucky Military Institute, Farmdale, Kentucky, in 1885, which high honor he wears with becoming dignity. He was elected the leading delegate to the General Conference by the Western Virginia Conference, in

1885. This was the more remarkable because at the time of the election he was barely eligible to that distinguished position. The General Conference met in Richmond, Virginia, May, 1886.

THE BURNS FAMILY.

THE Burnses, of Sandy, are of Scotch origin, and came along the same line of descent as Robert Burns, the illustrious poet. On the maternal side, Elizabeth Roland, of a family made famous in French Huguenot history, is their ancestor. Jerry Burns, who was the father of Roland T. Burns, was in the Revolutionary War. His father and uncle came from Scotland and settled in Maryland. Jerry married, and from his first union had two sons. They went South-west and became noted people.

After the death of his first wife, Mr. Burns, who was a noted Methodist preacher of his day, at one of his great preaching-places first saw Miss Elizabeth Roland, who was a devout worshiper at his meeting. In song she was wonderfully gifted. She was a brunette of a most perfect type; hair as black as a raven, heavy eye-brows, a curved lip, and a faultless figure. The preacher fell in love with her. She accepted his hand and heart, and they became one flesh. Some of their children were born in the valley of Virginia; others were born in Monroe County, Va., where they had moved about the commencement of the present century. The younger ones were born near the Mouth of the Sandy.

We have only space to note the more striking historical events in the career of the descendants of Jerry Burns and Elizabeth Roland, who were the founders of the Burns house in the Sandy Valley. No pair in the State has been so highly honored by the great number of descendants rising to distinction in law, theology, and official stations as Jerry Burns and wife. A son went to Missouri, where his descendants are in high official place. One was a representative in Congress. Another went to Oregon, and his descendants rose to distinction. California was invaded by another son. He, too, left a name above the common walks of life. A daughter married James M. Rice, who was not only a great lawyer, but a circuit judge and a senator besides. Judge Rice's youngest son, John M., is now the criminal judge of his district, after twice being congressman and State legislator; and the elder brother, Jake, was lawyer and legislator.

Roland T. Burns, the father of W. H. Burns, John M. Burns, La Fayette Burns, Roland T. Burns, and Elizabeth Handley, was a farmer, a preacher, lawyer and legislator. He owned and lived on the farm that is now the homestead of John Powers, on Bear Creek, Boyd County. He practiced his legal profession in a large district, and represented Lawrence and Morgan Counties for two terms in the Legislature. He preached often, and worked with his own hands on his farm. His wife, Miss Margaret Keyser, was a noble Christian wife and mother. Mr. Burns died at forty-three years of age, in 1834.

The youngest sister of Roland T. Burns was the wife of O. W. Martin, a lawyer from Virginia.

Of the children of Roland T. Burns and Margaret Keyser, his wife, Wm. Harvey was a fine lawyer, and lived in West Liberty, Ky., until the commencement of the Civil War, when he moved to Lebanon, Va., where he had great success in accumulating a vast fortune. He was serving as circuit judge in his district when he left the State, preferring the Southern cause. He had great ability as a lawyer, and was an able, upright judge. His brother, John M. Burns, is now serving on the bench as circuit judge of the same district, in his election carrying every county but one. Judge John M. Burns has a son, Roland C., who is at the front as a criminal lawyer in the valley. Another son is a physician, who, in addition, is possessed of literary gifts, showing the fire of his illustrious ancestor in Scotland. La Fayette Burns is a practical farmer, living near the old homestead of his father, greatly respected by his neighbors. Roland T. Burns, of Louisa, is an able lawyer, and is also engaged in merchandising. He is a man of great ability, and could reach almost any official position to which he might aspire; but, being a devout Christian, he ignores the shameful methods used by many seekers of place to gain office; and, furthermore, being a man of wealth and careful in business, he thinks "a bird in the hand is worth two in the bush." All the Burnses are Democrats, excepting Hon. John M. Burns and his sons; and most of them are Southern Methodists, John M. again proving the exception, he being a Regular Baptist. The only living sister of the illustrious Burns brothers is Mrs. Elizabeth Handley, wife of Alexander Handley, of Wayne County, West Virginia. She, like her father and brothers, is talented, and one of the most devoted wives and mothers.

JUDGE JOHN M. BURNS.

The Burnses, until the alliance with Elizabeth Roland, a French beauty of the perfect brunette caste, were all blondes, but the blood of the Huguenots has changed the type of the family to a full brunette.

We could name several more official places filled by this gifted family, but space forbids.

JUDGE ARCHIBALD BORDERS.

ARCHIBALD, son of John Borders, was born in Giles County, Virginia, in 1798, and came, with his father's family, to the Sandy Valley in 1802. His father intended going on to the Scioto country, but falling sick, stopped near the mouth of Tom's Creek, in what is now Johnson County, where he died, leaving a widow and eight children—four sons and four daughters. The oldest son settled on George's Creek, where he died in 1882, at the age of eighty-two. John, the second son, also settled on George's Creek. He died in 1879 or '80. He was a highly respected Baptist

JUDGE ARCHIBALD BORDERS.

preacher. He, too, lived to a great age. Hezekiah settled on the Sandy River at what is known, and has been for sixty years, as Borders Chapel. He and his wife were great Methodists, and no Methodist preacher ever passed by the chapel during their lives who did not call to see these pious people. They passed to their reward many long years ago; but a son of theirs, the now aged Joseph Borders—the father of Joe H. Borders, once a journalist of the Sandy Valley, but now a banker in Kansas—owns and lives at the old homestead, to represent his honored ancestors. The chapel has been rebuilt, and is the best-looking log church in the valley. Polly, the oldest daughter, married Isom Daniels. They settled on the farm two miles below Tom's Creek, now the home of Peter Daniels, one of their sons. She died during the Civil War. The father and mother left a large number of sons and daughters, who have come to honor. More than one of the sons is a Baptist minister. Betty married Joseph Davis. They settled on the banks of the Sandy, at a place well known as Davis Bend.

This branch of the family also rose to honor. The wife of Rev. Z. Meek, D. D., is a daughter of this honored pair. John Davis, formerly a leading business man of Paintsville, was their son. William Davis, the large land-owner in Lawrence and Johnson Counties, is another son. Daniel, the wealthy business man and prominent Republican politician of Johnson County, is a grandson. Jemima married Felty Van Hoose. Katie, the youngest, married John Brown, who became a wealthy farmer and a noted old-time hotel-keeper on George's Creek. She is the only one still alive of all the John Borders family, and, although over eighty, is a well-preserved old lady. Her husband died in 1875.

It will be seen that the entire household of the first Borders who came to Sandy have occupied the highest positions known to ordinary life; and without detracting from them any meed of praise, it is true to say that the brother who was the youngest outranked them all, if not in moral worth, in great business plans.

ARCHIBALD BORDERS,

WHEN a little past twenty-one, married Jane Preston, a daughter of Moses Preston the first, and a sister of "Coby" Preston. They settled near Whitehouse Shoals, and lived there until two of their children were born, when they moved down to the farm which he possessed when he died. He opened up a large and productive farm, ran a large store, a tannery, shoe-factory, and saddlery. Those branches of trade and industries, it would seem, were enough to occupy the full time of any one man; but he also was one of the largest tan-bark and timber traders then on the Sandy. Nor did he fail in either. In 1860 he built the steamer *Sandy Valley*, a boat equal to any of the Sandy steamers of to-day. He was not only a man of great industry and business capacity, but was a gentleman of the most refined tastes. He established a large park on his plantation, stocked with a herd of the native deer of the mountains, which not only supplied his table with venison, but the gambols of the beautiful creatures added pleasure to himself, his family, and others. He continued to attend to business up to within a year or so of his death, which occurred November 12, 1886.

He accumulated a vast amount of land and other property, leaving his children well off. During his busy life he was a friend of Churches and schools, and gave much to support them, yet never made a public profession of Christianity until within a month of his death. His conversion was miraculous. He prayed the Father to send him the witness of his Spirit, and make it so plain that he could have no doubt, as he was too weak to prove his conversion by an examination of the Word of God. He was satisfied, and then asked the great Jehovah to reveal to him how he should receive the ordinance of baptism, whether by immersion or sprinkling. He was told to be sprinkled. He immediately sent for his kinsman, Rev. Z. Meek, D. D., who baptized him and admitted him into the Methodist Episcopal Church, South.

Archibald Borders was more than an ordinary man, or he could not have borne so many burdens, and live up to the age of eighty-eight years. He was foreman of the grand jury that indicted one Walker, who forfeited his life on the gallows at Louisa for murder. He filled the office of justice of the peace in Lawrence County from 1834 to 1850, when it expired by the death of the old Constitution. The same year he was elected the first county judge of Lawrence, and was re-elected in 1854, serving for eight years. During the great Civil War the Borders family were Union people, but always conservative. Since the war the judge and his son David, a wealthy citizen of Lawrence, have voted oftener for men and measures than at the suggestions of party managers.

Judge Borders and his wife, Jane Preston, had five children—four sons and one daughter. Of the sons, John and Arthur have long been dead. David, to whom we have already referred, is a widower, living on a farm near his father's old home, and takes the world easy. Allen P. has one of the finest brick residences on the Sandy River. His wife is a daughter of the late Lewis Mayo, so well remembered for his noble traits of character. Julia, the only daughter, is the wife of J. W. Dillon, a leading man in the business circles of Catlettsburg. After the death of her father, Mrs. Dillon had her invalid mother brought down to her home, where she might better attend to her many wants until the candle of her life, which for twenty years has been flickering down low in the socket, became extinguished.

Among the most prominent contemporaries of Judge Borders in Lawrence, not yet named, the author may mention John D. Ross, Major Bolt, Neri Sweatnam, Walter Osburn, and Greenville Goble, the father of M. B. Goble, of Catlettsburg. All these, save Mr. Sweatnam, were called upon to fill official stations, and Mr. Sweatnam was as useful in private as he could have been in a public station.

Walter Osburn and John D. Ross are all that linger on the shore of time. These were, and are, honorable names.

THE LACKEY FAMILY.

OF the many noted families coming to the Sandy Valley in its early settlement, none were more conspicuous than the house of Lackey. Alexander Lackey, the founder of the house west of the mountains, came from Southern Virginia in 1804, and settled at the Forks of Beaver, in Floyd County. He married the daughter of David Morgan, a relative of General Daniel Morgan, of Battle of the Cowpens fame.

Mr. Lackey brought slaves and considerable property with him from his home in Virginia. Commencing the world under favorable auspices, with property, selecting one of the richest tracts of land in the valley, and backed by his clear judgment and iron will, he soon rose to distinction, both as a successful business man and as a public personage. He filled many offices of trust and honor, both county and State; was a representative in the Legislature, judge and sheriff, and rose to be a general in the militia of his district. He reared and educated, in the best schools obtainable, a family of sons and daughters who have added luster to the name they bore.

MORGAN LACKEY,

OF Prestonburg, son of Alexander, was a delegate in the convention of 1849, that framed the present Constitution of Kentucky, and filled other offices, civil and military, with honesty and fidelity. Most of his life he has been a successful merchant at Prestonburg, where he is regarded as a citizen of the highest attainments in every thing that constitutes true manhood. Like all of his family, Morgan Lackey has been not only a Democrat of Democrats, but has ever been regarded as a sagacious politician. But with all this urging him forward as a worker within the lines of his party, when he witnessed men of the brightest intellect and social standing in his town, county, and section falling into drunkards' graves, snapping asunder the heart-strings of mothers, wives, and sisters, he called a halt, and demanded of his fellow-citizens that party lines should be loosened until intemperance, the fountain of all wrong, was driven from the Sandy Valley forever. By marshaling the forces of temperance, law, and order, through his potent influence every grog-shop was driven from his town, where the poisonous fluid had for sixty-five years held one continuous carnival of death. Not satisfied with driving the monster from the town, the war was carried into every precinct in the county, and to-day (1887) not a drop of liquor is sold according to law in the county.

Morgan Lackey is unmarried, and lives with his sister, the widow of Hon. J. P. Martin. Being wealthy, he, as he grows in years, spends much of his time in leisure, cultivating those virtues which lead to a happy old age and a peaceful death.

GREENVILLE M. LACKEY,

ANOTHER son of General Alexander Lackey, has made a history as bright as that of his younger brother, Morgan. He has filled a seat in both Houses of the Kentucky Legislature, and has borne other official honors with credit to himself and profit to his constituents. For more than thirty years he has resided at Louisa, during all of which time he has been a prominent merchant there. He is, unlike his brother, a married man, and has two sons and one daughter. One son, Alexander, named after his grandfather, is a lawyer, rising to fame, while the other has been engaged in merchandising and official business. The daughter is the wife of Thomas R. Brown, a son of Hon. George N. Brown, a young lawyer of much promise. A daughter of General Lackey married

HON. JOHN P. MARTIN,

WHO came from Virginia about 1828, and commenced the practice of law in Prestonburg, where he soon rose to distinction as an able lawyer and eloquent speaker. He occupied a seat in both Houses of the State Legislature, and was twice elected to the Congress of the United States. Mr. Martin was one of the most brilliant men of his time, and his suavity of manners made him popular with his fellow-citizens of all parties. He died at Prestonburg in 1863. Mr. Martin left a son,

ALEXANDER L. MARTIN,

WHO, like his father, was an able man and a prominent lawyer of his native town. He filled the office of State senator, and received the honor of having the county of Martin named for him, and the county seat of Elliott to perpetuate his name. He married a daughter of Judge George N. Brown— a lady of rare grace and loveliness.

Mr. Martin had apparently started out on a long and brilliant life, when death, which loves a shining mark, claimed him as a victim, and in 1877 he ceased to live. His wife survived him a short time, when she, too, suddenly gave up the struggle for life, and joined the great throng on the shining shore. They left a bright little boy, whose sparkling eyes and manly form show signs of future promise; and a little daughter, of bright and winsome mien.

The eldest daughter of Hon. John P. Martin married a Mr. Trimble, a scion of the house of that name—a prominent family both in Kentucky and Virginia. Mr. Trimble died during the Civil War, leaving a widow and two sons, Malcolm and James. Both received the best of moral and intellectual training, and on arriving to young manhood engaged in merchandising in their native town, Prestonburg. But when the Catlettsburg National Bank was opened, the moral, social, and financial standing of the Trimble brothers was so fully known that James, the younger, was given a prominent position in the official directory of the bank, where he still is, respected and trusted by all.

Malcolm continued his mercantile course until disease preyed upon his constitution, and he was borne to the city of the dead, loved, by all who ever knew him, for his many Christian virtues and his manly bearing. He died in 1885.

The mother of James and Malcolm, several years after the war, married a gentleman from Virginia, named Armstrong, a lawyer. They soon after moved to Missouri, where, a few years ago, she died. The younger daughter, Miss Mousie, married Captain John C. Hopkins, who came of a prominent family of Tazewell County, Virginia. He is a lawyer by profession, but is engaged largely in the steamboat interest on Sandy. The family lives in Catlettsburg. Mrs. Hopkins, like all of her father's children, received a classical education at college.

SAMUEL DAVIDSON

MARRIED another daughter of General Lackey. Mr. Davidson was a bright man from Virginia. He reared a large family of sons and daughters, who married into prominent families of the valley, strengthening the house not only in numbers, but in influence. One son, especially, rose to be one of the most popular and influential men ever living at Prestonburg.

JOSEPH M. DAVIDSON

WAS a man of a high order of talent. He had received a fine scholastic training; after which, by study and travel, he so polished his nature and enriched his mind that few men in Eastern Kentucky were more finished than he. He had been in the Legislature of the State, and was one of its shrewd, bright politicians. He was a merchant and trader of great prominence, and for some time a banker in connection with his cousin, Green M. Witten, at Catlettsburg. He was a large land-owner in his county, and took a deep interest in his county's welfare. He was a very handsome man, and as manly as he was handsome. He died in the vigor of his manhood in 1883, leaving a widow and several grown-up daughters. The oldest married Mr. Fitzpatrick, the clerk of the Floyd courts. Walter S. Harkins, a brilliant attorney of the same place, married another daughter. Frank Hopkins married one of the daughters, and Mr. Schmucker still another. No man ever died in Floyd whose death created such a void as Joseph M. Davidson's.

THOMAS WITTEN,

From Tazewell County, Virginia, married another daughter of Alexander Lackey. They lived principally in Tazewell County, although Mr. Witten, for many years, was a business man on Sandy. They had two sons, who were well educated in Tazewell, and trained in mercantile affairs. The youngest son died fighting on the Southern side, believing it was his sacred duty. The other son, Green M. Witten, spent most of his youth and younger manhood in merchandising at Prestonburg, Ky.; and for many years he was a noted banker of Catlettsburg, where he now lives. He is one of the best informed men on most topics to be found in the valley. The father has long been dead, and the mother more recently quit the shores of time, dying on her way to her home in Tazewell County, Va., from a visit to friends in the Sandy Valley.

General Alexander Lackey, the founder of his house in the Valley of the Sandy, was a Baptist, but was liberal to all Churches. He often spoke at religious meetings, although but a layman. The greater part of his descendants are adherents of the Southern Methodist Church. Mrs. Captain Hopkins and Mrs. Thomas R. Brown, granddaughters, are Presbyterians. The general and every one connected with the family, to the fifth generation, have been Democrats; and Mrs. Mousie Hopkins informs us that, in time of the war, she was a rebel. Most of the men are Masons.

HON. M. J. FERGUSON.

The Fergusons of the Lower Sandy Valley are of Scotch-Irish descent. More than two hundred years ago a Ferguson went over to the North of Ireland from his Scottish home and married a Miss Jemison, an Irish lady. From this pair have descended the Ferguson family to whom we now refer. The given name of so many of the Ferguson family is derived from their Irish maternal ancestor. The Fergusons are a plucky, progressive people, and have held a conspicuous place in the public affairs of their country and a prominence in business pursuits.

Joseph Ferguson, of Ashland, is a prominent man. He

JUDGE MILTON J. FERGUSON.

served as captain in the Confederate army with distinction; but, like his great brother, when the war was over he accepted the results with grace, and settled down to business, doing all he could to make up for the waste the war had brought upon the land. Charles, too, is a true man. He is a merchant and farmer at Wayne Court-house, West Virginia.

Colonel M. J. Ferguson was the great representative of his house. He was born in 1833, in Wayne County, Virginia, a few miles from Cassville, and when but twenty-six years old was looked upon as the foremost man of his county. He was county attorney; but, in addition to the duties of his office, he had an immense business in settling up estates, and other delicate and responsible trusts of great magnitude were committed to him, which he managed with such consummate ability as to receive the plaudits of the wisest financiers. He married a daughter of Samuel Wellman, a wealthy citizen of Wayne.

When the call sounded to arms in 1861, Jemison Ferguson, as every one called him, being a man of ardent temperament, rushed into the thickest of the fight. His education and feelings leading him to take sides with the South, he raised a regiment and was mustered into the Confederate service, and served with bravery and honor during the great struggle. When the war was over he held no spite against those who had been successful in ending the conflict in favor of the old Government, but went heroically to work to smooth over the places made crooked by the war, and it was hard to decide who admired his political liberality most, those who fought with him or those who were arrayed against him. He soon settled in Louisa, and in 1868 ran for circuit judge of the Big Sandy Judicial District. He was overwhelmingly elected, and served with great distinction and ability the term of six years. He then retired, to look after his great material interests and to practice his chosen profession. Few men did more to encourage the building of the Chatterawha Railroad than he. He favored every enterprise which was calculated to add to the material, educational, and moral wealth of the valley. He was cut off in the midst of his usefulness and busy labors, dying on the 22d of April, 1881. Few deaths could have produced a greater sorrow than did that of Judge Ferguson. He was a Free Mason of high standing, and was an adherent of the Methodist Episcopal Church, South. His motto, all along life's journey, was to do justice to all the world, never to forsake his friends, and fear no man.

He left a wife and two sons. The eldest, Henry Ferguson, is a lawyer at Louisa, having been educated at the University of Virginia. He is a talented young man. He married an educated and lovely lady of his town—Miss Burns, a daughter of R. T. Burns, Esq. The youngest son, Lynn Boyd Ferguson, is the editor and publisher of the Louisa *News*, a sprightly Democratic paper. He has for a partner a young Mr. Conly, son of Asa Conly, a scion, on his mother's side, of the house of Leslie.

The artist has brought out every lineament in the features of Judge Ferguson.

THE GARRED FAMILY.

DAVID GARRED and Jennie Graham, his wife, moved from Monroe County, Virginia, stopping awhile in Kanawha, and settled at the Falls of Tug, about 1820. James, their oldest son, married Polly Wilson. Ulysses married Lydia Stafford, daughter of John Stafford, the wealthy farmer and noted Methodist of Whitehouse Shoals.

Hon. Ulysses Garred has, since coming to manhood, been ranked as one of the foremost citizens of his section. He is a model farmer and trader, and as a hotel-keeper "Garred's Stone House" has for a quarter of a century maintained a reputation second to no other hostelry in the valley. He has been a member of the Legislature, and has filled many other offices of note in his county, always with satisfaction to the people. His wife died a few years ago, greatly regretted by all who knew her; and to her family the loss was irreparable. He has but one son, who married a daughter of Captain A. P. Borders. The son is a farmer, merchant, postmaster, and hotel-keeper at Richardson.

David, the youngest son, married Nancy, daughter of Owen Dyer. This pair have reared a large family. One son is a prominent physician in West Virginia. One is the clerk of the Circuit Court of

Lawrence County. Another is the owner and landlord of the Chatterawha Hotel at Louisa. David has a fine farm on the Sandy, adjoining his brother Ulysses, nine miles above Louisa. Flora married Garred See, a cousin, before the family moved to the Sandy Valley, and moved to Indiana, but soon came to Kentucky. Polly married Richard Chambers. He was a man of good reading and sprightly mind. William Vinson married a daughter of his, and it has been said that, while the Vinsons are a smart people, much of the dash of William Vinson's children came from the Chambers side. Mr. Chambers was a noted Whig politician. Elizabeth married Ira W. Goff, who became the father of Felix and Captain John B. Goff, of Big Creek, Pike County, Kentucky. Felix Goff lives in quiet at Louisa, having a farm in Mississippi, where he once resided. He is a very intelligent man, and a great student. He is an ardent Democrat, and takes great interest in State affairs.

JOHN B. GOFF.

John B. Goff lived a few years in Mississippi, but returned to Sandy in 1858, and has been ever since a citizen of Big Creek. We give his picture, first alone, and then in connection with his two handsome daughters. When the Civil War broke out, he, being an ardent Southern man in feeling, raised a company of men for the Southern army. The company was known as the "Pine-knot" company, from the fact that the captain proposed to arm his men with pine-knots to drive back the Northern soldiery who might come down to invade Southern soil. This step was taken before the captain had obtained a census of the Northern men; but when the "Yanks" began pouring in like Egyptian locusts, Captain Goff, who never was a one-idea man, placed the best of arms in the hands of his brave mountaineers, and used the "knots" for kindling camp-fires. No braver man fought on the Southern side than John B. Goff. He was taken prisoner one year after entering the service, and sent to Camp Chase and to Johnson's Island. He was exchanged, and reached home on the 17th of March, 1865.

JOHN B. GOFF.

The father of the captain and of Felix W. Goff removed to Mississippi before the boys were grown, where he died. The mother died in Louisa, Kentucky.

John B. Goff married Mary E. Small, at Louisa,

in 1858. He has seven children, all daughters but one. The son is at home with the family. Sarah married David Young. Dixie married Floyd W. Murphy, a bright business young man in the neighborhood.

Captain Goff has been, and is still, engaged in merchandising, farming, and general trading. He has a competency, and, like all the Goffs, is liberal in Christian deeds. No one is turned away from his castle who is in need, without being supplied by his liberal hand.

JOHN B. GOFF AND DAUGHTERS.

Jane Garred married Harve Ratliff, and moved to Missouri. Hannah married Charles Wilson. Sarah Ann married Burgess Fitzpatrick, of Patrick's Gap. Minerva married C. C. Kise, who is referred to in another place. Maggie died, on arriving at womanhood, unmarried. Another daughter married William Ratliff, the father of Mrs. William Bartram.

It will be seen that David Garred and Jennie Graham, his wife, raised thirteen children, three sons and ten daughters, all of whom and their descendants, now alive, are living in the valley, except Harold Ratliff and wife, who went to Missouri, where they did well.

The elder Garreds were ardent Whigs in politics, and during the Civil War took sides with the Union. Since the war, they and most of their descendants have allied themselves with the Democratic party. In religion most of them are Southern Methodists, while some are Baptists and of other faiths. It is estimated that over three hundred voters on Sandy have Garred blood in their veins.

The ancestors of the Garreds were Presbyterians before coming to Sandy. David Garred and wife are buried on the high bluff overlooking the farm of their son, Ulysses.

REV. R. D. CALLIHAN.

By the request of my friend, Dr. Ely, I will make a brief statement relative to my entrance into the Valley of the Big Sandy, in which I spent many happy years. In December, 1827, I visited the home of the Hon. F. Moore, who lived on the Virginia side of the said river, about one mile below its forks, or the town of Louisa, the county seat of Lawrence County, Ky. The object of my visit was in search of remunerative labor. I found employment in this family, and during my stay there I found a pleasant home. Mrs. Moore proved to me next to my own dear mother, kind, amiable, pious, and devoted. Perhaps I ought, in vindication of my history in after life, to say that the employment in which I engaged at Mr. Moore's was the distillation of whisky, a business not then regarded as disreputable. For this I was paid so much per gallon. In this labor I remained for about three months, and this closed not only my labor as a distiller, but my employer also abandoned the business.

I refer to this period of my life because it has been circulated by some of the citizens of this date that by selling whisky and other intoxicants I made large amounts of money. This report is untrue. I never drank nor sold any vinous or malt liquor, but for at least sixty-five years have been opposed to the use of every thing that would cause intoxication.

My fidelity to the interest of my employer proved to be a prelude to my future avocation in life. I had acquired his confidence to that extent that he introduced me to the only commercial house of any note in the town of Louisa, or, indeed, in the valley. This I regarded as an advance into a higher state, not only of social, but business life, and with it greater obligations were placed in my hands. The business of this house was conducted under the style of A. Beirne & Co. Mr. Beirne, who lived in the county of Monroe, and State of Virginia, furnished the capital, and three young men of Louisa were regarded as the active business partners, one of whom moved to Pikeville, the county seat of Pike County, Ky., with an assortment of mixed merchandise; and it would have been a valuable branch to the main store at Louisa if it had been conducted prudently. These men, unfortunately, soon formed habits of dissipation and kindred vices, rendering it necessary to close up the business of the firm; and, in doing this, new and greater responsibilities were acquired by me, in becoming the agent, by the mutual consent of the partners, to close up the business; and consequently the firm placed notes and accounts in my hands for collection, amounting to about $17,000. To do this work required at least two years, as I had to travel on horseback over parts of six counties in Kentucky and three in Virginia. After having accomplished this, there being a vacancy of a clerkship in the Pike County Circuit Court, caused by the death of Mr. Honaker, my friends, uniting with the gentlemen of the bar, recommended me to the Hon. Silas W. Robbins, the presiding judge, who, under the old Constitution, appointed his own clerk, and he had the kindness to appoint me as the successor of Mr. Honaker to the office of Circuit Court clerk of said county of Pike. This office I held for twelve years. I then resigned, and the Hon. Kenas Farrow, who succeeded Robbins, appointed Martin Mims as my successor.

My desire then was to engage in merchandising and settle in Pikeville, which I did in April, 1832. But my means were scanty. I had formed the acquaintance of Harry B. Mayo, who lived in Prestonburg, Floyd County, Ky., a gentleman of high and influential standing, with money. Hearing of my wish, he solicited a partnership, which I gladly accepted, and this connection was both harmonious and profitable. Our first purchase was made in Maysville, Ky., April, 1832. We got all safely to our home, and opened our goods. We had a trade beyond our expectation. Our collection of produce, etc., was very satisfactory, so much so that we were induced to seek a different city to make our purchase for the Spring of 1834. My benefactor, Colonel Beirne, visited Pikeville and Louisa, and to him we made known our desire. He approved of it, and kindly and generously gave us an open letter of introduction to the merchants of the city of Philadelphia, on which I could have purchased an unlimited amount of merchandise. But a prominent trait of my life has been that of cautiousness, and hence the purchase was circumscribed to about $3,000.

The business of this year was more gratifying than the preceding; and I must say that our customers showed to us a noble trait of character, which, in all my business life, I have not known excelled—a native promptness in the payment of debts.

I remained in the business of selling goods in that place until the Spring of 1844. During these years I was the humble instrument of redeeming two young men from lives of dissipation, and I had the pleasure of seeing them become sober, discreet business men—men of wealth, ornaments in society, and useful members of the Church of God. In the Spring of 1844 I returned with my family to Louisa, the starting-place of my business life.

I could extend this sketch of my humble life; but I forbear. The more interesting part would be that of my conversion to the religion of our Lord Jesus Christ, which occurred on the 29th of August, 1829, at a camp-meeting, held on what was then called Farmer's Camp-ground, about eight miles south of Ashland, now Boyd County, Ky. But I decline this at present, with this significant truth, that I owe all I am worth to the effects of our holy Christianity, and the fostering care of the Methodist Episcopal Church, with my united industry, economy, and cautiousness in life.

THE HAGER FAMILY,

OF the Sandy Valley, like the Auxier and Moore families, is of the German race. John Hager and Mary Schaefer, his wife, spoke the German language, and used the German Bible to find out God's ways to man. We first hear of them in Amherst County, Va., where their sons, Daniel, George, and John were born, as well as their daughter, who became the wife of James Layne, the father of Judge

THE HAGER FAMILY.

Lindsay Layne. They moved to Floyd County and settled on the Sandy, near the mouth of John's Creek, when their son Daniel was but a few years old. Their other sons grew up to be useful citizens.

George, the eldest, living to a great age, died several years ago in West Virginia. He was the father of Mrs. Van Horn, recently deceased. He was a very religious man, and a great Methodist. Another son was also numbered among the leading people of the valley. But Daniel, by his energy and superior mental endowments always ranked as the leader of the house of Hager. When he came to manhood, in 1820 or 1821, he married Miss Violet Ventrees Porter, daughter of John Porter, of Russell County, Virginia. His wife was a lady of great kindness of heart, and strength of character.

GEN'L DANIEL HAGER.
(Taken in 1846.)

Six sons and six daughters were born to them, all of whom are still living but John J., Henry G., and Ventrees. The sons and daughters, without an exception, married into families of the highest respectability; and the descendants of Daniel Hager, to the third generation, maintain the reputation of their ancestors for intellectual vigor and great energy.

Captain Elijah Patrick, of Magoffin, Captain Frank Preston, Dr. Turner, William Stafford, of Johnson, and Dr. Martin, of Ashland, are all sons-in-law of General Daniel Hager and wife—all foremost men in their communities.

Ventrees was the wife of E. W. Brown, of Morgan. She died some years ago. The sons all grew to manhood, and entered the busy race of life; and each one of them, to this day, has never, by any wrong act, stained the fair escutcheon of the house of Hager. They all developed into wise business men and sterling citizens. John J. went South with the Confederate army, and lost his life. Captain Henry G. was merchant and steamboat-owner, and died in the prime of his busy life. He left three sons and a daughter, who reflect the image of his person and strength of his mind. The daughter is the wife of Captain D. M. Atkinson, a prominent citizen of Salyersville. The second son, John F. Hager, is one of the most prominent lawyers of East Kentucky. He lives in Ashland, and is recognized as one of the leading men there. Milton, the younger brother, is a fine business man at Salyersville, and is a man of intellectual force.

General Hager became comparatively wealthy, and did nobly by his children, not so much in a pecuniary sense as in raising them to think and act for themselves, and to depend on their own efforts to succeed in life. He was for many years a brigadier-general in the militia, was the first sheriff of Johnson County, and served in the Legislature of the State, and in many other places of trust and honor, with great intelligence and integrity.

When the war came upon the country in 1861, General Hager, having all his life been a Jefferson Democrat, logically took sides with the States in rebellion against the General Government, and expressed his sympathies that way. But when his own State refused to go with the South, he quietly settled down in charity to all, and awaited the result. His sons, save the oldest, were either Union men or had the good sense to follow the example first set by their State, and remained neutral.

Daniel, the youngest son, served a term in the Union army. Dr. Martin acted as surgeon in the same cause. Captain Reuben Patrick, another son-in-law, was active as an officer in the war. Captain Henry G. did service, also, as a carrier of supplies during the great struggle.

General Hager has always been a decided Democrat, and most of his sons follow in his footsteps, though Daniel, the youngest, is a Republican. Four of his sons-in-law are Republicans—Captain Patrick, Dr. Martin, Dr. Turner, and E. W. Brown. William Stafford and Captain Preston are Democrats; but the family never let politics destroy personal friendships.

The Hagers are Methodists in religion, and favor all reforms calculated to raise the race to a higher plane of happiness. They are all sober, temperate people. The general and his male descendants are great Masons.

When General Hager was in middle life he was fond of fine horses, as were also two friends of his, Dr. Hereford and Samuel Porter; and the trio often engaged in testing the bottom of their fast horses. Sometimes hundreds of people would be in attendance at these places of amusement; and those three determined men kept down every thing like disorder, which speaks well for them and for the people who attended the early-time races.

General Hager grows quite feeble, being now (1887) in the eighty-sixth year of his age; but he is happy in the consciousness of having faithfully discharged his duty through his long life. Death has no terrors for him. His noble wife died in 1876.

His portrait will call to mind for many years one of the noble characters, who, with other pioneers, has done so much to develop the Sandy Valley, and make it the abode of wealth and culture.

L. D. WALTON

CAME to Catlettsburg about the time of the arrival of E. C. Thornton; but, unlike the latter, who was popular with every body, Walton was so churlish that he was almost hated by every body. And yet he was a useful man. In buying lots and placing cheap houses on them, he did much to increase the material wealth of the town. He, like Thornton, came from New York State, first going to the upper part of the Sandy Valley to erect a mill for a New York company.

His wife dying, he married for his second wife a lady of great respectability, a daughter of one of the most prominent families of that entire section. They moved to Catlettsburg soon after it was made a town. Mr. Walton owned or leased the saw-mill which stood below the entrance to the wood on the bank of the Ohio, on the road to Ceredo. He floated the lumber down with which he built so many houses, and sold enough to maintain his family, besides paying for the hardware which was used in putting up the buildings. He rented out the buildings as he finished them, until he found a cash purchaser, when he let them go, even sometimes at a low price. For two years or more before he left the town he was engaged in store-keeping in the house on South Front Street, which afterwards became the beginning of the Sherman House, established by Captain Job Looman, who married the widow of John Layne.

In 1860 Walton gathered up his personal effects, having already disposed of all of his real estate, and moved to Arkansas or St. Louis. No one regretted his departure; but every one was sorry to see his amiable wife leave the town. She was a noble

Christian lady, connected with many of the best people of the valley, and admired for her many amiable qualities of mind and heart. The two little boys, the children of Walton's first wife, left a good name behind. The second Mrs. Walton had no children.

Not long after the family arrived at their Western home news came back that Mrs. Walton was dead; and, after the sad intelligence was corroborated, no one since has cared enough of Walton to inquire after his whereabouts. It was thought by many at the time that he took away with him a large sum of money, as he worked hard, traded close, and hoarded what money he took in. He was a singular man.

THE WILLIAMSONS,

OF the Sandy Valley, are of Welsh descent. The first ancestors came to America long before the Revolution. They were patriots, and fought for independence. The family, on coming to America, settled in Pennsylvania, but after the Revolutionary War moved South into Maryland and Virginia. The immediate ancestors of the Sandy branch settled in Russell County, Va., from whence Benjamin Williamson, the grandfather of Wallace J. Williamson and Mrs. Marr, *née* Williamson, came in 1795, and settled on the Tug River, near the mouth of Pond. John Williamson, about the same time, settled in the John's Creek country. John was the ancestor of Hibbard Williamson, so well and favorably known in Pikeville.

Another one of the family pitched his tent on Rock Castle, now in Martin County. The Williamsons, like most of the early settlers, were a brave, determined set of people, impressing their strong individuality upon all with whom they came in contact. They practiced virtue and morality, and were early patrons of religion in their neighborhoods.

While all of the old stock of Williamsons were forceful people, Benjamin, the son of the first Benjamin that came to Tug River, was the leader. He, like his father before him, was a woodsman and hunter, and this circum-

BENJAMIN WILLIAMSON.

stance no doubt caused him to purchase the boundless tract of land which he owned. His portrait accompanies this sketch. He grew rich in lands and herds of cattle, and before he died provided amply for all of his children. Two of these had died before him. He left Floyd, Wallace J., Benjamin, three sons, and one daughter, Mrs. Thomas Marr, of Catlettsburg. His wife was a Deskins, of a prominent Sandy family. He died in about 1880, at an advanced age, loved by his children and grandchildren—for he was extremely fatherly to them all—and respected as an upright man by the entire community in which he had so long been a leader of the people.

His sons are well-to-do in material wealth. W. J. Williamson is one of the great business men of Catlettsburg. Mrs. Marr, the only daughter, is a model wife and mother, and highly respected for her lady-like bearing. The other branches of the house of Williamson have spread, until the family tree is one of the largest in the valley, keeping fair the bright escutcheon as it was handed down to the younger generation by the early ancestors of the house.

SAMUEL T. WALKER

Was among the early arrivals in the John's Creek Valley in an early day. He was a great hunter, and, like many of the old-time bear-hunters, was a noted gunsmith and blacksmith. He was one of the early Methodists in the valley. His descendants are among the most respectable in the country. A grandson is a merchant of the valley at this time.

HON. ROBERT M. WEDDINGTON.

HENRY and his brother, Jacob Weddington, the founders of the house on Sandy, came from Virginia when mere boys, in 1790. The Weddingtons were original North Carolina people. The two plucky boys went to work with the determination to succeed. They stopped in what is now Pike County. They had but little education; but, what was better, they had good native sense and intellect. Henry, the grandfather of Robert M., soon became a merchant, while Jacob farmed and traded in live stock. They both succeeded well in business.

In 1800 Henry married Elizabeth Garrell. From the union two children were born—James and William. The latter was Judge Weddington, the father of Robert M. Weddington, whose name heads this sketch. Henry died in 1836, and was buried on Shelby, where the Weddingtons first settled. His wife survived until 1860, living with her son, the judge, seven miles below Pikeville, where she was buried. James, Henry's other son, married Katie Mead, who was the daughter of a prominent old settler. They had born to them twelve children, eight boys and four girls.

In about 1866 James Weddington, then quite an old man, left his home, and started west. He has never been heard of since. It is supposed that he was killed or met with some mishap. His widow still lives in Pike County, with her sons, Jack and Marion, with an unmarried daughter in charge.

James's children married and settled mostly in the Sandy Valley, and are doing well. The brilliant South G. Preston, of Paintsville, married a granddaughter of James Weddington. What is remarkable, William Weddington, like his brother James, was also the father of twelve children—five sons and seven daughters. His wife was a daughter of Rhoads Mead. The children all married. The eldest son, Martin, married a Miss Tipton, and lives in Arkansas. Rhoads, another son, lives in Texas. His daughter is the wife of John Owens, great-grandson of "Dad" Owens, who laid off Pikeville in 1821. The son whose name heads this article married a daughter of Hugh Harkins, the grandfather of Walter S. Harkins. Harry, another son, is a business man in Pike County, Ky. Another son, C. C., lives in Arkansas.

The eldest daughter, Lucinda, married Dr. S. M. Ferguson, the large capitalist and land-owner of Pike and Floyd Counties. J. Lee Ferguson, of Pike, is their son. Elizabeth is the wife of John L. Hatcher, of Pike. Catherine married James A. Porter, of Johnson County. Mr. Porter has represented his county in the Legislature. He is a bright man, a son of Samuel Porter, of Miller's Creek. Nannie married A. J. Scott, of Pike County. Amelia is the wife of Washington Cloud, of Pierce City, Mo. He is the editor of the Pierce City *Democrat*.

HON. ROBERT M. WEDDINGTON.

Judge William Weddington died in 1878. His widow still lives. Jacob Weddington, the granduncle of Robert M., was married three times, and left a large family of sons and daughters, who have married into the prominent families of the valley, and are amongst the prominent people. One of Jacob Weddington's daughters married John Hargiss, the grandfather of Thomas Hargiss, the chief justice of the Court of Appeals. Captains William and Harry Ford, and their brother Jackson, were half-brothers of William and James Weddington. After the death of the father, she married a Ford, by whom she had the three bright sons named. William and Harry were both captains in the 39th Kentucky, Union army.

ROBERT M. WEDDINGTON.

Captain William Ford died while in service at Lexington, Ky. After serving faithfully for two years, Harry was compelled to resign on account of poor health, returned to Pike, and became a large trader and merchant. He died in 1880, leaving a widow and several children. Three of his sons, Moses Ford, S. King Ford, and John Ford, are popular traveling salesmen for first-class wholesale houses. A daughter of Captain Ford married J. Crittenden Cecil. After his death she became the wife of Mr. Phergo, a journalist.

The Weddington-Ford family is one of the strong houses of the valley; but want of space forbids much that is historic.

DR. S. M. FERGUSON,

A SON-IN-LAW of Judge Wm. Weddington, and brother-in-law of R. M. Weddington, is one of the prominent physicians in the Sandy Valley. He is a man of wealth, and great energy. He was lieutenant-colonel in the 39th Kentucky Infantry, United States army. He came from Virginia to Sandy in about 1843. He is a strong Republican in politics. Nearly all of the Weddingtons are Democrats, though some are ardent Republicans. In religion they are mostly Methodists. A few of the family, however, are Baptists. R. M. Weddington has been a bright newspaper man, having, with Mr. Leslie, founded the Prestonburg *Banner*, a Democratic paper of ability. He ranks among the ablest lawyers of the valley. The influential family of the Morgan and Elliott County Weddingtons are descendants of the Sandy house of Weddingtons.

THE WARDS.

This family came to the valley soon after the first settlement on the Sandy. James Ward was the pioneer of the family. He settled on Rockcastle Creek. The family has increased in numbers until but few families in the valley outrank it in multitude. They have all along been noted for their quiet dispositions, and for their good citizenship. The old stock were noted hunters, having been trained in Indian warfare.

The Ward family has sent out a number of preachers and professional men. The mother of Rev. Z. Meek was a Ward, and a noble woman. Dr. Joseph Ward, of Martin County, is a descendant of Solomon Ward. William Jefferson Ward is one of the solid men of business in Johnson County. In religion they are generally of the Baptist persuasion; in politics, mostly Democratic.

The Ward family are noted for naming their children after their ancestors. Of Jim Wards there have been quite a host; and in order to designate them they were nicknamed. Hence we had Big Foot, Nine Toes, White Head, Bit Nose, Jimper, Little Jim, Jim's Jim, Hawkum, etc. To call a man Jim Ward, no one would know which Jim was meant.

JOHN I. WILLIAMSON

Came from Maine long before the Civil War. On his way out, on stopping at Pittsburg, his trunks were broken open, and he was robbed of all his money, a considerable sum. He had heard of the great openings in the Sandy Valley, and to Catlettsburg he and his young wife came. Without means, he opened a small merchant tailoring establishment, and went cheerfully to work. In ten years he was one of the principal merchants in the town. His wife died in about 1881, leaving him one son, Adelbert, who is his father's helper in the large business.

Mr. Williamson is a popular man. He is a Mason, an Odd Fellow, and a member of the Methodist Episcopal Church. He is a man of great benevolence, for his means.

THE VINSON FAMILY.

In 1800 Benjamin Sperry, Peter Loar, and William Artrip, three brothers-in-law, came from the Shenandoah Valley, Virginia, and settled on the Sandy River, near where Cassville and Louisa are now located. On their way out, James Vinson, a young man of sprightly mien and good address, from South Carolina, joined the party, and proceeded with them to their destination.

It was not long after the families composing

the little colony had settled down in their primitive homes when young Vinson, who had wooed and was promised the hand of a fair daughter of Mr. Sperry, asked permission of the parents of his betrothed to have the rite of matrimony solemnized. The appeal was granted, and the young couple were married. From this alliance has sprung the house of Vinson in the Sandy Valley—a family destined to fill a large scope in the history of this section.

Two daughters and six sons composed the family of the second generation. One of the daughters was the last wife of Hon. William Ratliff, of Wayne County, West Va.

Captain William Vinson, the oldest son, attained to a popularity but seldom found in any man. He was an extensive farmer and saw-log dealer, and filled many positions of trust. When the Civil War came upon the country, he with alacrity flew to the standard of his country, and gave valuable assistance in filling the ranks of the 14th Kentucky Volunteer Infantry, and while not able to do personal service in the field, he was a good loyal Union man until the war closed. He had been an ardent Whig before the war, and afterwards generally voted the Republican ticket. In the latter part of his life he united with the Christian Church, and died within its pale.

William Vinson was brave, noble, and just. He, like the rest of the Vinsons, was quick to resent an insult, but as ready to do a kind act or charitable deed to any who might stand in need. He died in 1883, at his home in Lawrence County, Kentucky, about sixty-four years of age.

Samuel S. Vinson, another brother, while not the oldest of the living brothers, has, by his great ability and indomitable energy, placed himself at the front of the family. He now resides on his large farm, two miles above Ceredo, Wayne County, West Va. He is the senior member of the large timber-trading firm of Vinson, Goble & Prichard, located at Catlettsburg. Mainly through Mr. Vinson the buying, measuring, and transfer of the timber to market was reduced to scientific book-keeping in the carrying on of the business. Mr. Vinson has, besides his farming and timber trade, other financial ventures under his watchful eye. A man of such ability as he possesses will, by force of circumstances, come to the front in public affairs; and while he has never aspired to official position for himself, he has made

S. S. VINSON.

his influence felt in placing those in office whom he chose to see there. He has the ability to fill with credit any office in the gift of the people, and his friends expect to place him in some high official trust at no distant day.

The other brothers are all prominent men of business, and occupy a good place in social life. They live on the Tug River, some in West Virginia, and others in Kentucky. They are all Democrats in politics, and adhere to the Christian Church. in religious belief.

Among the children of the third generation are to be counted a number of prominent men. Richard F., son of William Vinson, is a prominent business man and lawyer of Louisa, who married the only daughter of Dr. P. S. Randle and Malinda May, his wife. Z. C. Vinson, another son, is a prominent business man of Catlettsburg. The entire family of William Vinson are found among the leading people of the valley. Samuel S. Vinson has a son who graduated at a leading college, and is a practicing lawyer.

The Vinson family represent a large landed estate in the Sandy Valley.

THE ULEN FAMILY

Is ANOTHER of the old houses which was here before the Catletts had gained a foothold at the Mouth. The grandfather of Ulba and Charles S.

was a daring frontiersman, whose fearless deeds, enacted at the mouth of the Kanawha in Indian warfare, are recorded in several books of Western adventure. Dr. Ulen, the father, was among the old settlers of the East Fork region, from whence came his two sons, in the time of the Catletts, to the Mouth.

Elba, the older of the two, was sheriff of Greenup County in an early day, and did the business of that office in the Sandy region of the county more than a generation ago. He has lived continuously in Catlettsburg since it was a town, and has always ranked as one of Catlettsburg's useful and prosperous citizens. He had charge of the England Hill property from the time it was turned over to be managed by a local agent until the English owners sold it in 1870. He owns and runs a nice little farm three miles out on the pike. He has a very comfortable brick dwelling. While Mr. and Mrs. Ulen have no children, they are popular with the young people of the place, and at their home many young folks are made welcome, and enjoy the good cheer of the host and hostess. Mr. and Mrs. Ulen are prominent and useful members of the Methodist Episcopal Church, South. Mr. Ulen is among Catlettsburg's oldest men, as well as citizens.

Charles S. has lived at Portsmouth, but finally drifted back to the place of his first love. He was a manufacturer, but has been for some time, and is now, a merchant. He is blest with a family of bright children. A daughter, the oldest, is the wife of one of the ablest preachers of the Kentucky Conference of the Methodist Episcopal Church, South, although her father and mother are Presbyterians. All the daughters are well educated, and are esteemed for their many graces and virtues. The oldest son is a newspaper man.

EZRA C. THORNTON,

BY his great talents as a preacher, teacher, lecturer, writer, editor, mechanic, and business man in general, did more to develop the latent resources of Catlettsburg in the field of education, morals, and material wealth than did any other citizen living in the place, from the time of his arrival on the ground in 1851 to the day of his leaving in 1858. He was a New York man, who had married and settled in Ohio. He was a Methodist preacher, and joining the Western Virginia Conference of the Methodist Episcopal Church, South, settled in Catlettsburg, and entered upon a ministerial career which, though short in duration, was one of the most brilliant in the annals of the conference.

Most men can only do one thing well. Not so with E. C. Thornton, who was a genius. He was a thorough scholar, not only trained in the solid English and mathematical branches, but in Greek and Latin as well. He founded the Thornton

Academy, the leader among high-school institutions in Catlettsburg. Even the building in which he conducted the school was the workmanship of his hands. His own commodious residence, where S. G. Kinner now lives, is a monument to his labor and ingenuity. But not stopping here, he erected by contract several houses in the town, not merely directing the workmen, but joining with them in all branches of mechanical labor, from digging for the foundation to giving the finishing touch with the painter's brush.

It is not out of place to say that Captain A. C. Haily, Catlettsburg's noted sign-writer and house-painter, caught the inspiration of his noble calling from Mr. Thornton.

But the grosser pursuits of manual labor failed to interfere in the least with the higher pursuits, which he was carrying forward for the intellectual and religious elevation of the people. He went far and near, delivering lectures on Education, Free Masonry (for he was an enthusiastic Mason), Temperance, and kindred subjects, great crowds listening spell-bound to his matchless eloquence.

Not satisfied with cultivating the fields of usefulness we have already named, to him belongs also the honor of founding and publishing the first newspaper in Catlettsburg in 1854. The printing-office was in the building which is now the residence of Noah Wellman.

After seven years of constant toil and labor in

the fields of intellectual, moral, and material industry, he concluded to bid adieu to the scenes of his many triumphs at Catlettsburg, and seek a larger field, where he might give fuller scope to his varied talents. In 1858, leaving his family in Catlettsburg, he took a trip to the State of Wisconsin, to seek a location, intending to return, sell off his property, and move his family to that young and vigorous commonwealth. While there, stepping hastily aboard the train, he fell, and was instantly killed. The news of his sudden death not only overwhelmed his wife and children with grief, but made it a sad day for all. The people of the town, but more especially the members of his Church and his Masonic brethren, had felt that it would be sad to have him leave them in health, and go to a distant field of labor, but the thought that they never would look on his face again was almost beyond endurance.

An administrator—Morris Wellman, his brother-in-law—was appointed to settle up his estate. The academy building and dwelling-house were sold to the late Judge Jerry Wellman, Mrs. Thornton, through the administrator, buying the property, and moving into it (now the home of Columbus Prichard).

Mrs. Thornton, the widow, died in 1860, and also one of the children. John Wesley, the oldest son, married the daughter of a prominent citizen of Grayson, and is in business there. Bascom, the second son, is said to be a Southern Methodist preacher in Mississippi; and Ezra, the youngest, went to live with his uncle in Wisconsin, in 1870. The oldest daughter married Colonel R. M. Thomas. They moved to Texas in about 1873 or '74. He engaged in the foundry business, but afterwards published a newspaper at Dallas. His wife is now dead. Another daughter, at last accounts, was engaged in literary pursuits in Virginia. One was afflicted, but tenderly cared for.

The Thornton children were bright, and, like their illustrous father, well educated.

BYRON OBRIAN

WAS never a dweller in the Sandy Valley; but some of his descendants came to the Sandy country, intermarrying with prominent families, which has interwoven his own history with theirs. He was of Irish descent, and moved from one of the Northern States to Tennessee, and became a prominent citizen there. Daniel Jones married a daughter of his in Tennessee. Mrs. Garrett, afterwards Mrs. Davenport, now of Ashland, a sister of Mrs. Jones, is the mother of Rev. Theodore Garrett, a prominent preacher in the Methodist Episcopal Church, Kentucky Conference. Mrs. W. F. Moore, Mrs. "Tip" Frederick Moore, Jr., and Miss Hannah Obrian, a former teacher at Louisa, are half-sisters of the former; James Obrian, their brother, is a prominent citizen of Louisa. He married a daughter of John Van Horn, the prominent old citizen of the Lower Sandy Valley. Daniel Jones and Mr. Garrett both settled at Prestonburg. The former, about 1840, moved to Louisa with his family, where he soon after died. His widow, now venerable in years, and greatly respected, still lingers on the shores of time. Mrs. Medley, wife of Rev. J. F. Medley, one of the ablest and best known preachers in the Methodist Episcopal Church, South, in the valley, is her daughter. The wife of Major D. J. Burchett, is also a daughter of hers. Mr. Garrett died at Prestonburg, and her second husband, Mr. Davenport, now resides in Ashland, where they have a happy home.

THE SHORTRIDGE FAMILY.

COLONEL JOHN SHORTRIDGE was of English lineage, whose ancestors came to America in an early day, and settled in Virginia. Colonel Shortridge was a brave soldier and skillful officer in the War of Independence. He came to the Sandy country in about 1792, and settled on the land now called the John Ewing farm, three miles above Catlettsburg, in Boyd County, Kentucky. He was not only a brave man, but a brainy one as well.

His sons George and Eli, like their father, were men of strong mental endowment. Eli was a lawyer by profession, and for a time was a district or associate judge. As a lawyer he was once called on to prosecute a man accused of murder. He labored hard to convict the accused, and succeded in gaining a verdict of guilty, although he had doubts of the prisoner's guilt. On going home he told his mother he never would appear as a prosecutor against one charged with a capital crime again. "For," said he, "how dreadful it would be to hang an innocent man!"

Colonel John Shortridge's daughter, Melinda, became the wife of William Hampton, the father of Dr. Henry Hampton, Jr., Wade Hampton, Levi J. Hampton, William Hampton, etc. John Chadwick married another daughter.

All the land located between Horse Branch, two miles below the mouth of the Sandy, and running up to Blaine, and above so as to include what is now Edmund M. Smith's farm, had been forfeited for taxes. The Shortridges formed an arrangement with David White to redeem the vast domain, by paying the taxes, and thereby becoming owners of the same. White went to Frankfort in 1798, and paid off the tax which amounted to the sum of $64.50. The Shortridges got by this purchase all the land below Campbell's Branch, while White took all above that stream. Each owner divided with his sons and sons-in-law, giving each a large farm. John Chadwick got the part now known as England Hill, running up Chadwick's Creek, which took its name from him.

The Shortridge family impressed their mental and physical vigor on their descendants in a remarkable degree. The Hamptons got much of their dash and energy from the Shortridge house. They have all died. Most of them went to Missouri before they crossed the stream of death.

THE CATLETTS

WERE Virginians. Sawny, the father of Horatio, came with his family to the Mouth" early in the century. He brought negro slaves with him, and was a well-to-do man. The creek running through the town of Catlettsburg bears the Catlett name, in addition to the name of the live, busy mart of trade, often called the Gate City—the only monuments commemorating the once proud family.

Sawny Catlett's bones lie buried in the old Catlett burying-ground, near the barn of Colonel L. T. Moore. His son, Horatio, was the first prominent hotel-keeper at the Mouth. He was also a merchant, postmaster, farmer, ferryman, and general trader. A line of stages ran through the place from Lexington, Ky., to Charleston, Va., in early times, and Mr. Catlett had the honor of entertaining such notable personages as General Jackson, Henry Clay, and Felix Grundy. While the Catlett House was only a plain log building, the splendid *menu* spread for its guests, with the charming loveliness of the ladies of the household, made it a hostelry far in advance of its day. Several of the present matrons of Catlettsburg, who were young misses in the days of the Catletts, tell us that the Misses Catlett were the most charming and lovely maidens they ever knew.

As the outgoes of the Catletts were greater than their income, they got badly in debt, and to extricate themselves they sent away one by one of their numerous slaves, and then followed on after them to the west of the Mississippi, hoping, no doubt, to raise enough money by the sale of the negroes to lift the mortgage from the Catlett estate at the Mouth. But, like nearly all such cases, the scheme failed.

FRY AND SISTER,

Who inherited from Wilson, the mortgagee, the title to the property as the mortgage had been closed, came upon the scene.

Fry was a sickly, irritable man, and for some time would neither sell the land as a whole or lay it off into town lots. But in 1849, being in sore need of ready cash, he laid out the town of Catlettsburg from Catlett's Creek to Division Street, and in less than two years sold the remainder to a syndicate consisting of John Culver (who had already bought and occupied the now fine homestead of Colonel Laban T. Moore), William Hampton, William Campbell, Frederick Moore, and W. T. Nichols, who, in 1851, laid out that part of the town which lies above Division Street.

In 1847 Horatio Catlett returned to the Mouth. Hearing, before he came, that the valuable property was about passing from his ownership, caused his rage to boil over on reaching the hotel, at the time kept by Levi J. Hampton, but formerly his own, and he died so suddenly that an autopsy was deemed necessary. Dr. James, a physician of the hamlet, found, on examination, that the sudden severing of the wind-pipe had instantaneously stopped his breathing, caused by a long standing blood trouble. So before the unfortunate man could look around on the objects made dear to him by a long former residence, and renew old-time acquaintanceships, he was called, without a moment's warning, to that bourne from whence no traveler returns. His remains are interred by the side of his father and two of his daughters. Thomas E. Henderson, now of Ashland, but then a small lad, was on a visit to his brother-in-law, L. J. Hampton, the hotel-keeper, when Catlett died. The death of Horatio Catlett ended the Catlett dynasty at the Mouth. They will long be remembered as giving their name to the creek running through town, and to the town itself.

JOSEPH EWING,

THE father of John C. and Colonel T. J. Ewing, about 1812, came to the Mouth, having inherited from his father-in-law all the land between Catlett's Creek and Horse Branch, running back for a mile. He married a daughter of John Chadwick, a son-in-law of Colonel Shortridge. Colonel Shortridge was the grandfather of Rev. William Hampton and brothers.

Mr. Ewing came from Monroe County, Va., as the business representative of the Beirnes Bros., a noted wealthy firm, dealing in ginseng, furs, pelts, etc. The business of the great house extended to New Orleans and to London, England. Mr. Ewing sold goods on the Point in an early day, and afterwards moved over to Catlettsburg and sold goods just below the iron bridge. For a time he had charge of a store at Louisa. In 1853 he sold the remainder of his lands (not previously disposed of to several iron men, who went from Catlettsburg to Ashland in 1847, and started that thriving city). Mr. D. D. Geiger, the purchaser, made a handsome fortune by laying the bottom off into town lots, and disposing of them at good prices. It is the seat of many of the fine residences for which the Gate City is noted.

Mr. Ewing, after disposing of his property, went three miles up the Sandy River, and became owner of the farm now owned by his eldest son, John C., Ransom Hatfield, Asa Runyon, and John C. Richardson. Mr. Ewing was a notable man in his day, being very handsome in person, coupled with a grace of manners showing off to good advantage. He gave his sons a good education, sending the two oldest to Marshall College to be trained, and no doubt would have sent the younger away to be educated had he lived.

John C. Ewing is a prosperous and scientific farmer of Boyd County, while Thomas J. is a lawyer, giving most of his time to the pension agency business.

The daughter first married John Creed Burks, a very popular business man, who died in 1863. She afterwards married Dr. Cromwell, and moved to Arkansas, where she died.

John and Thomas J. are the only children living.

THE HAMPTONS

WERE here in early days, and have always been regarded as one of the most notable families of the valley. They are of English descent, some of them coming to the New World before the Revolution, and have spread from New York and Pennsylvania all over the Southern and Western States.

Henry Hampton was the ancestor of the Sandy Valley Hamptons. He settled in Wayne County, Va., about the beginning of this century. His son William married a daughter of Colonel Shortridge, who lived where John C. Ewing now lives. This alliance makes the Hamptons, the Chadwicks, and Ewings kinsfolk.

The father of William Hampton (the latter still living) reared a large family of sons. Two of them are physicians, still on the stage of action.

One is in California, one in Texas, and another, not a doctor, is in Iowa. Rev. William Hampton, named above, has, from a time long before the laying out of Catlettsburg, been one of its most useful and honorable citizens. For nearly fifty years he has been a useful lay preacher in the Methodist Church. The wife of Rev. William Hampton came of a noted house, a Miss Buchanan. The Buchanans, from whom Mrs. Hampton descended, are an ancient and honorable family of Scotland, and of the same lineage as President James Buchanan. Mrs. Hampton's many superior qualities as wife, mother, neighbor, and friend proved the high origin of her lineage, all crowned with the graces of the true Christian heroine. She died in about 1874. Mr. Hampton then married Mrs. Salena Mason, a lady of great respectability. From the latter marriage no children were born; but from the first, six sons and a daughter. One of the sons died in young manhood. George, the

REV. WILLIAM HAMPTON.

oldest, and Wade, the youngest, are farmers in Missouri. W. O. Hampton is a lawyer, but is engaged in commercial pursuits. He lives in Catlettsburg, as does his brother, C. H. Hampton, who is a large capitalist and trader. John W. Hampton practiced law with great success until 1882, when he laid aside his law business, took up the Bible, and went to proclaiming the Gospel to a dying world. He has filled the pulpit of the Methodist Episcopal Church, South, in Charleston and other places, with great acceptability, and is now the popular pastor of the Ashland Church of his denomination. His wife is the daughter of Hon. W. C. Ireland. She is a lady of rare intelligence, having received her education at Vassar College. The daughter married Dr. Barnett. Both husband and wife are dead, leaving two bright sons in good financial circumstances.

MRS. WILLIAM HAMPTON.

Levi J. Hampton, like his brother William, was a remarkable man among the old pioneers at the Mouth. He came along about the same time, and led, as long as he lived, as busy a life as did William. He was a man like Miles Standish, of wonderful force of character and determined will. He lived for a while in Brown County, Ohio, where he married Elizabeth Henderson, a lady of intelligence and great force of character, and, like her other six sisters, who all married men that became prominent in the higher active business pursuits of life, she was a lady who filled the relations of wife, mother, friend, and neighbor with a luster of undimmed brilliancy.

Mr. Hampton, soon after marriage, came back to the Mouth of the Sandy, which was about 1845 or '46, and ever after made the place his home, being some time engaged in timbering, timber-dealing, general trading, and hotel-keeping. He was a man of ardent temperament, and when he made up his mind to do any thing, he did it with his might. While he was a strong Whig in politics, as most of the old settlers at the Mouth were, he was equally ardent in his devotion to Southern institutions, and on hearing of the struggle going on in the Territory of Kansas between John Brown, leading the Free State party, and Stringfellow at the head of the pro-slavery or Southern host, Mr. Hampton rushed to the scene of conflict and identified himself with the Southern side. In the struggle, John Brown and his party gained some advantages over the side Mr. Hampton was on, and, seeing it was necessary for his personal safety, he retired from the field and hurried to his home, being shortly after pursued by agents of the then dominant party in Kansas, who demanded his immediate return to Kansas to answer a charge made against him for some offense committed when in the conflict. Mr. Hampton's friends and neighbors gathered about his person, and determined that he should not go with the posse unless they could show that he was a violator of the laws of the Territory. As they left without taking Mr. Hampton with them, it is presumable that his offending was more technical than real. His business affairs, however, suffered by this episode in his life, from which he never fully recovered. But he would, no doubt, had he lived a few years longer, have again come to the front in business prosperity. It is a little epigrammatic that while contending for Southern rights in Kansas, when the cry of secession was raised in the South, he raised his voice against the cry and declared for the old flag. He enlisted in the 39th Kentucky Regiment Volunteer Infantry in 1862, was appointed quartermaster, and, being in charge of some stores for the command stationed above on the Sandy, when near Prestonburg he was fired upon by the enemy, and was killed, bravely fighting to the last.

Mr. Hampton was always a warm friend of education, and desired above all things to see his children and neighbors' children have provided for them the means to obtain not only a common-school education, but a training only to be obtained in the higher academies, and hence, by word and means, he did much to start Catlettsburg forward to the high position she attained many years ago as an educational center.

Mr. Hampton left a widow, five daughters, and one son. The widow died a year or two after his untimely taking off. Of the daughters, all are happily married to worthy men. Julia, the oldest, married Henry J. Witman; Amelia, P. O. Hawes; and Minnie, the youngest, married Mr. Hayden. All three families reside in Omaha, Nebraska, where Mr. Witman carries on the tin and stove business. Mr. P. O. Hawes practices law, and has been in Congress, and Mr. Hayden is engaged in banking. Mary, the third daughter, married Captain Matthew Scovill. They live at Shreveport, on the Red River. Captain Scovill is a prominent steamboat commander and owner. Millard F., the son, finished his education at Asbury College, now DePauw University, and for a while engaged in mercantile pursuits. Subsequently he entered the circuit clerk's office of Boyd County as deputy under his cousin, W. O. Hampton, and at the end of the term of the principal, Millard was elected to the office, which he has filled for twelve years with great acceptability to the court and general public. He is an ardent Odd Fellow, and through the medium of that benevolent order does much to alleviate the wants of the sick and suffering. He is a working member of the Presbyterian Church, and is an officer in the same. He married the oldest daughter of Captain Washington Honshell, a lady of great amiability, suavity of manners and kindness of heart.

Mr. Millard F. Hampton, like his father, is fond of politics, but, unlike him, he is a Democrat of the strictest sect, yet by no means a bigot.

Before we bid adieu to Levi J. Hampton and descendants, it is not amiss to say that, in addition to the many other evidences of his industry and local patriotism, stimulating him in pushing forward substantial improvements in Catlettsburg, in 1850 he built the fine brick mansion now owned and occupied by Robert J. Prichard as his residence. Mr. Crum, the brother of the now venerable Baptist preacher of that name, made the brick and laid the walls; the wood-work of the same building was executed by Shade Casebolt, then a young man and carpenter, now almost venerable in age and a wealthy capitalist of Ashland. Mr. Casebolt performed the entire job by hand-work alone, as that was a little before the era of machine-work dawned upon the realm of labordom. Mr. Hampton sold the place in 1854 to the late John D. Mims, who occupied the same for more than a quarter of a century, when it fell into the hands of the present owner. His fourth daughter, Lizzie, married, and is in the West, doing well.

JOHN CLARK

WAS another prominent figure in Big Sandy affairs. He was a highly educated Scotchman, and came to the Sandy country previous to 1837. He was a great book-keeper. He was book-keeper and financial director of many of the most prominent manufacturing enterprises located at or near the Mouth of Sandy. He was a great Freemason. He had but one child, a daughter, Elizabeth, who married Marcus L. Kibbe. The wedding of Mr. Kibbe and Miss Elizabeth Clark was the most fashionable and high-toned that ever occurred at the Mouth. The ceremony came off at the Catlett House, the "Alger" of that day, where the Clark family had rooms. The beautiful bride was attended by Miss Catlett, a lovely daughter of the host, while the dashing groom had for his "best man" the celebrated and able lawyer, Rochester Beaty. Rev. Conditt, father of the able Presbyterian minister now at Ashland, officiated on the occasion.

Mrs. Clark and Mr. Clark have been dead nearly a generation. The beautiful bride of fifty years ago—for the wedding took place in December, 1837—has for many years rested in the tomb; but the children, the fruit of the marriage, live to bless the memory of their grandparents and mother, and to cheer their father, who still lives, as hale and rugged as a man of fifty.

A daughter, Miss Emma Kibbe, and her sister Mary, are teachers in a noted female college, while another is a popular teacher in the Catlettsburg graded school. The other daughter is the wife of R. B. Rigg, a nephew of William Biggs, the youth who in 1818 dipped the gourd of water from the Sandy River to wash the dough from the hands of Mrs. Moore, while transporting passengers up the noted stream.

L. L. Kibbe is the present sheriff of Boyd County; his brother is a saddler. Both are sons of M. L. Kibbe and Elizabeth Clark.

THE MURPHY FAMILY

CAME from Pennsylvania to the Big Sandy in 1837, and settled on a farm two miles from the Mouth. Mr. Murphy was a tailor, and carried on the business quite largely for many years. The whole family, consisting of husband, wife, and four daughters, were noted for their great intelligence and pleasant manners.

Mr. Murphy died in about 1849. The wife, who was one of the most amiable and strong-minded ladies ever living in the community, died about 1875. The married daughters, as well as most of their children, have passed away.

For many years previous to, and after the Civil War, the Misses Murphy, Anna and Julia, were the fashionable mantua-makers of Catlettsburg. They made up with artistic skill the trousseau for the blushing brides of that day. They had a monopoly in the business. Not only this, but a wedding in Catlettsburg among the better class was considered incomplete unless the Misses Murphy graced the festive occasion. At funerals their presence was always demanded to perform the solemn duties of preparing the robes for the dead, and suitable mourning apparel for the living. Their sympathy went out to all the distressed, both rich and poor.

Miss Anna has long since passed away, and Miss Julia alone, of all the family, is left. She is in comfortable circumstances, and spends much of her time visiting her friends. She has legions of them. She is as blithe as a girl of sixteen. She has gathered up the dust of all of her family who have passed away, and had it placed in a lot in the new cemetery, decorating the graves with flowers and shrubs. No one ever left the door of the Murphys without feeling that they were Christians; not that they professed so much, but because they acted as Christ told the people to act.

JAMES McCOY

CAME to Catlettsburg in 1847, and was a wagon-maker. He was a good citizen. His family are connected with many of the leading people of this section. He died in 1881, leaving a widow and several daughters. Mrs. F. R. French is a daughter of his.

JAMES AND JOHN FALKNER

CAME to the Mouth from Virginia about 1847. They carried on the blacksmith business in a shop on the ground where the opera-house now stands. James married a Miss Ratliff, of Pike. He died fifteen years ago. John is still alive, and as active as ever, although he served in the Mexican War. He is a warm-hearted, generous man.

THOMAS CLINEFELTER

WAS an early settler. He came from Hanging Rock. He was a builder. He died in about 1857, leaving a widow, with three children. One of the children died in childhood. The mother has proven herself to be a lady of great courage and perseverance. She educated her two daughters in the best schools, and prepared them to hold their own in the circles of the best society. The elder daughter is the wife of Captain Wallace J. Williamson, the rich trader and banker. The younger is the wife of James W. Damron, a prominent Front Street merchant. It is an open secret that Mrs. Clinefelter has a handsome balance in her favor at the bank, all of which she made by her own industry in making fine coats and vests.

PROMINENT PHYSICIANS.

The medical men, no doubt, were a useful and ill-paid class of men, in an early day of the Sandy Valley history. It is hard to find out who the early doctors were. In fact, skillful old ladies, to a great extent, took the place of male physicians in administering to the sick.

Dr. Hereford was practicing at Louisa as early as 1830.

Dr. James was located at the same place not long after, or about the same time. He moved to Catlettsburg long before the town was laid out.

Dr. Cushion went to the Falls of Tug and practiced medicine late in the thirties.

Dr. Yates, of Louisa, followed in the forties.

Dr. Steel practiced medicine at Prestonburg as far back as 1836.

Dr. Draper, of Pike, was a long time in the harness, dying at a great age, in 1885.

Dr. Johnson came to the Tug River country in 1837, and has practiced there ever since, until within a few years.

Dr. Strong has practiced more than thirty years at Paintsville, and Dr. S. M. Ferguson near forty years on the line of Pike and Floyd.

Dr. P. S. Randle commenced the practice of medicine at Prestonburg in 1838, moving first to Louisa, then to Catlettsburg. He was surgeon in the 5th Virginia Infantry during the war. He married, for his second wife, Miss Mahala May, of Prestonburg, his first wife having died. His only daughter by the second marriage is the wife of Richard Vinson, of Louisa. The doctor died soon after the war, near Maysville, Kentucky. His widow and only son, P. S. Randle, Jr., moved to Wisconsin, where Mrs. Randle had a brother living.

DR. J. D. KINCAID

WAS born and raised in Greenbrier County, Va., where he received his literary and medical training. In 1847 he came to what is now Catlettsburg and commenced the practice of his profession, which he has pursued without a single break ever since, for a period of forty years. During the forty years of his practice he never took a vacation of six weeks, and never took any until within the last few years. No physician in the valley has had a larger continuous practice than Dr. Kincaid. He is a man of fine literary taste and ability, not only keeping well in hand the lit-

DR. J. D. KINCAID.

erature incident to his profession, but is well read in the higher grade of general literature. Dr. Kincaid is as familiar with English and American classics as the child is with its primer.

He married Miss Chapman, a lady of great worth, who bore him two daughters and one son. The son, Dr. James W. Kincaid, graduated in medicine at the Ohio Medical College, Cincinnati, afterwards taking clinics in another noted college of medicine, which brings to his aid every thing needful for the successful practitioner. He is married to a worthy young lady, and bids fair to make a leading physician. The elder daughter is the wife of D. D. Eastham, a prominent lawyer of Catlettsburg. The younger daughter, a very intelligent and refined young lady, although quite young for such an undertaking, presides at the head of her father's home since the death of her mother in 1884.

Dr. Kincaid has nearly approached his three-score and ten mile-stone, on his annual tour of life's journey; yet he looks as young and fresh as most men do at fifty. He was a Whig before the war, but since that time has been an uncompromising Democrat. The Kincaids are Methodists, and are all members of the Methodist Episcopal Church, South.

Dr. Yates is still practicing at Louisa. He has grown wealthy.

Dr. Strong, at Paintsville, still lives, but is very old and feeble. He, too, is wealthy.

Dr. Steel moved from Prestonburg to Cannonsburg about 1850, where he continued to practice till 1861. He and his wife died soon after at the home of their son-in-law, Hon. W. J. Worthington.

Dr. Johnson still lives, though very feeble.

Dr. Carnahan has been practicing at Round Bottom for forty years. He was always a popular physician, as well as a popular man. He is now quite feeble, but holds out to practice yet.

DR. A. P. BANFIELD.

We produce the portrait of the gentleman whose name heads this article as a specimen of the young physicians of the Sandy Valley. The Banfields are a prominent people. While not directly of the Sandy Valley, they are found all over the interior of the eastern portion of the State, filling the higher walks of life. Many of them, like their kinsman, Dr. A. P. Banfield, are physicians also. But on the maternal side he comes of an old Sandy house, noted for the intellectual brilliancy of one branch of the family and for the solid financial grasp of the other. His maternal great-grandfather Prichard came from Tazewell County, Va., in an early day, and settled on Sandy, one-half mile from what is now Rockville, Lawrence County. He left two sons, Lewis and James. Lewis Prichard and his sons and daughters, all grew rich by strictly attending to business according to the laws of trade.

James Prichard, the grandfather of Dr. Banfield, was a very bright, well-read, intellectual man. He was for many years magistrate, first of Carter, then of Boyd, and was recognized as the ablest member of the County Court on the bench. He raised a family of sons and one daughter of remarkable intellectual endowment. Hon. K. F. Prichard, of Boyd, is one of his sons, and an uncle of Dr. A. P. Banfield. Dr. Allen Prichard, one of Boyd County's most noted physicians and capitalists, is another. Hon. G. W. Prichard, of Carter, is also one. Wily Prichard, the strong-minded man and heavy capitalist, is another; and a very bright son is a physician in Indiana; two other sons are farmers, and intelligent men. Mrs. Banfield, the sister of the bright sons, and mother of Dr. Banfield, is not behind the sons in intellectual vigor. She was born within two hundred yards of where her gifted son keeps his office at the mouth of Bear Creek, or Rockville, Ky.

DR. ALLEN P. BANFIELD.

Coming of such an ancestry, he could hardly fail of success. But he does not depend on the prestige of ancestral blood to achieve success, but rather on his own exertions. He studied medicine with his uncle Allen Prichard; afterward he attended the best seminaries of learning in the country, and graduated from one of the best colleges of medicine in Cincinnati, and immediately commenced practice at Rockville, Ky., where he has had great success. His practice, which is very profitable, is more than he can attend to. Like his kinsfolk, he is equally at home in financial affairs. Although so young, he is often called on to settle up large estates, from the well-known fact that he is just and accurate and trustworthy. He is a strong Democrat in politics, and an intelligent politician; but under no circumstance will he run for office, preferring, rather, to dictate good men to fill official stations than to hold them himself. He is unmarried, but is a great society man. He boards at the Rockville House, kept by Dr. J. F. Hatton. He is not thirty-seven years old, yet has accomplished more than many men who have lived to three-score and ten.

JOB DEAN

Was an early settler on John's Creek. He was very eccentric, but a good scholar. He wrote a splendid hand, and was well versed in history. Late in life he often wandered from home, and left his wife, who was an excellent woman, to look after the house and farm. He was of Irish descent. Notwithstanding his many oddities, his children turned out well, the mother giving them wholesome training. One of his sons, Dr. William H. Dean, practiced many years in Pike. Thomas, another son, is a physician at Salyersville. James R. Dean, the oldest son, is one of the most prominent citizens of Lawrence. For more than a quarter of a century the people, without cessation, have kept him in office. He has been surveyor, school commissioner, county judge, and again surveyor. He is a large farmer on Blaine. The lady whom he married was a daughter of Robert Walter, a granddaughter of Neri Sweatnum, and a sister of the author's wife.

THE DIXON FAMILY.

HENRY and Joyce Dixon, two brothers, came in 1814 and settled on the land where Paintsville now stands. Henry was born in 1774, and died in 1854. Joyce was born in 1772, and died in 1856. They came from Grayson County, Virginia. They intermarried with the Farmers, a prominent family by that name in Virginia. The brothers were leading people in their section for a half-century nearly. They were in good circumstances. Their descendants are regarded as among the leading people there.

Among the descendants are Dr. H. F. Dixon,

Captain George W. Dixon, Joseph K. Dixon, and others. The Dixons are Republicans in politics and adherents of the Methodist Episcopal Church, generally.

The town of Paintsville was laid out on the land of the Dixons.

THE CANTERBURYS

CAME from North Carolina or South-west Virginia in 1800. There were three brothers. Reuben, the most prominent, lived for several years where the widow Newman now resides. The place is on the old maps as Canterbury. He was postmaster there. Another brother lived near where Rev. Joseph Wright now lives, and still another at the Durney place. They were a bright people, with a restive nature. Previous to 1837 they had sold out, and gone West.

THE ELLINGTONS

ALSO came from North Carolina, in the year 1800. Pleasant Ellington was a noted bear and wolf hunter of his time. He trapped many wolves on what is now known as Ellington's Bear Creek, called after him. Wolf-scalps were legal tender in those days. Each scalp was worth five dollars, paid by the State. But few if any of the Ellingtons are now found here.

THE NEWMAN FAMILY.

PEYTON and Joseph Newman, the grandfather and grand-uncle of Joseph Newman, of Catlettsburg, came along with the Ellingtons from North Carolina. They settled near the Sandy River, and have multiplied until the family is very numerous. Many of them have become well-off. Joseph Newman, of Catlettsburg, is one of the prominent citizens there. His father, Peter Newman, who died near thirty years ago, was a leading man of the valley.

The Newmans are Democrats, and generally adhere to the Methodist Church.

The old stock intermarried with the Ballengers, Hazeletts, and other noted families.

THE DEERINGS

CAME to the Little Sandy country about this time. Richard, the father of the noted preachers, Rev. Richard Deering and S. S. Deering, was a genius. He was an inventor. He built a little furnace near where Hopewell Station now is, but, not doing well, came to the Big Sandy in about 1832. He built a mill on Abbott, near Prestonburg; but the country was too slow for him. He pulled up stakes and moved to Louisville some time in the forties. He invented a peculiar fish-trap, which caught many fish as they passed up and down the chute over the falls at Louisville. Other fishermen, through envy, demolished the trap.

Mr. Deering and wife were brilliant people, and raised a family of children who have been long noted for brains and culture. The celebrated Rev. John R. Deering, the newspaper writer and minister, is their grandson. Mollie, the daughter of Richard Deering and wife, married David Grace, and moved West.

THE CHAPMAN FAMILY.

WILLIAM CHAPMAN, the ancestor of the Chapmans of the Sandy Valley, came from Giles County, Va., in 1806, and settled in what is now Lawrence County, Ky. Mr. Chapman was followed in 1810 by William McClure, who was his son-in-law. The latter came from Botetourt County, Va.

Mr. Chapman's grandson, Lieutenant George R. Chapman, now holds a patent for land inherited from his frandfather, issued by James Monroe, then governor of the commonwealth of Virginia, afterwards President of the United States. The patent was issued to David French, who afterwards transferred it to William Chapman, dated April 19, 1782. It calls for four thousand acres of land. The deed from French to Chapman, bearing date of 1802, calls for one thousand acres of aforesaid patent. When the patent was issued it was for Kanawha County, this part of Kentucky then being in that jurisdiction. This was before Kentucky

County had been established. The tract of land embraced in the Chapman purchase from French, now owned by Lieutenant Chapman, is situated on the west bank of the Sandy, five miles above Louisa, and is known as the Gavitt Place.

Mr. Chapman died at a ripe old age, in 1840, on the farm where he first settled after leaving Virginia. The wife of his youth lingered on the shores of time till 1863, dying at the great age of ninety-seven years.

The descendants of William Chapman are very numerous in the Sandy Valley, and have spread out into various localities and States. When we count the descendants in the male and female lines, we find but few families in the valley more numerous than the William Chapman family. The descendants of William Chapman have brought no stain on his fair character and upright life. If they have not become as noted as some other families, they have certainly added much to the material, intellectual, and moral wealth of the country. They may not be money-gatherers, but are good livers. The family is noted as knowledge seekers.

One grandson is a skillful physician; another is a professor in a State college; one, who was educated at a university, is at the head of a classical school; and another fills the office of superintendent of common schools in his native county. A granddaughter was for several years a teacher in a prominent female college.

Lieutenant George R. Chapman, a grandson, now past middle life, was an officer highly spoken of in the war for the Union. He resigned his position on account of sickness before the war ended. He was in the 14th Infantry Regiment, Kentucky Volunteers, Union army. He is a leading citizen of Louisa. The Chapmans are either members or adherents of the Methodist Episcopal Church. In politics they are nearly all Republicans, although some are Democrats.

THE CECILS,

OF the Sandy Valley, are of English ancestry. Lord Baltimore, who founded the Maryland colony, was a Cecil.

Kinzy B. Cecil came in an early day, and settled in the John's Creek Valley, where he raised a large family, the members of which have always held high rank in the business, political, and social affairs of the country. When quite an old man he moved down into the Rock Castle country and opened up a large plantation. He died there many years ago, and his last resting-place is marked by a stone tomb inclosing his grave, erected by his dutiful sons.

Two of his sons are still living—Samuel, near Pikeville, a farmer; and Cob, who is one of the solid men of the valley.

The Cecils have ever been noted for their great

individuality and tenacity to what they believe to be right, their motto being to do justice to all the world, never to forsake their friends, and fear no man.

A grandson, Cob Cecil, Jr., is one of Catlettsburg's most prominent business men. A son, Hon. William Cecil, filled the office of county judge of Pike with great credit to himself and profit to his people, besides many other places of trust and honor. Cob Cecil, Sen., was for many years a leading merchant of Pike. He, too, has filled official stations with honor to himself and usefulness to the people. He has been for many years the most potent and well-known Democratic politician in the Sandy Valley. He married a daughter of General Wm. Ratliff, of Pike.

The Cecils are generally adherents of the Methodist Episcopal Church, South. As a family they have been staunch advocates of temperance and good morals.

THE CYRUS FAMILY.

ABRAHAM, Thomas, William, and Smith Cyrus came to what is now Wayne County, West Virginia, about 1806. They came from North Carolina. They were hard-working, energetic men, and obtained a competency of this world's goods, and were useful citizens. Abraham Cyrus and Ross Cyrus, of near Virginia White's Creek, are sons of Abraham Cyrus, Sen. They are a Baptist family; Democratic in politics. Abraham Cyrus is one of

Wayne County's most highly respected citizens. Ross is a large farmer and stock-trader. Abraham is connected with the Hatton family by his first marriage. Ross married a lady of the old house of Lockwood. The other branches of the family are numerous, living in Wayne County, West Virginia, and in other localities. Jesse Cyrus, a brother of Abraham and Ross, is a wealthy farmer of Boyd County, Ky. John Smith, father of Lindsey T. Smith and Edmund M. Smith, was a cousin of the Cyruses, and came with them from North Carolina.

ALEXANDER E. ADAMS.

THE subject of our sketch was born in Lee County, Virginia, August 15, 1835. At the age of ten years he came to Whitesburg, Letcher County, Ky. He entered, as store-boy, the service of his brother-in-law, D. I. Vermillion, who was a prominent merchant of that place. The country was new, the public buildings constructed of logs, the staples in trade of the country being ginseng and fur skins, the farmer often paying his county and State revenue in coon and opossum skins. The people were generally kind and clever, especially to strangers traveling through the country, a night's entertainment for man and horse frequently being not more than ten to twelve and a half cents, entire bill, old peach and honey included.

Young Adams soon became an expert in the fur-trade, and at the proper seasons was mounted on horseback, fully equipped by his employer as a traveling fur-buyer. His usual route was over the counties of Letcher, Perry, and Harlan, in Kentucky; Lee County, Va., and Hancock, in East Tennessee. But learning after considerable experience, that all could not be John Jacob Astors (though they be fur-buyers), he abandoned the fur-trade, and bent his energies in the pursuit of useful knowledge. He attended for some time a good country school in Lee County, Virginia, and next entered Sneedsville Academy at Sneedsville, East Tennessee. At the expiration of his term at the latter institution, he found his supply of school-funds exhausted. He then returned to his former employer at Whitesburg, Kentucky, and engaged with him as clerk at a good salary, all of which he carefully laid by until his funds were sufficient to again enter school. This time he started out on foot, and soon after

CAPT. ALEXANDER E. ADAMS.

found himself a student of Mossy Creek College, Tennessee, at which place he remained until he finished the course of studies he had so long desired. He then left Mossy Creek for his now adopted home in Kentucky, and he and his brother-in-law, Vermillion, entered into a co-partnership under the style and firm name of Vermillion & Adams.

Some time after the above firm was organized Mr. Adams went to Baltimore, and became a student of the Baltimore Commercial College, at which place he graduated with high honors in 1861. He returned to his home in Kentucky to engage largely and earnestly in the business for which he was now so well qualified. But, to his great disappointment, in place of his former prosperous business, he found that bitterness, hatred, and strife were raining down from the great war-cloud of the Rebellion among his people. The time had come that all men must take sides, and Mr. Adams promptly espoused the cause of the United States Government.

At a convention of Union men, held at Pikeville, Ky., in 1861, Mr. Adams was declared the nominee of the party to represent the people of his district in the next Legislature of Kentucky. Mr. Adams made several public speeches in the district, and was threatened with instant death at some points if he attempted to speak; yet he made the race without receiving personal violence, and was beaten. Then he was notified by a friend to leave the country or he would be taken to Richmond, Va. He then set about raising a company of soldiers, for the purpose of aiding in the suppression of the Rebellion. The company was raised, and joined with the 19th Kentucky Infantry. Mr. Adams was elected and commissioned as captain of Company D, the company he had raised, and marched to camp at his own expense. He was engaged in the battles of seven days in the rear of Vicksburg, on the Yazoo River. The United States troops were defeated, Captain Adams, with his company, composing the rear guard on the retreat of the army to the gun-boats. The next move of the troops (which was immediately) was on Arkansas Post, which place was captured with all the Confederate troops, eight thousand in number, and all of their arms and munitions of war. Captain Adams, in charge of one hundred men, assisted in the destruction of the fortifications. The army then returned, to renew the fight on Vicksburg, this time in front of the city. Captain Adams's health was now so much impaired that he was unable to longer command in person his much-beloved company, and under orders of General Grant relieving the army of all permanently disabled soldiers, in order to make a decisive assault on the enemy's stronghold, Vicksburg, Captain Adams tendered his resignation, which was accepted.

In 1863 he was married to Miss Georgie A.

Dils, eldest daughter of Colonel John Dils, Jr., of Pike County, Ky. Soon after his marriage he was elected by the people of his old district to represent them in the Kentucky Legislature. Next in order he was appointed United States assessor of his county, but soon after resigned. In 1870 he was appointed assistant marshal for Pike County, to take the census. In March, 1876, Mr. Adams was appointed by President Grant, consul at Port Said in Egypt, and received his commission April 3d, following. But after waiting in Washington City, for three months, on Congress to make an appropriation for his, as well as many other similar missions, which Congress failed to do, disgusted at the non-action of Congress, Mr. Adams resigned his position, and returned to his home in Kentucky. A short time after his return, he was tendered the United States marshalship of Kentucky, but declined the position. He was elected State senator from the Thirty-third District in 1879, which position he filled with honor to himself and entire satisfaction to the people of the eight counties composing his district. During his term of office as senator, he was chosen as a delegate to the Republican national convention, June, 1880, at Chicago, which nominated James A. Garfield for President of the United States. He also holds a medal, commemorative of the thirty-six ballots of the Old Guard for Ulysses S. Grant for President of the United States.

Mr. Adams since, and during a portion of his public career, was engaged in mercantile pursuits, in which he was successful; but owing to bad health he retired from the latter, went on a farm, and is to-day the pioneer tobacco farmer of Eastern Kentucky, being the first to raise the weed in quantity for export. He is also the first to manufacture wines in quantity for export from native wild fruits, all of his wines taking gold premiums. Mr. Adams has devoted much of his time, both public and private, to develop the vast natural wealth of Eastern Kentucky, having at all times favored internal improvement, never having failed as a law-maker to favor the granting of railroad charters throughout the State, and the building by convict-labor great State turnpike roads through Eastern Kentucky. He favored free education to all classes within the school age, regardless of color or previous condition.

HOWES FAMILY.

AMONG the numerous families whose planting in the valley was unheralded by early fame, yet whose progeny has increased so rapidly as to become a strong family, must be mentioned the descendants of Alexis Howes. Mr. Howes came into the region of country about where Paintsville now stands, as early as 1815. He and his family were Methodists of the pioneer type; and for more than a quarter of a century he exercised his gifts as a local preacher. He had several sons and daughters.

Among the sons, John Howes, who for more than twenty years was clerk of the courts in Johnson County, was also a local preacher in the Methodist Church, and one of the most highly respected citizens of his county. He died near the close of the Internal War, greatly loved and venerated by his family, and lamented by the entire community. Another son, Wiley Howes, is a noted lawyer of Salyersville, Ky. John left a large family of sons and daughters, several of whom are still living in Paintsville, where all were born and came to manhood and womanhood. The sons, together with their brothers—Rev. Charles J. Howes, presiding elder on the Covington District, Methodist Episcopal Church, and Rev. George W. Howes, now pastor of the Methodist Episcopal Church at Catlettsburg—have all filled high positions of official trust or honor at the hands of the people of Johnson County. One of the daughters is the wife of Rev. William Childers, a member of the Kentucky Conference, Methodist Episcopal Church. Rev. G. W. Howes voluntarily gave up official position in his county, and renounced the practice of the law to become a Methodist preacher. Their mother was a highly respected Christian lady, and died about the same time as the father.

The other descendants of Alexis Howes are

scattered over several States, and are highly respected people. The Howes are a brainy and cultured people.

THE HATFIELD FAMILY

HAD a small beginning on coming and settling in the great valley, but has increased in number and influence until it is a mighty host. Ephraim Hatfield, the founder of the house in the Sandy Valley, came from Russell County, Va., in 1795, and, with his wife and children, settled on the waters of the Tug River, in what is now Pike County. Ephraim left a son, George, who became the father of Madison, Polly (who married Alexis Music), Ransom, James, Alexis, Anderson, Johnson, Bazell, Wallace, Elias, and Floyd. Brothers and cousins of Ephraim, the founder, settled in Logan County, now West Virginia, whose descendants have become exceedingly numerous. When the West Virginia branch is added to the thrifty Kentucky house, the Hatfields outnumber most other families in the Sandy Valley. A few years ago, at a large gathering of the people of the Tug region to listen to a political discussion, it was found out that over three hundred voters in the crowd were either Hatfields or had Hatfield blood coursing through their veins.

Prominent men have appeared from time to time in the family, who rose above the average walk in life. Several preachers have emerged from the house, and become noted in their vicinity, whilst others have been called upon to fill important official stations. Bazell made an excellent judge of Pike County, and is now the model sheriff of the same county; and most people in Pike concede that the affairs of the county were never better administered by judge or sheriff than they have been under the *régime* of Bazell Hatfield.

The Hatfields are noted for physical development and strength, and, while by no means ignoring scholastic learning, depend largely upon common sense to carry them through. They read the book of nature more critically than they do the text-books of the schools, although many of them are well versed in scholastic training. They are a high-spirited family, but are kind, neighborly, and just to all who treat them justly. An enemy, however, might as well kick over a bee-gum in warm weather, and expect to escape the sting of the insect, as to tramp on the toes of one of these spirited, tall sons of the mountains, and not expect to be knocked down.

Ransom Hatfield has been a resident of Boyd County since 1877. Although he moved down from Pond Creek, in Pike County, and had never read an agricultural book or paper in his life, he has done much by his industry, and correct judgment applied to farming, to help educate his neighbor farmers in the science of husbandry. He is a man of great strength of character and kindness of heart. Sheriff John Richardson, who is his son-in-law, appointed him as the chief guard to attend Henry Freese from the jail to the scaffold, on which he suffered the extreme penalty of the law, in August, 1885, at Catlettsburg. Mr. Hatfield exhorted the doomed man to exert every power of mind and muscle, as well as to call on God for help, to enable him to meet his end with becoming fortitude, and the encouragement given the culprit by Mr. Hatfield so nerved him up that he met the awful shock with heroic composure.

The Hatfields were originally nearly all Democrats in politics, but since the war they have become strong Republicans, with but few exceptions. Bazell Hatfield, sheriff of Pike, is a Republican; Ransom, of Boyd, is a mild Democrat. They are a strong Baptist people in religious matters. Physically, they are tall and muscular, with a good share of brains and will-power.

THE HOLBROOK FAMILY

CAME from North Carolina early in the present century, and mostly settled on the head-waters of Blaine. They were a well-off people, who brought their slaves with them. Many of the family now (1887) are numbered amongst the well-to-do people of the valley. Alonzo Holbrook, of Flat Gap, Ky., is a scion of the family.

THE HATCHERS,

WHILE not among the first settlers in the valley, are by no means late arrivals. James H. Hatcher married a Miss Peery in Tazewell County, Va., and settled at the mouth of Mud Creek in about 1830. They had born to them a large family of sons, who early developed into business men, and have for forty years occupied a conspicuous place in the mercantile affairs of the valley. By the mother's side of the house they are connected by consanguinity with many leading families of the valley. Mrs. David Borders, Mrs. "Coby" Preston (afterwards Mrs. Dr. Strong), Mrs. K. N. Harris, and Mrs. Arthur Preston were sisters of Mrs. Hatcher.

Mr. Hatcher died in the prime of life, about 1845, and his widow not until 1886, at quite an advanced age. All the sisters are now dead but Mrs. Harris, who lives with her daughter in Utah. Andrew Hatcher, a son, and his sons, are very prominent business men at Pikeville. James, another son, married Mary C. Herriford, daughter of Dr. Herriford, and merchandises at the mouth of Abbott. Kenes F. and Ferdinand are both prominent citizens of the valley. Mrs. Frank Morrell is a daughter of Jas. H. Hatcher. The Hatchers have always been identified with the Methodist Church, and now most of the family are working members in the Methodist Episcopal Church, South. They are Democrats.

JOSEPH GARDNER.

Joseph Gardner, an American, went to the Island of St. Domingo, West Indies, and married a French lady. Soon after the blacks rose in rebellion against their white masters, engaging in indiscriminate slaughter of all whites, whether citizens or sojourners. Mr. and Mrs. Gardner escaped with their lives, bringing away with them, in their hasty flight, one little negro slave. They came to the Sandy Valley, or rather Greenup County, and started out in life anew.

Mr. Gardner was a brave, bold man, of great force of character, and brainy withal. He bought on the waters of the Big Sandy, great cargoes of bear-skins and other pelts and furs, took the stock to Pittsburgh in keel-boats, and sold out to the agents of foreign houses at great profits. He accumulated much wealth. These transactions occurred in the early part of the present century.

WASHINGTON GARDNER,

His son, married Nancy, daughter of Joseph Bloomer, of Bloomer's Bar. Washington Gardner was the father of Hon. Joseph Gardner and Captain Henry Gardner, of Salyersville, Magoffin County. The family has from its foundation been noted for the high social and financial positions occupied by its members. They are connected with the Raisons, of Kentucky, and the Samuels, of West Virginia.

Henry Gardner served as captain in the Civil War on the side of the Union. The Gardners are mostly Democrats in politics.

JOHN HENRY FORD

CAME from Fluvanna County, Va., and settled in Prestonburg about 1840. He moved his family to Catletttsburg in 1852. He was a blacksmith. His wife was a Friend, a prominent family of Floyd County, who came from Monroe County, Va.

Many of the Friends have held high official positions. R. S. Friend, of Prestonburg, is now filling one with rare ability. The Friends have intermarried with many of the best families of the valley.

Mrs. Ford still lives to bless her children; but her husband passed away in 1886. He left a family of children, all grown. Charles Winston and Tandy Lewis, two of the sons, are among the leading business men of Catlettsburg. Winston is a leading Democratic politician, and his brother, Tandy, is equally strong as a Republican; and while the brothers give each other no quarter in party strife, they are as lovable in the social amenities of life as were Jonathan and David.

When Mr. Ford died, the hearts of the old settlers were touched, and his funeral was largely attended. He was a relative of the Mayos, of Sandy.

J. LEE FERGUSON,

The publisher and editor of the Pikeville *Times*, a Republican paper, started by him in 1885, and still conducted with ability, is a son of Dr. S. M. Ferguson, a leading capitalist and physician of Floyd County, Ky., and was born in 1852. He received a good common-school education in his neighborhood, and afterwards obtained a collegiate course in a Virginia institution; studied law, and graduated at the Law University of Iowa City, Iowa; obtained license to practice, and opened an office in Pikeville, Ky., and rose to prominence. He is now the county prosecutor, although the county is politically largely against him. He is a good writer, and bids fair to take a high rank as an editor and lawyer. He is unmarried. It is needless to say that he is an ardent Republican.

J. LEE FERGUSON.

HON. JOHN M. ELLIOTT

WAS so well known to the Sandy people, that they have his eventful life indelibly pictured both in their memory and on their hearts. He, too, like so many others, added luster to the bar of Prestonburg. The high position to which he attained, the many official stations he adorned, and the tragic manner of his death, will always keep his name embalmed in the memory of Sandy people. It is a small consolation to his widow and to his friends, now the mists have been swept away by time and circumstances, to believe that his slayer was a crank, scarcely responsible for taking the life of one of earth's warm-hearted sons, and a jurist as pure as a Marshall or a Story. His widow lives in Catlettsburg, keeping green in her memory the goodness and greatness of her great husband.

THE ENDICOTTS

OF the Lower Tug Valley are quite an old family. Samuel, the father of the large family of Endicotts now living in Wayne County, West Virginia, and in Martin County, Kentucky, came from Southwestern Virginia in an early day, being attracted to the country by the great number of bear and deer found on the Tug. He was a great hunter in his day. He succeeded in procuring a title to considerable land, which his children inherited.

The Endicotts have always been noted as a mild-mannered people, governed by the precepts of right and justice, although one of the Endicotts (not, however, of the Samuel Endicott branch), killed a man in the Rock Castle country in 1860, which caused an intense excitement at that time. Samuel Endicott's descendants are generally moral and trustworthy, and good citizens.

THE LESLIE FAMILY

BELONGS to the Celtic race. William Leslie came from Ireland to America before the American Revolution, and settled in the valley of Virginia. He was a patriot, and fought against the king. Robert, his son, came to Sandy with his family in 1798, settling at the mouth of Pond, where he made a crop. He, however, was driven off by the Indians before he had been there a year. He, with his family, returned again in 1800, this time settling on John's Creek, at a place now and from that time known as the Leslie Settlement.

Robert's son, Pharmer Leslie, was the first male child born on the waters of John's Creek. The event occured soon after the family came to the country. Pharmer became one of the prominent men of the Sandy Valley. He was a model farmer and grew rich at farming, stock-raising, and timbering. He was a man of high character. He was the father of seven sons, four of whom are still living. A granddaughter married Dr. Jackson, a noted physician of Pike County. The sons, like the father, were men of mark, noted for energy, honesty, and fair dealing. They married into leading families of the valley, and now the Leslie family is one of the largest as well as one of the most noted in the valley. Doctors and lawyers are representatives of the house, as well as merchants and traders. One, a scion of the house, came to the front as a newspaper man several years since.

In early days, when the plank in the upper John's Creek country was sawed by hand, and used as fast as sawed, William Leslie died, at seventy-three, and no plank could be procured to make a coffin to bury him in. Nor could a whipsaw be procured to saw enough. His relatives and friends were determined to give him a decent burial; so they had a nice poplar-tree cut down, and chopped off a log of proper length, squared it up, and with ax and adze, shaped it into a coffin, digging out a trough. They took clapboards and shaved them, with which they made a nice lid for the trough-like casket, and in this unique case the remains of William Leslie, of John's Creek, were consigned to mother earth.

Pharmer Leslie died in 1883, at nearly eighty-four years of age. One feels sad that a man like Mr. Leslie could not have been spared to witness the coming of the railroad up the valley. In childhood he had many times heard the growl of the bear, the howl of the wolf, the scream of the panther, and the savage yell of the Indian. What a contrast would it have been to him to have listened to catch the piercing scream of the locomotive, and to see the smoke and fire issuing from the nostrils of the fiery steed, as he drags in his wake scores of iron chariots, laden with the wealth of all climes—all traveling faster than the winds of old ocean! But God is good, and we must bow to the incidents of locality and circumstances.

The Leslies are Democrats in politics, but are not office-seekers. In religion they are mostly Southern Methodists.

THE KINNER FAMILY.

Mr. Kinner came from South-western Virginia at quite an early period of Sandy history, and settled near the mouth of Bear Creek, Ky. He procured land in the vicinity sufficient to make a good farm for each of his numerous children. The sons and daughters, as they grew up, married into the leading families of their community. Hansford H., while not the oldest, at an early age became conspicuous for the energy and talent displayed as a timber-trader on the Sandy. He married a Miss Curnutte, the daughter of an old-time citizen, always respected for his good qualities. About 1856 Mr. Hansford H. Kinner moved from his place in Lawrence County to the vicinity of Catlettsburg, where he has ever since resided, being engaged during that period in coal-mining, timber-trading, merchandising, and milling. He has always sustained the highest reputation for honesty, integrity, and energy. A great reverse overtook him the past Summer in the utter destruction by fire of the saw and planing mills and furniture factory of Smith, Mitchell & Co., in which he was part owner.

The Kinners were all Union men during the Civil War. Since then they have been Democrats.

HON. S. GIRARD KINNER,

THE only son of Hansford H. Kinner, was well educated at the schools in his neighborhood. He afterwards spent some time at Center College, Ky., and at South Bend, Ind., and finished his collegiate course at Wesleyan University, Delaware, O. Soon after leaving college, he married Miss Ceres Wellman, youngest daughter of Judge Jerry Wellman, and settled in Catlettsburg. On finishing his study of the law, which he chose for a life profession, he at once entered upon its practice. He was appointed, by the board of trustees of Catlettsburg, town attorney; he was afterwards nominated by the Democratic party of Boyd as a candidate for county attorney, and elected by a handsome majority over his Republican opponent. This was in 1874. In 1882 he was elected prosecuting attorney for the Sandy Valley Criminal District. Having served in all these places so ably, the people, without much regard to politics, re-elected him to fill the same office for another term.

Mr. Kinner is a pronounced Democrat in politics, and in religion is a liberalist, with a leaning to the Southern Methodist Church. His father and mother are leading members in that communion.

THE JOHNS FAMILY,

WHILE not so numerous as some, has age and respectability on its side. Thomas Johns, the founder, came from Virginia in an early day, and helped to clear out the valley and make it the fit dwelling-place of men. His descendants are now found scattered along the banks of the Sandy from Pikeville to Louisa, all occupying a high position in life. John Johns, the merchant at Prestonburg of that name; Daniel Johns, now of Minnesota; James Johns, of Louisa; Harvey Johns, of Mud, as well as many with Johns blood in their veins, inheriting it from their mother's side,—are all prominent people.

THE HATTON FAMILY.

SAMUEL HATTON, the early progenitor of the Sandy Valley branch, was born in London, England. On the day George III was crowned king of Great Britain was Samuel's anniversary, being eleven years old at the time. He received a number of presents on this his natal day, which caused him to feel quite hilarious. Under the excitement, he made some disparaging criticisms on the new king, which came to his master's ears (for he was apprenticed to a paper-hanger), who gave the little rebel a flogging for his temerity. Smarting under the blows, he ran away, leaving his widowed mother and brothers and sisters, and went to Ireland, where, boy as he was, he obtained work at his trade, of a ship-owner in one of the sea-ports of that island.

After remaining one year, his employer prevailed on him to take passage on one of his vessels bound for America. He landed in Alexandria, Va., three months after leaving Ireland.

He drifted about until the Revolutionary struggle commenced. True to the instincts of his boyhood, he enlisted in the army, and fought all through until the surrender of Cornwallis at Yorktown.

He married Rosannah Queen, of Loudoun County, Virginia, where sons and daughters were born unto them. Of these sons, Samuel and Josiah came to the Lower Sandy Valley in 1790, and settled near what is now known as Turman's Ferry, in West Virginia, just below Round Bottom. Philip, another son, came out a year or so later.

These brothers were single men when they came west; but each, soon after arriving, finding it not good to be alone, took a wife, and established a home.

Samuel Hatton married Nancy Campbell, whose father's family came to the country from Redstone. Campbell's Branch, a streamlet emptying into the Sandy River five miles above Catlettsburg, was named in honor of Nancy Campbell, whose father lived upon the stream, and gave his daughter a farm on its banks.

Jonah Hatton married Margaret Wallace, and Philip married Jane Cardwell.

In a few years after Philip's arrival, another son of Samuel, Sen., came on, and soon after married Elizabeth McGinness.

David, a twin-brother of Elijah, came soon after, having married Sally Purgett in Virginia. The last-named two brothers settled near where Samuel, Jonah, and Philip had located.

From these five brothers have sprung all the Hattons of Boyd County, Hentucky, and Wayne County, West Virginia, and many have moved West—a numerous host, numbering more than four hundred souls.

The Hattons have ever maintained a reputation for industry, honesty, and integrity. In searching the records of crime, no Hattons' name is found on the black catalogue. They are generally farmers, although numbers of them are engaged in commercial pursuits. Joseph F. Hatton, a grandson of Jonah Hatton, is a noted merchant of Rockville,

Ky. Strother Hatton, who is known as the Egyptian corn-merchant and farmer of Elijah's Creek, West Virginia, is a man of wealth. Samuel K. is a bright business man, lately gone to Illinois. Wily Hatton is one of the wealthy farmers of the Sandy Valley, living three miles from the Mouth, in West Virginia.

Allen Hatton, now a venerable old man, carefully attended to by his nephew, Joseph F. Hatton, at Rockville, Ky., is one of the best informed men living on Sandy. Allen is a son of Jonah Hatton. Allen Hatton was, in his younger days, a steamboatman, and in 1843 piloted the first steamer that ever went above Louisa. He says mothers rushed to the bank on hearing the steam escape, bringing their offspring along to see the wonder of their lives. Chickens and geese ran from the barn-yards on the banks in great affright. Horses and cattle were seized with fear, and dashed away to the hills to escape the awful calamity that seemed to threaten them. But now how changed! Steamboats pass up and down the Sandy almost daily, laden with merchandise going up, and returning with the products of the farm, the forest, and apiary, in exchange.

The Hattons were nearly all Union people during the civil strife. Since the war most of them have acted with the Republican party, while some, however, are strong Democrats. In Church relation they are mostly Methodist, although a few are of the Baptist faith.

The author forgot to state that Jonah Hatton was a soldier of the War of 1812, serving in the same company with William Cyrus, an uncle of Abraham and Ross Cyrus.

THE HARRIS FAMILY,

Of Sandy, are a brainy set. James P. was the early ancestor. He married a daughter of Judge Graham. They are connected with the Harmons, of Virginia, an intellectual family. Many of the Floyd Harrises have filled public offices. Some have been lawyers; some are now members of the bar.

Henry C. Harris was a brilliant man. He went to Newport some time in the forties, where he died.

K. N. Harris was an eccentric man, but had a solid education. He once lived in Catlettsburg; but after the great fire, made his home in Prestonburg, but left there and went to Paintsville, where he died in 1885. His sons, living in Utah, were very good to him in decrepitude and old age. Unlike the most of the family, he was a Whig in politics, and an aggressive Union man during the Civil War.

JOHN S. PATTON,

One of the prominent citizens and an able lawyer of Martin County, was born in Lawrence County about thirty-four years ago, where he resided up to about fifteen years ago. His parents came from Virginia just before his advent into the world. They were honorable people, and possessed good mental powers, which the son inherited. Not being rich, they could furnish their bright boy with but few books in his youthful days; but he made good use of all coming in his way.

When eighteen years old he was found teaching school, and soon after commenced the study of the law. In 1869 he was admitted to the bar at Greenup, Ky., under Judge R. H. Stanton, having previously passed a creditable examination before Judge M. J. Ferguson at Louisa. The same year Mr. Patton settled in the then new county of Martin, and entered upon the brilliant career that has distinguished him ever since. Mr. Patton's personal popularity is so great that twice the people of Martin have elected him their county attorney, although the county is overwhelmingly opposed to him in politics.

JOHN S. PATTON.

Soon after going to Martin County, he married a daughter of Dr. Hinkle, a lady well qualified in every way to journey with him through life. They have no children.

In starting out on professional life, Mr. Patton was of a jovial turn of mind, but for eight years has been a model of sobriety and Christian virtue. He is a humble Christian, and does much to help the cause of morality and Christian progress in his section. He is a working member of the Methodist Episcopal Church, South, but his liberality takes in all Christian people.

ARTHUR PRESTON,

ARTHUR PRESTON, JR.

Whose portrait appears in this book, is a descendant of Moses Preston, Sen., and Isaac Preston, his son. He is a young merchant, and one of the younger timber-traders on Sandy. He is quite a student, and has read and digested much; is a leading Democratic politician of his section, but not an office-seeker, being too much absorbed in business to spare the time to hold an office were it thrust upon him. He is a potent factor, however, in shaping by his counsels the destiny of his party, and is popular with his own party and well liked by his opponents. He is a coming man, if no check interposes his progress to fame. He belongs to several benevolent orders, but is a liberal in his religious belief.

THE PATTONS,

WHILE not an old-time Sandy family, have for thirty years been identified with the business interests of the valley. William M. Patton, the father of the three Patton Brothers of the drughouse carried on by them, was for many years a prominent figure in the social, moral, and material interests of Catlettsburg. He died fifteen years ago, greatly respected for his noble Christian qualities, leaving not only material wealth to his descendants, but, better still, a name above reproach. His aged widow still lives in the spacious Patton mansion, one of the most elegant homes in Catlettsburg, An accomplished daughter is a fitting companion to her mother in her graceful passage down the declivity of life.

The three sons, George B., James, and Dr. W. A. Patton, have, by skill and energy, built up the largest drug-trade in Kentucky, outside of Louisville.

Judge Joseph Patton, a brother of William M. Patton, commenced the milling business at Catlettsburg in 1862, and he and his enterprising sons have successfully prosecuted it ever since. The judge died in 1885, but the business goes along all the same under charge of the sons. Joseph Patton was a public man, filling the offices of town trustee and county judge, and occupying a seat in the Kentucky Legislature before he moved to Boyd. He was a sterling Democrat, while his brother, W. M. Patton, was an equally strong Republican.

The Pattons are mostly Presbyterians, especially W. M. Patton's family, while the judge's family are adherents of the Methodist Episcopal Church, South.

JOHN W. LANGLEY

Is the son of Joseph R. Langley, a prominent citizen of Floyd County. At fifteen years of age John W. Langley declined his father's offer to educate him at college, preferring to depend on his own exertions to win his way in life. At sixteen years of age he received the highest grade in the county to teach school. He passed the civil service examination, and was appointed an examiner in August, 1882. He was promoted for efficiency, though only nineteen years old when appointed. He entered Columbia Law University in 1882, where he took the junior course. Next year he entered the

National Law University, from which he was graduated in 1884, receiving the degree of Bachelor of Law. He then entered the post-graduate course in the institution, and in June, 1886, received the degree of Master of Law, and won the prize for the best essay upon a legal question, standing second for the class medal. His subject was "Married Women under the Law." He then passed the bar examination, answering 90 per cent of the questions, and was, upon motion of one of the faculty of the university, admitted to the bar of the Supreme Court of the District of Columbia. Since Mr. Langley's return to Prestonburg, his home, he has been admitted to the bar there.

JOHN W. LANGLEY.

Mr. Langley has a genial, sunshiny nature, and makes friends wherever he goes. He is a Republican in politics of the most pronounced type, but is liberal in his treatment of those who differ from him. In age, he has just commenced ascending the steps of twenty.

MAJOR BURCHETT.

Major Drew J. Burchett's great-grandfather and grand-uncles, who came to Floyd in an early day, were all fighters on the side of freedom in the Revolutionary War. The grandson and grand-nephew inherited the pluck of his ancestors. In 1861 he was found with his whip in his hands, driving oxen and hauling saw-logs; but when the tocsin was sounded, calling on the young to rally round the Old Flag, young Burchett threw down his whip, turned out his cattle, and enlisted as a private in the 14th Kentucky Volunteer Infantry, United States Army. His grit, boldness, and daring soon elevated him from a private's position to that of major of the regiment. He served with great courage on many a hotly contested field in Georgia, and, while as brave as Cæsar, was as popular with his comrades as any man in the regiment.

MAJOR D. J. BURCHETT.

At the end of the war he returned to Louisa, bought a splendid home, and married Miss Jones, a daughter of Daniel Jones, formerly of Prestonburg. By industry and perseverance, he became one of the solid citizens of his town and section, owning many houses and lots, and is now successfully engaged in a large leather and shoe establishment.

He has twice represented Lawrence and Boyd in the Legislature, and ran for the State Senate in the district composed of Lawrence, Boyd, and Elliott. Though the district was very largely Democratic, he was nearly elected, notwithstanding the popularity of his opponent.

Major Burchett had the nomination for a seat in Congress tendered to him by the Republicans of his district in 1886, and had flattering prospects of an election had he accepted the nomination.

He has a lovely family, noted for their refined enlightenment. He is a leading Mason and a humane man; is the friend of temperance, and the promoter of religion. He is about forty-seven years of age.

THE BURGESS FAMILY,

OF the lower Sandy Valley, is of Scotch origin, the ancestors coming over to Virginia before the American Revolution.

Edward, the founder of the house on Sandy, came from Giles County, Virginia, about 1800, or before. The Burgesses are kinsmen of the Colonel Ralph Stewart family, who came from the same section in the Old Dominion.

Edward Burgess had two sons, Edward and William. William's sons were George R. and Edward (who were twins), Reuben, Strother, and John (who was killed by the falling of a tree when a young man). Edward met his death, when eight years old, by being scalded to death in a kettle of boiling sugar-sap.

The daughters were Clara and Rebecca, who were twins. Clara married Edward Winfield; Rebecca married Louis Riggleston. They moved to Iowa, and did well. Permitta, another daughter, married a McGranahan; Nancy, married a Mr. Williams, and went West. Sarah, the youngest, married a Mr. Donohoe, and moved to Kansas and got rich.

The William Burgess branch have all come to the front as good citizens and fine business men and women. Reuben was a little "off," but never lost his integrity. George R., who married into the noted family of Spurlocks, is perhaps the best representative of his father's family. At least he is better known in the valley than his other brothers and sisters. For forty years he has been a magistrate, and has represented his county in the Legislature of the State. He is now an old man, stricken in years, and full of honors. He reared a large family of children, many of them now occupying a front rank in the mercantile, professional, and social walks of life. Two sons are doctors; one is a lawyer and State senator in West Virginia, while still another was a minister in the Methodist Church, South, though now dead.

Mr. George R. Burgess and wife enjoyed their golden wedding in the Summer of 1886.

Edward Burgess, the brother of William, was at one time sheriff of Lawrence County, and like his brother, reared up a large, respectable family, who, together with their descendants, are among Lawrence County's best and most prominent citizens. George Burgess, who married into the prominent family of Johns, was a man of rare integrity and honor, and left to his large family of children a priceless name and much wealth. Edward and Gorden were noble men, and left large families to bless the county. The Burgesses are Methodists. In politics, they are divided. Most of them, however, are Democrats. A promising son of Edward Burgess, the third in line of that name, was an officer in the Union army and fell in defense of the stars and stripes.

THE BARTRAMS.

DAVID BARTRAM, when a boy, began his Sandy Valley career near the forks of the Sandy and the Tug. He came to the locality in 1810. He hunted, fished, made shoes, and farmed. Every body liked him for his good qualities. He was the father of James and William Bartram, two men of prominence in the Lower Sandy Valley.

James Bartram was no ordinary man. He struggled along, as most boys were compelled to do in the rugged country where he lived; but, by industry and perseverance, he rose to be a large merchant and timber-dealer. He had a good business education, picked up as he could spare a little time from pressing work.

When the Civil War set in, James Bartram owned the great farm at the Falls of Tug, where he also had a store, and was largely engaged in trade. He had, at the time, valuable property in Catlettsburg. He lost heavily by the war. He moved to Catlettsburg, and for awhile was engaged in buying horses for the government.

At the close of the war he went back into the timber business and merchandising. Although doing a large business, he was unsuccessful. He lost most of his property, and kept hotel for a living until he died in 1883.

His son William was a captain in the 14th Kentucky Infantry, Union army. He is now a prominent citizen at the Falls of Tug. He married a daughter of Judge William Ratliff. A daughter of his married James Peters, a bright business young man of Lawrence.

Captain John A. Bartram, another son of James Bartram, is a noted steamboat clerk and captain at the Mouth of Sandy. He is a son-in-law of Abraham Cyrus. Lindsay is in business there, while the hotel is run by the widow and Miss Fanny, a very worthy daughter of James Bartram.

William Bartram, another son of David Bartram, was a well-to-do farmer on Mill Creek, West Virginia, who raised a respectable family, and died about 1880. David, the ancestor, died in Catlettsburg in 1863, at an advanced age.

The older Bartrams were ardent Democrats; but when the war came on, they declared themselves for the Union, and since that time have been among the most pronounced Republicans. They are members or adherents of the Methodist Episcopal Church in religion.

Captain John A. Bartram has been a seeker of public favor, and, though not successful, ran ahead of his ticket.

THE BRYANS.

JOHN AND ZEFFIE BRYAN, two brothers, whose ancestors were English, settling in Vermont, but subsequently moving to Virginia, came down the Ohio in 1798, and in 1800 settled on the Blaine Bottoms, near Rove Creek, Lawrence County. John married Sarah Lakin, widow of James Lakin, and daughter of Samuel White.

The Bryans were cousins of the wife of Daniel Boone, and were relatives of the Bryans at Bryan's Station. John Bryan was one of the first to throw away his hand-mill and take his corn to the Falls of Blaine, to the water-mill there. While catching fish with a gig, just below the falls, he was attacked by a panther, which he wounded with the gig, and afterwards killed with his hunter's knife. His granddaughter, now living, has a little spinning-wheel which was made in 1806. It is still in good running order. The wheel has a scar or scratch on it made by a mad dog, while the mother of Mrs. Sloan was spinning. Her father killed the dog with a stick.

The old man, when quite one hundred years old, cut, split, and laid up one hundred rails in a day. In 1799, while in a hunter's camp on the Kanawha, he cut on a rock the date of his birth, which made him, in 1867, when he died, one hundred and fifteen years old. He is buried at Cummins Chapel grave-yard, near where he lived after coming to the Sandy.

Of Zeffie we hear but little; but he, too, must have been a man of energy, as we find his son, Recy Bryan, now an aged man, one of the wealthy men of Boyd County.

THE BROWNS, OF BOYD.

RICHARD BROWN, the founder of the family in the Sandy Valley, came in an early day from Eastern Virginia, and settled near Guyandotte, Va. About 1836 he moved to Lawrence County, Ky., and settled on the farm at the junction of the Sandy with the Tug. He raised a large family, mostly daughters, who were destined to fill conspicuous places in life, as the wives of noted men. His daughter Matilda became the wife of Judge James M. Rice. Three of the daughters are now widows, living in Catlettsburg, highly esteemed by all who know them.

George N. Brown, a son, has for thirty years been one of the foremost men in the law and business in the valley. He was educated at Augusta College. He commenced his career in Pike County, where he filled several official positions. He married a lady who was daughter of Thomas Cecil and granddaughter of Kinzy B. Cecil. She died, leaving a son and three daughters, and he married, for his second wife, a Miss Poage, daughter of William Poage, a distinguished early settler near Ashland, Ky. William Poage's wife was a Miss Van Horn, a niece of John Van Horn and Mrs. Frederick Moore. The issue from that union all became distinguished people.

Mr. Brown moved to Catlettsburg in 1860, where he has ever since lived. He has been one of the leading practitioners at the bar ever since, save the six years he served as circuit judge of his district. He was elected judge in 1880, defeating John M. Burns, who in turn defeated him for the same office in 1886.

Judge Brown had made some enemies in his

action in the Ashland horror case, though all believed he acted from a sense of duty. He also had, from some cause, raised up a large crop of personal enemies while judge, who determined on his defeat at all hazards when he should run again, which was made good by the election of his competitor, Burns, by an immense majority. Leaving Judge Brown's defeat in abeyance, it is hard to find a man to say that he did not make an able and upright judge.

Judge Brown appears unsoured by the sting of defeat, and many think he will come to the front again. He is a man of wealth, owning a great many houses and lots in Catlettsburg and a greater number of farms in the country.

He has a son, Thomas R. Brown, who was educated at the University of Virginia, and is now one of the leading members of the Catlettsburg bar. He is a leading member of the Presbyterian Church, and is the champion of temperance and good public, as well as private, morals. A sister became the wife of Alexander L. Martin, of Prestonburg, both now dead, while another married the Rev. Dr. McClintock, an eminent Presbyterian divine, who has since died.

The Browns were once Whigs, but on the breaking out of the Know-Nothing craze in 1854, they joined the Democratic party, and have been its strongest pillars.

THE BROWNS, OF JOHNSON.

This family is of English origin. Their early ancestors came to America before the Revolution, and settled on the north branch of the Potomac. As early as 1789, Nathaniel and Thomas C. Brown moved to Kentucky and settled in Fleming County, but soon moved to the Sandy Valley, settling on the river, nearly opposite Paint Creek. A daughter of Nathaniel married Samuel Auxier, the grandfather of Major J. B. Auxier, thus connecting the two houses, by a matrimonial alliance, at an early day in the history of Sandy Valley.

Of Nathaniel we hear but little after his coming to the valley. His brother, Thomas C. Brown, became the founder of a house noted in the annals of Big Sandy. Thomas had a son named Francis Asbury Brown, who became the father of Hon. W. W. Brown, Judge Thomas Brown, Judge Nathan Brown, and others. Wallace W. Brown is a lawyer of Paintsville, but, being engaged in merchandising and general trading, gives but little attention now to the practice of law. He is a brainy man and well read, not only in law, his chosen profession, but in science and general literature. He is a Democrat of the strictest sect, but is a genial friend and neighbor. Mr. Brown has often been called upon to fill offices of great responsibility, among these the offices of State senator, and member of the Lower House. He has served his county as prosecuting attorney, and occupied other official positions of trust and honor, all of which he filled with fidelity and good judgment. His brother Thomas was a lawyer, also, of the Paintsville bar. He served his county four years as judge, and on the expulsion of John M. Elliott from his seat in the Lower House of the State Legislature in the beginning of the Civil War, he was elected, from Johnson and Floyd, to fill the vacant seat.

At the time Brown took his seat in the Lower House, the great question under discussion in the Legislature was whether the State should remain in the Union or join the Confederate Government. Mr. Brown made a speech in favor of the Old Government and the Old Flag that was remarkable for brilliancy as well as sound logic. It carried all doubters with him, and settled the question for all time. The potency of Mr. Brown's speech was more apparent from the fact that he had always been a Democrat. Afterwards he ran for Congress, but was not successful. Shortly after the close of the war he moved to the North-west, but soon returned, and quietly settled down at Paintsville, where he lived until about 1884, when he moved with his family to Utah, where he now lives.

The Browns were, from their first ancestors, Methodists, and Thomas was for a great many years a preacher in the Methodist Church; yet, in his old age, he swerved from his ancient faith, and joined the Latter-day Saints, or Mormons. He is an erratic but brilliant man.

Nathan, another son of Francis Asbury Brown, was a lawyer. He, too, like Thomas, served a term as judge of his county, and was a local preacher in the Methodist Church. Like the Browns of Johnson, he was a brainy man. He died in 1884, leaving a family of children. William and other sons were farmers and store-keepers.

News has come back from Utah that Thomas Brown renounced Mormonism as soon as he reached Utah.

WILLIAM AND FRED. BRUNS.

THE two Bruns brothers are old settlers at the Mouth. The younger of the two, William, is engaged in the fancy goods business, while Frederick, the elder, is a shoe manufacturer and dealer. Frederick's family are mostly sons. One of them is a bright young doctor. The others are engaged in the shoe-trade. William's children of the elder set are girls, who show great skill in all kinds of bric-a-brac work done by ladies.

The heads of both families, as well as most of the children, are members and workers in the Methodist Episcopal Church. They are all Republicans and prohibitionists. The two brothers are of the Teuton race, and came from Prussia.

DANIEL BLOOMER

MARRIED a daughter of Edmund Price, who was one of the first settlers in the valley. Mr. Bloomer lived in the Kentucky Bottom, opposite Bloomer's Bar, which took its name from him. He was owner or part owner of the salt-works on Taber's Creek. He came there before the War of 1812.

The Bloomer name has disappeared from this region, although Bloomer blood courses through the veins of many of the best people in Eastern Kentucky. Washington Gardner's wife was Daniel Bloomer's daughter, and the Gardners are among the foremost people in Eastern Kentucky.

JAMES McSORLY,

JOHN'S father, came to the salt-works when he was a young man, and clerked for the company. He married a sister of Daniel Bloomer's wife. Mr. McSorly was a good scholar, and after the works went down engaged in school-teaching, which he followed until he died in 1875.

THE McCALLS.

WE first hear of the father of Hon. R. B. McCall at the Taber's Creek Salt-works in 1825. He married a Miss Hardwick, whose father was one of the principal men there. He had sons and daughters. Of the latter, Mrs. Hugh Honaker is one, living at Catlettsburg.

ROBERT B. McCALL,

A PROMINENT citizen of Catlettsburg, is a son, who has by energy and perseverance attained to eminence. He was a captain during the war in the 5th West Virginia Volunteer Infantry, where he rendered distinguished service in putting down the Rebellion. Since, and even before the War, he has filled nearly continuously, either the office of town marshal or police judge of Catlettsburg. The man has not yet appeared who could beat him in the race, so long as he chooses to contest for the place. He has accumulated a handsome property, and is a warm-hearted man, and personally very popular. He is a Mason and an Odd Fellow. He belongs to no Church, but is friendly to all. Before the war he was a Whig, but since then has acted with the Democrats. Many Republicans always vote for him when a candidate. He is about fifty-six years old, is married, and has a wife and two children.

THE BEVINS FAMILY.

JOSEPH BEVINS was born in Ireland, and came to America and settled in Virginia before the War of the Revolution. He was a patriot. In 1812 he came to Pike County, then Floyd, where he lived until his death, which occurred in 1824. He left sons and daughters behind him.

John married a daughter of William Justice, who came with his family from Pittsylvania County, Virginia, to the Sandy Valley in 1787, and settled on the lands ever since known as the Justice Bottom, ten miles above Pikeville.

The Justices were, in their earliest days on the Sandy, large slave-owners, and had an eye single to the importance of owning, not only negro slaves, but a great deal of land also. The Justices of the valley are still large owners of land, and many of them leading citizens in the community. The descendants of William Justice and wife, Miss Bevins before her marriage, are found in every county bordering on the Sandy River.

John Bevins, Joseph's son, died in 1867, and John's son, James, who was the father of J. M. Bevins, died in 1864. J. M. Bevins is among the prominent business men of the valley. The Bevins family is not only among the ancient houses of the valley, but is one possessing intelligence and respectability, and keep clean the escutcheon of the ancient Bevinses of the Green Isle.

THE ANDREWS FAMILY.

This family came to the Mouth of Sandy, from Illinois, at the laying out of Catlettsburg. The younger brother, N. P. Andrews, was married before coming to Sandy. G. W. Andrews married the eldest daughter of George R. Burgess. They were always quiet business men and good citizens. N. P. Andrews is in mercantile business with his son-in-law, C. W. Sheritt. N. P. Andrews is a Presbyterian in religion, and a Republican in politics. Dr. W. A. Patton, of the drug-house of Patton Bros., married a daughter of Mr. Andrews. His only son, Ralph, is engaged in railroading.

G. W. Andrews and his only son, Watt, are leading dry-goods dealers. Watt married a Miss Prichard, daughter of A. J. Prichard and granddaughter of George Burgess, of Lawrence County.

In politics they are Republicans and in religion hold to the Methodist Episcopal Church.

REV. J. F. MEDLEY,

THE eccentric but talented preacher of the Methodist Church, South, for forty years traveling up and down the valley, is one of the most noted men of Sandy. His first circuit was the Harlan Mission. For his yearly salary a liberal-hearted steward gave him a pair of new yarn socks, while an outsider helped the young preacher along by shoeing his horse "all round." But he was the recipient of still greater favors while on that noble Mission. A very liberal old bachelor, who by thrift had accumulated much of this world's wealth, by some mishap had failed to contribute of his abundance to the parson's support. As Mr. Medley hurrying off to Conference rode by a farm-house, at which the old bachelor was staying, the latter spied his preacher friend, and sallied out to pay his quarterage. The preacher was out of sight before the man of means had time to pass into the road; but, being both liberal and conscientious, he started on to overtake the "man of the cloth," and though fleet of foot, he passed several miles over hill and dale before he overtook the fleeing parson. Yelling at every jump he made, he at last brought the preacher to a stand, who waited impatiently for the caller to catch up. At length the parson and his parishioner were face to face, when the strings of a well-tied purse were loosened, and the brother, with what was to him a great stretch of liberality, took out a bright silver quarter, saying to the preacher as he passed him the money, that others might do as they pleased, but he never would let his preacher leave the circuit without contributing of his means to his support. Mr. Medley was soon after sent to the Louisa work, where he married a daughter of Mrs. Jones, who was the widow of Daniel Jones, whose name is so often mentioned in this book. He lives at Catlettsburg, though often serving districts, circuits, and stations. He has been a preacher, and a worker too, in the Sandy Valley for forty years. He is a man of great physical endurance, and as a builder will do more work than men of thirty, and as good. He has always taken a deep interest in developing the moral, material, and educational interest of the Sandy Valley. He has two daughters, both married, who live in Catlettsburg. Their husbands are engaged in contracting and building.

THE CRUM FAMILY.

ADAM CRUM and wife came from Bedford County, Va., in 1806, and settled on Rock Castle, in what is now Martin County, Ky. From this pair have descended all the Crums of Martin, Lawrence, and Johnson Counties, Ky., and Wayne County, West Va. The family has been noted for its industry and for the good morality maintained by its members. They are mostly farmers, yet many have been, and some are now, merchants and traders.

WILLIAM CRUM.

Two of the grandsons, William and Nathan, were very extensive merchants at Warfield. Nathan is a storekeeper at Eden, Ky. William, whose portrait is given, is an extensive dealer in timber and lumber, whose operations extend from the Sandy River to Brooklyn, N. Y. He spends considerable time in the latter place, giving his personal attention to the sale of his lumber. William Crum and his brother Nathan were left orphans in childhood, but struggled, like brave boys as they were, to better their worldly condition, going away from home to a good school that they might be qualified to intelligently conduct business in after life. They both taught school and saved a little money to commence business with. Success has smiled upon them. They have a brother who is a lawyer.

The Crums are a Baptist family, and several preachers have gone out to bless the world. They were originally Democrats, but were loyal to the Government during the war, and since that time have nearly all acted with the Republican party.

THE LOCKWOOD FAMILY.

About 1770, when the people of the Colonies were being stirred by the encroachments of the British Crown upon their liberties, a little cabin was situated on the hill-side of the land skirting the Susquehanna in ——— County, Pennsylvania. The inmates of this plain little home bore the name of Lockwood. A sweet little new-born babe brings joy to all households, be the inmates rich or poor, but the cup of joy at this time, in this romantic homestead, ran full to overflowing; for instead of one little stranger to gladden the hearts of the young father and mother, God sent triplets; and as the Lockwoods were Christian people, they felt that the three little darlings were his good gift to them, and gave no heed to meddlesome young uncles or aunts, who suggested many odd names to be given the little triplets. Reverently the father named them, in their order of seeing the light of day, Abraham, Isaac, and Jacob, after the three illustrious patriarchs of Bible history. The mother struggled along, and reared the children in the principles of virtue and truth, and, on the three boys coming to young manhood, the neighbors all said that the Lockwood boys were models to be followed by old and young.

Jacob, the younger, like his namesake of old, went away from home to better his condition; and still, like Israel, the man he served, down in Bracken County, Kentucky, had many daughters; but one of them in particular caused the young man's heart to throb whenever she appeared in his presence. It was an affair of love, and soon Sarah White, daughter of David White, became Mrs. Jacob Lockwood, wife of Jacob Lockwood. From this honored pair have descended the family of Lockwoods, so well and favorably known in the Lower Sandy Valley. David White, his father-in-law, as is stated elsewhere, having become the sole owner of all the land on the Sandy River, from Campbell's Branch, three miles above the Mouth, to the mouth of Blaine, was able to give all of his sons and sons-in-law a large farm, and then have enough left to make almost a Texas ranch. Jacob Lockwood again showed a resemblance to Jacob of old, by selecting the best land for his portion of the vast domain, and accordingly settled on that part now owned by his grandson, John Lockwood, of Lockwood Station, on the Chatterawha Railroad, opposite Virginia White's Creek, said by many to be the best and most valuable farm on the Big Sandy River. Jacob Lockwood lived to a good old age, as did also his wife. They left many descendants, who have borne good names in the community where they were born and raised.

Residence of John Lockwood, Staley, Ky.

Jacob Lockwood opened his doors to the preachers of the Gospel who at an early day traveled up and down the valley, warning sinners to flee the wrath to come. Mr. Lockwood and wife were Methodists, and their descendants still hold to that faith. Party politics never gave them much trouble; but when the Civil War came on they were found on the side of the Union.

John Lockwood, grandson of Jacob Lockwood,

married a daughter of the well and favorably known John Van Horn, who was brother-in-law of Frederick Moore. Mr. Lockwood has one of the most complete farm-houses in the Sandy Valley, furnished in a style of exquisite taste, and presided over by his wife, a lady of sense and refinement, who dispenses her hospitality with a grace and dignity almost queenly. They have but one child, a son, now eleven years old, whose expectancy of material wealth outranks that of most boys in the valley.

THE McCLURE FAMILY.

WILLIAM McCLURE, one of the old settlers of what is now Lawrence County, came from Giles County, Virginia, where he married Lucretia Chapman, and settled on the Sandy, about five miles above the Forks, where, or near where, he continued to reside until his death in 1861. His faithful wife died the same year. From this pair have descended a large family of children, grandchildren, and great-grandchildren.

Among the first and second generations, from William McClure and wife, are found some of the prominent people of the valley. Some are well-to-do farmers, while others are teachers and professional men and women. One grandson is a noted doctor in the interior of Kentucky; another a high-school teacher; another a professor in a deaf and dumb asylum; and still another is at the head of the educational department of his native county. A granddaughter was, for several years, a teacher in a noted college of the State.

The McClure family has always maintained a respectable standing among the people of Lawrence and the adjoining country. They were Methodists from the beginning, and most of them are now in communion with the Methodist Episcopal Church. They are Republicans in politics; and have contributed to the material, moral, and intellectual wealth of the valley.

THE WELLMANS.

BENNETT WELLMAN was the founder of the Wellman family of the Sandy Valley. He settled near Cassville, Va., about 1792. His descendants are now a great host in numbers. He ranked as one of the greatest huntsmen of his day. The Wellmans always liked the woods, and the liking caused them to procure large boundaries of land. Many of the family have risen to note in the business and official world.

Samuel Wellman, of Wayne County, West Virginia, who died in Louisa about 1870, was a man of wealth, and had filled many official positions of trust and honor. He was the father-in-law of Judge M. J. Ferguson.

Jerry Wellman, a brother of Samuel, was for many years one of Wayne County's most honored citizens. He filled the office of sheriff of his county, and was a representative in the House of Delegates, at Richmond. He moved to Catlettsburg in 1857, occupying a high place there as a merchant. He filled several offices in the town and county with great faithfulness. He was noted as a great advocate and friend of common schools and internal improvements, and gave liberally of his means to encourage manufacturing enterprises in town, though ever so humble. He was a great lover of Odd Fellowship, to which order he belonged. He died in about 1872.

Fred. Wellman, son of James Wellman, who is a nephew of Samuel and Jerry Wellman, is the chemist in the drug-house of Patton Bros.

THE HARKINS FAMILY, OF PRESTONBURG.

HUGH HARKINS, the father of John Harkins, and grandfather of Walter S. Harkins, came of old Pennsylvania stock, emigrating from that State and settling in Prestonburg some time in the thirties. He received a good English education in his youth, and learned the saddlery trade; but having an aptitude for the legal profession, he studied law, and became a practitioner at the Prestonburg bar during life. He worked more or less at his trade, however, during his long residence in Prestonburg. Mr. Harkins was a man of refinement and considerable reading, and was much respected for his many good qualities as neighbor, business man, and citizen. In 1869 he died, leaving a son, who, although merely having reached manhood, had already given promise of the brilliant future which was so soon to crown his life.

John Harkins, the son, was fairly well educated, and being especially endowed with the mental qualifications requisite to become a good lawyer, took high rank as an attorney almost immediately on his entrance to the bar, which occurred in 1860. From that time until the commencement of the fatal sickness which ended his short but busy and useful life, he constantly rose in the estimation of the people as one of the brilliant lawyers of the valley, Prestonburg contributing her full share. Had Mr. Harkins lived he would no doubt have reached as high and honorable distinction in political preferment as he attained as a pleader at the bar. Although in possession of a splendid physique

JOHN HARKINS.

and a strong constitution, insidious disease attacked the citadel of life; but, thinking the enemy expelled, he left his home in Prestonburg and went to Pikeville, where the attack was renewed, terminating in his death August 25, 1871. His unexpected death created a sensation in the valley; for no man had warmer and truer friends than John Harkins, the genial man and brilliant lawyer. He was unmarried, but was betrothed to a highly respected and worthy young lady, who to this day holds herself bound in the silken cords of undying love by refusing the hand and heart of all other suitors. In politics Mr. Harkins was an ardent Republican. The portrait we give of Mr. Harkins is a very good one, and will be readily recognized by his friends.

WALTER S. HARKINS.

Walter S. Harkins, whose likeness is found in this connection, is a grandson of Hugh Harkins and a nephew of John Harkins, who, following the bent of his mind as inherited from his grandfather and uncle, before he had passed the years of childhood, resolved to become a lawyer. And to this end he applied himself in his studies, whilst in and out of school, with such diligence that, on reaching manhood, he was regarded as one of the best educated young men in his town. The good training he had undergone enabled him to make rapid strides in the study of the law, resolving at the start to use all honorable means to climb to the highest position attainable as a lawyer in the Sandy Valley, noted for the number of its able attorneys. Walter S. Harkins was admitted to the bar in 1877, and at once entered upon a lucrative practice

Law Office, Walter S. Harkins, Prestonburg, Ky.

in his native town. Mr. Harkins has not only proved himself to be a good lawyer, but is equally at home as a correct business man. The cut of his office, perhaps the most complete as well as imposing in the valley, proves his good taste and judgment in architectural design; and its internal arrangements testify to the great order governing him, not only in his routine business, but in the methodical manner of conducting his law practice. Mr. Harkins married a daughter of the late Hon.

Joseph M. Davidson, who was one of the foremost men of his county. This alliance connects Mr. Harkins with many of the most ancient and honorable families of North-eastern Kentucky. In politics Mr. Harkins is a Democrat, and a Methodist in his religious views.

WILLIAM POAGE'S FAMILY.

WILLIAM POAGE, of the prominent family bearing that name, living in Northern Kentucky and Southern Ohio, married a sister of John Van Horn and Mrs. Frederick Moore. This was soon after the Van Horns and Moores settled on the Sandy River. Mr. and Mrs. Poage, while not settling immediately in the valley, located less than four miles below the Mouth of the Sandy, on the Ohio River. Their children, however, or at least four of them—two sons and two daughters—have, since coming to manhood and womanhood, occupied conspicuous places in the affairs of Sandy. Their older son, George Bernard Poage, for many years prior to 1861, was one of the most noted and popular preachers in the Methodist Episcopal Church, South, within the bounds of the Western Virginia Conference of that Church. He was for a time the clerk of the courts of Lawrence County. In 1862 he moved to Bracken County, and soon after was elected clerk of the courts there, and has filled the same office ever since. Meantime he has continued to preach as a local minister. Dora Poage, his brother, soon afterwards moved to Bracken County, also, where he married a Miss Holton, who, as well as her numerous sisters, is celebrated for personal beauty. He is a tobacco-planter. John T. Sullivan, a wealthy Covington tobacco-dealer, married a daughter of William Poage and wife. The wife of Hon. George N. Brown is another daughter, and so is also the wife of Judge John M. Rice, of Louisa.

FELIX A. BARBEE

Is a son of the Rev. J. R. Barbee, known as the "Old War-horse" of Baptist ministers in Kentucky. He was born and raised in Cynthiana, Ky., his birth occurring in 1855. Since 1866 he has constantly been engaged in the printing business, learning his trade in the office of the Cynthiana *Democrat*, and working there without a break from 1866 until 1883, when he came to Catlettsburg and was made foreman in the office of the

FELIX A. BARBEE.

Democrat, filling the place with credit to himself and satisfaction to the owner of the paper.

In 1885 he commenced, in conjunction with Joseph J. Emerick, the publication of the Catlettsburg *Leader*, but has for some time been sole proprietor. He is a sound Democrat, and a member of the Baptist Church. His paper has a fine local patronage. He is a genial, popular man, and a leading Odd Fellow. His portrait is placed in the book, to represent the journalists of the valley, who, as a class, have done, and are still doing, much to develop the material, intellectual, and moral wealth of the Sandy country.

THE HENDERSON FAMILY.

BEFORE Catlettsburg had become a town, a noble matron, with seven bright daughters and two sons, appeared at the Mouth, when the houses round about were few and far between. The name of the mother was Henderson. Duncan Henderson, her husband, had fallen into decay and desuetude, and left the mother to care for and educate the children. She was able to bear the burden. How grandly she succeeded the reader must judge when the narrative is completed. Through Mrs. Henderson's veins coursed the blue blood of the Churches, a talented family, which, by the well-developed intellect of its members, has made the history of New York State more renowned than it would have been had the Church family not lived within its borders. Elizabeth, Mrs. Henderson's second daughter, married Levi J. Hampton, who, as has already been said, was of an ancient Sandy house. Mr. Hampton was not only in those days a man of means and business thrift, but he was equally conspicuous for his benevolent actions, and, as the son-in-law of Mrs. Henderson, helped substantially in bearing her material burdens. But, after all, Mrs. Henderson depended on her own efforts to rear and educate her loving offspring. She was endowed with a strong mind, a firm will, industrious hands, and a heart consecrated to God by faith in the Redeemer's blood. Armed with these strong weapons, she succeeded. Her daughters, on coming to womanhood, were better trained and educated than were many of the daughters of the more favored in worldly wealth. The two sons received not only a good education, but to that was supplemented a business training.

This worthy mother may have sown some seed in tears, but long before old age overtook her on life's journey she gathered in the sheaves. All of her daughters married happily and well. Two of them married noted steamboat owners—Captains Sharp and Nelson. One married D. W. Eba, the long-time merchant and projector, builder, and owner of the "Alger House;" while another is the wife of C. S. Ulen, a member of an old respected family and a leading business man of Catlettsburg. Mrs. Geiger, whose husband is a prominent merchant, farmer, and capitalist of Ashland, is one of her honored daughters; while the youngest is the wife of the graceful W. H. H. Eba, a prominent citizen of Ashland. Such a parallel of matrimonial success would be hard to find.

Major John Henderson, the elder of the two sons, made a fine record in the war as an officer in the Union army, and is now engaged in business in West Virginia. He is married. Thomas E. Henderson, the younger, lives in Ashland, where he does business. He is also married, and has a smart wife and bright children. All of the daughters and both of the sons of Mrs. Henderson are living, except Mrs. Levi J. Hampton.

Mrs. Henderson in early life was a Presbyterian, but became a member of the Methodist Episcopal Church, in which communion she died, at Catlettsburg, in about 1873. Her daughters and sons-in-law are Christians, and members of some one of the leading branches of the Church of God. Mrs. Hampton was a Presbyterian, as is also Mrs. Ulen; while Mrs. Sharp, Mrs. Nelson, Mrs. D. W. and W. H. H. Eba are members of the Methodist Episcopal Church. Mrs. D. D. Geiger and her brother, Thomas E., are members of the Methodist Episcopal Church, South. All are prominent Christian workers.

What a wonderfully successful life was that of Mrs. Henderson!

THE PELPHREYS

CAME from Virginia in 1804, and settled in Johnson County, where many of the descendants now live. One of the old stock, James Pelphrey, has been for fifty years a Baptist preacher. Other members of the family have come to the front as office-bearers and business men. They are Baptists, and most of them are Democrats.

DAVID MORGAN FAMILY.

DAVID MORGAN married a daughter of Judge Graham, and settled on the left-hand fork of Beaver, in Floyd County, in 1799, between Christmas and New-Year. He was not only a hardy and adventurous man, but was one of fine sense and acquirements. His family married into the best families of the country, and from the Morgans are descended many of the noted people of the Sandy Valley. General Alexander Lackey was Morgan's son-in-law.

ANDREWS FAMILY.

G. W. and N. P. Andrews, two brothers, came to Catlettsburg in 1851. They were born and raised at Portsmouth, Ohio, but went to Jerseyville, Illinois, where they were engaged in the business of general store-keeping and lumber-dealing for several years; but the country there being unhealthy, they concluded to sell out and try the pure air and sparkling waters of a more hilly region than the slashes of the low Mississippi bottoms. Arriving at Catlettsburg before any houses worth naming were erected on Center Street, they procured a lease of the ground on the corner of Division and Center Streets, where the National Bank now stands, put up a one-story frame building, and commenced the business of dry-goods merchants, which has been continued uninterruptedly to the present time, no change in the style of the firm occurring until 1877, when the younger brother, N. P., retired, leaving George W. in the old stand on the corner of Division and Front Sreets, who addmitted his son into partnership with him, who now conducts the business under the firm name of G. W. Andrews & Son.

The firm of G. and N. Andrews remained for a year or two at the corner of Division and Center Streets, bought the lot now the property of G. W. Andrews & Son, and erected, in 1854, a commodious three-story brick store-house, in which, from that time to the day of the firm's dissolution, they carried on a large general mercantile business. N. P. Andrews, on withdrawing from the firm of G. and N. Andrews, built a nice two-story brick building on Division Street, where he carried on a large dry-goods and furniture business, until, like nearly all other business men, he was burned out in the great fire of 1878; after which he re-built and resumed business, but was again burned out in the disastrous fire of August, 1884. He again re-built a much better store-house than any that had preceded it, but leased it to William Nickels & Son, who use it as a clothing-store, Mr. Andrews retiring from mercantile life. He held the office of treasurer of Boyd County, a position of great trust and responsibility, and is also engaged in the insurance business.

Mr. N. P. Andrews has always stood high in the community as a man of strict integrity and business honor, and has often been called to fill places of great trust by the town and county authorities, although he differed from them in political matters. The people of Catlettsburg are indebted to N. P. Andrews for the uniform system of sidewalks that line the streets of the town, and for the general leveling of the lots in the place. Had he not persisted in carrying out the plan laid down by the board of which he was chairman, Catlettsburg to-day would look hideous by the pavements varying in width from three to twelve feet, instead of the uniform gauge of eight feet as now. Mr. Andrews always took a lively interest in the material, educational, and moral developement of the place in which he had so early in its history cast his lot.

Mr. Andrews was married when he came to the Mouth. His wife, although an invalid most of the time since, has had such determination and courage as to direct well her household, and has by no means failed to give to society the benefit of her sunshiny nature, carrying into the social circle the most refining influences. They have three children living, two daughters and one son. The elder daughter is the wife of W. A. Patton, the head of the noted wholesale drug establishment of Patton Brothers. The youngest is the wife of C. W. Sherritt, the ex-popular county clerk of Boyd County. The son, Ralph H. Andrews, is married, and is engaged in railroading.

Mr. Andrews and family are working members in the Presbyterian Church. In politics Mr. Andrews is a Republican. He owns and lives in a fine, modern-built brick house, corner of Main and Broadway.

On returning to George W. Andrews, we find him and his son, Wat, carrying on a large wholesale and retail dry-goods business. Mr. G. W. Andrews married the oldest daughter of Esquire George R. Burgess, of Boyd County. To this marriage have been born four children, one son and three daughters. The oldest daughter, Lizzie, married Alberto Wolf, a prominent wholesale stove and tinware merchant of Catlettsburg. The other daughters are single. Wat, the son, married a prominent young lady of Louisa. Mrs. Andrews for many years has had the misfortune of being nearly blind, which has deprived her of the pleasure of mingling to any great extent in society; yet, with all her disadvantages, she has filled well her part as wife, mother, and neighbor.

Mr. and Mrs. Andrews belong to no Church; but the children are connected with the Methodist Episcopal Church, and all the family are liberal contributors to that denomination. In politics, like his brother, Mr. Andrews is a Republican. He owns a fine place just above the corporation line, where he resides.

FOLLOWING close upon the arrival of Dr. Kincaid at the mouth of Sandy came Captain Washington Honshell, James McCoy, Thomas Clinefelter, A. C. Hailey, William A. Foster, Casper Kastner, L. D. Walton, James R. Ford, Hugh Honaker, R. B. McCall, K. N. Harris, George W. Andrews, N. P. Andrews — most of whom are still prominent in the history of Catlettsburg. There are no better means of information as to the history of these early settlers than their deeds and acts, known to all good Sandians.

Captain Honshell is an Ohio man. He married near Burlington, Ohio, and soon after moved to Catlettsburg, purchasing the lot on the south-west corner of Main and Broadway Streets, and erecting a neat and comfortable frame cottage there, where he continued to reside until 1863, when he bought the beautiful and substantial Geiger residence, which he has since greatly modified and improved, where he now resides. Captain Honshell long ago came to the front as one of the foremost steamboat commanders and owners on the Ohio River, and by great industry and perseverance, as well as following the true laws of business, has not only carved out for himself an honored name, reflecting credit on his business integrity and sagacity, but has, as a reward for a long life of labor and toil, accumulated quite a fortune. Captain Honshell's career as an Ohio steamboat commander covers more years than the town of Catlettsburg. The Captain's splendid packets were always the pride of Catlettsburg and Sandians. He made it a rule to build the best boats that plied upon the Ohio, to furnish them in the most comfortable and tasteful manner, and when it came to the *cuisine*, he had a *menu* prepared more like unto a wedding-feast than the fare of many first-class steamboats. To crown all, he always manned his boat with officers whose politeness, like his own, was of the most refined and gentlemanly type. The trips made by the Honshell line of steamers, twice a week for a quarter of a century, between Catlettsburg and Cincinnati, were so regular, observing such close time, starting and arriving with the promptitude of a dial, that the ringing of their bell or the sound of their whistle served to mark the time of day and day of the week. Promptitude has been one secret of his success. Through the liberality of Captain Honshell, the merchants of Catlettsburg had all the advantages of a first-class express company. He has carried on his boats untold thousands of dollars, remittances of business men to wholesale dealers in Cincinnati and other towns below, without charging a cent for the labor and responsibility; and so carefully were these treasures guarded that the author has never heard of a single package failing to reach its proper destination.

Of course, though a very hale man, and by no means incapacitated to stand on the hurricane roof and command a boat, his great experience in steamboat affairs and management called him to a more important, if not so active a field of usefulness. For quite a number of years past he has been one of the leading owners and managers of more than one important line of steamers. For some years his business called him to temporarily reside in Cincinnati, yet he never ceased to make Catlettsburg his real home from the time he pitched his tent on the ground before Fry had finished the plat.

The captain for a year or so has grown more local in his movements, and is doing much to add to the prosperity of the town by the erection of a number of first-class tenement-houses; setting an example for some capitalists to follow, supplying tenants with the conveniences of a first-class homestead; proving that he believes they have some rights which even landlords should respect. But this is just like Captain Honshell.

Captain and Mrs. Honshell are the parents of four children—three daughters and one son. They are all married. The oldest daughter is the wife of Millard F. Hampton; the youngest married Mr.

R. F. Williamson; and both live in their beautiful homes in Catlettsburg. The other daughter is the wife of Lindsay Kelly, a gentleman well-known and esteemed as a prominent business man and social gentleman of Ironton, Ohio. Augustus, the son, is also, like his sisters, happily married; he lives in Cincinnati, where he holds an important position in the steamboating business.

The excellent and thorough training of their children, both domestically and in the best schools, has brought back a handsome return to the parents for their trouble, by the honorable positions their offspring occupy in life.

Captain Honshell's family are active working members of the Presbyterian Church; and he also takes a deep interest in its success, liberally contributing of his means to aid in carrying on its material work. The captain is a liberal Republican in politics, but will vote for no unfit man for office, whatever his political professions.

THE MURPHY FAMILY.

In the year 1837 the Murphy family, destined to fill an honorable position in society in the early days of Catlettsburg's history, moved to their farm at Beech Grove, two miles from the Mouth of the Sandy, where Floyd Runyon now lives (1886). James K. Murphy, the husband and father, was of Irish lineage, while his wife, as her maiden name,

Gordon, indicates, came of Scotch or Scotch-Irish ancestry. Both were natives of Western Pennsylvania. Mr. Murphy in religion was a Catholic, while Miss Gordon was a strict Presbyterian. In Shippingsport, the town where she lived and was educated, the inhabitants were in an early day not only members of that influential denomination, but were great sticklers for implicit belief in the doctrines of Calvin and his coadjutors. Miss Gordon became dissatisfied with the doctrine, and adopted the Arminian system of belief. She left the Church of her ancestors, greatly to their sorrow, and united with the Methodists, in which communion she died. Her history would be incomplete without this reference to her religious views; for it shows up the main features in her long and useful life; a trait more than any other in the make-up of her symmetrical character was her great devotion to what she considered truth. She was the widow of —— Mundus, whom she had previously married; but he, dying soon after, left her with the care of children.

When Mr. Murphy met her at her home in her native town, he was charmed with her grace of person and mental culture, sued for her hand and heart, and soon wedded her as his wife. They shortly after came to Catlettsburg, where Mr. Murphy carried on the business of tailoring, working himself and employing journeymen up to near the time of his death, which occurred in 1849.

Mr. Murphy erected good, comfortable buildings for his dwelling and shop, planted fruit-trees, shrubbery, and flowers, and made the place in that day look like a home for the fairies, such exquisitely good taste did his accomplished wife and their young daughters display.

Four daughters were born of the union of Mr. Murphy and Mrs. Mundus (*née*) Gordon. The eldest daughter married a Mr. McClure, of Burlington, Ohio. She died in middle life, leaving a family of children, who, under their father's faithful watch-care, came to man's and woman's estate clothed in honor and respectability. The next daughter married George Chappell, and, like her eldest sister, died leaving ungrown children, four in number—two boys and two girls. The father, Mr. Chappell, being a man of poor health, could do but little in providing for the support and training of his offspring. So this onerous duty fell on the family of the Murphys, and was shared bravely alike by the grandmother and the aunts, Misses Anna and Julia. And no people ever were more faithful to a self-imposed trust than were they.

Mr. Murphy failed to leave great wealth to his widow and children at his death, although they were by no means destitute, owning a good little farm and surroundings; but they possessed that kind of wealth more valuable than stores and bank-stock, the legacy of willing hands to work, educated intellects to guide and direct, and hearts full of love going out after the dependent ones, causing them to feel that no labor, be it ever so hard, was too great to perform, if, by their sacrifices, the four children might grow to places of honor and usefulness in the world.

Mrs. Murphy was housekeeper and manager; Miss Anna was the teacher of the Chappell children, and also taught many of the neighboring children. It was a busy home, but by no means a dull one. Books on Science, Biography, Travels, Theology, and the range of general literature were found in the library of the Murphys; and, what is still more to their credit, they were not only read but studied.

Mrs. Murphy was a fluent conversationalist, and would discuss propositions in theology and political economy with the experts in those problems in a keen, logical way that was rare in a woman. The entire family kept abreast of the times by reading the current literature of the day found in books, magazines, and papers.

We have stated that the mother was the controlling power of the household after her husband's death, and that Miss Anna applied her mind and energy to teaching, while Miss Julia, as if catching the inspiration from her father, applied herself to the work of the needle, not in the construction of men's garments, but in making the fine dresses for the ladies; and while the fashionable dress-makers of the present time stand high as correct *modistes*, they have no better reputation for first-class work than had Miss Julia, assisted by her mother and sister Anna. From 1850 to 1865 they were at the very head and front in fashionable dress-making. The trousseaus of many blushing brides of Catlettsburg and the neighboring towns were the tidy work of these ladies. Not only were they the artists who prepared wedding garments for the better-to-do people, but their philanthropy caused them to volunteer to prepare habiliments to enrobe the dead. They were invited and welcome guests at the weddings of the rich and prosperous, and were thrice welcome at the house of mourning, where they administered words of consolation to the drooping, relieved the sick, and smoothed the pillow of the dying. Their social qualities were of a high order. For many years after the war many of the most wealthy and refined people of Catlettsburg thought it fortunate to spend a day at the delightful country home of the Murphys, so hearty was their welcome and so well did they know how to entertain.

With all their broad philanthropy, the family, including mother and daughters, had one great object in view above all else, which was to educate and train for usefulness in life the two sons and two daughters left to them by Mrs. Chappell. To this end they made many sacrifices, even moving to Ironton, Ohio, for a time, that the children might enjoy the advantages of the schools of that place. Under such training, of course, the children, on coming to mature age, were well educated. Albert served a term faithfully in the Union army. William, the younger, engaged in clerking. The young ladies, Georgia and Julia, two beautiful girls, engaged in teaching. Their aunt, Miss Anna, died in 1867; both brothers and sisters soon followed the aunt, each dying within less than a year of the other, in 18—, leaving the aged grandmother, Miss Julia, and William Murphy, an old bachelor brother of James K., who lived with the family from the time of his brother James's death in 1849, until his own, in 1877.

Mrs. Murphy died about 1876, leaving no one of the once numerous family but Miss Julia, who has since sold the place, and now lives in town, still fresh and bright, carrying sunshine wherever she goes. She has a competency sufficient to chase dull care away, and passes along life's pathway, gathering flowers in the performance of acts of kindness and deeds of love and mercy, and weaving all into a garland more bright and fragrant than the great possessions of the uneducated miser.

Towns of East Kentucky.

CATLETTSBURG.

GREAT FIRES.

On the 22d of July, 1877, at twelve o'clock, noon, a fire broke out in Peter Paul Schauer's bakery, on South Front Street, and destroyed all of the business part of the town. The fire only raged three hours, but its work was complete. Every business house (including every hotel), save Coon Wait's grocery, was destroyed. In six months most of the "burnt district" was built up with substantial brick edifices. No one received the slightest injury to limb in contending with this great conflagration.

SECOND GREAT FIRE.

At one o'clock A. M., during the latter part of the month of August, 1884, a fire started in the great drug-house of Patton Bros., and spread on one side to Prichard & Wellman's wholesale grocery, D. H. Carpenter's wholesale dry-goods house, and a small brick adjoining, and on the other side to N. P. Andrews's dry-goods store, all of which were consumed, with most of their contents.

James McKenzie, a young tinner, and David Kinner, a young business man of Williamsburg,

Ky., at Catlettsburg on a visit, were caught in the flames in saving goods from the Andrews building; the latter was burned to a crisp, and his charred remains were not found for twenty hours after his death. The former was taken out alive, and lingered ten days in great agony before death came to his relief. John Graham, a negro stone-mason, and another well-liked colored man, also perished in the flames while carrying out goods from the burning building.

All Catlettsburg was horror-stricken. The funerals of Kinner and McKenzie were attended by a vast concourse of people, Rev. Mr. Jackson, of the Methodist Episcopal Church, South, delivering a great sermon on the death of young Kinner, who was the hope of his family, and Rev. Mr. Hanford delivering an oration on the death of young McKenzie, the stay of his family. The colored men were buried with great ceremony also, rich ladies laying flowers on their caskets, because they died in discharge of duty.

FIRE-ENGINE AND HOSE.

In six months after the great holocaust, Catlettsburg procured a first-class fire-engine and hose, equal to any found in the State. The people spent $12,000 in taxes for that purpose. It would be hard to find a better drilled company of firemen than the brave boys who risk their lives in manning the *Gate City* fire-engine and hose.

SANDY WASH-OUT, JULY, 1875.

In the early part of the month of July, 1875, the Big Sandy suddenly rose forty feet, and as the Ohio River was at that time much below the ordinary low-water stage, the waters from the raging Sandy poured into it like a mighty avalanche, reaching to the north shore of that river, lashing boats tied there from their fastenings, and sending them adrift as though they were shingles. The force of the water was so great that South Front Street, from Division to two hundred feet above Franklin, was in less than twelve hours carried into the stream, together with all of the buildings on the street, excepting two; and from one of those left, the front rooms, the principal part of the house, which was a large one (the Bartram Hotel), were carried with the others into the river. The houses destroyed were among the best in the town at that time. The loss to individuals was $50,000, besides the damage done to property below Division Street fronting the Ohio River by the bank giving way. This caused a great decline in the price of the property, and an ultimate loss to owners hard to estimate.

The loss to the corporation could not have been less than $20,000, to say nothing of the inconvenience to the people at large by the great wash-out. A good-sized steamboat, the *Sam Cravens*, was at the time held in execution by the sheriff of Boyd County, Andrew Hogan, who had tied the craft to the shore below the mouth of the Sandy River, there to remain until the day arrived to dispose of her by public outcry. But the swirl produced by the mad waves ingulfed the stout craft, and tore her cabin, keel, and hull into thousands of fragments, with as little ceremony as if she had been a partridge-trap. The destruction of this boat by the rushing waters was the cause of a vexatious law-suit, brought by the owner of the boat against the sheriff for failure to save the craft. After a controversy running through seven or eight years, the sheriff gained the suit.

OHIO RIVER FLOOD OF 1883.

The February flood of 1883 was many feet higher than the river had attained since December, 1847, and was even higher than in that great overflow. The indications for several days previous to any thing like a very high river, as well as telegraphic reports from the head-waters above, gave ample warning to the citizens of Catlettsburg to set their houses in order, to prepare for a great inundation.

When the waters of the great flood appeared on the floors of the houses on the lower streets of the town, the occupants, while not welcoming the watery messenger as a willing guest, submitted to its silent entrance with a grace and resignation most commendable, knowing that no protest would or could prevent the god of waters from making pantry, kitchen, and parlor the haunts of his revels for at least several days; and so the inhabitants made this overflow a time of social enjoyment. Boating, sailing, skiff-riding, and social calling by the gay belles and beaus were indulged in to an extent almost unparalleled in the history of the town. The waters came into most of the houses not situated on or near the bluffs. They endured the siege good-humoredly. After a week's besiegement, many who had been driven to the second stories of their houses, and those who abode in one-story houses to other more favored retreats, were once more enthroned in their homes, which were made nicer by the thorough wash-out given them by the flood; and in three months it would have been difficult for one not a resident of the place to have known by ocular proof that any thing like a great overflow had visited the place.

Of course the people were greatly inconvenienced, and business was suspended for the time; but no great loss fell on any one, and had not the greater flood of the next year visited the place, the people would have looked back to this one as, in many aspects, a forced gala-day.

DELUGE OF FEBRUARY, 1884.

THE immense snow on the ground in the early part of February made the people restive; but when the heavens were darkened with clouds ominous of rain, followed by twenty-four hours of one continual down-pour, the people felt their doom had come. They rallied as best they could, and set their houses, stores, factories, shops, and barns in order, to meet what was apparent to them, the coming of the greatest flood which had ever invaded their borders. By the tenth of the month the muddy waters had invaded all the houses in the lower portions of the town, and at the expiration of three more days, most of the houses in town were under water, some from one to four feet in the second story. Many inmates of two-story buildings had to abandon their homes, and seek shelter, which in many instances was most hospitably offered by the fortunate dwellers on the highlands of the town. Others took refuge on boats, both steam and flat, tied to trees growing in the town. This great deluge kept the people imprisoned for seven days. It was so far-reaching in its destruction that, for several days, many people suffered for the want of fire and food. But the famine was at length broken, as supplies came in from many quarters.

The people of Ashland, always noted for humane acts, early came to the rescue with provisions and coal. Colonel Jay H. Northup, passing up to his home at Louisa when the flood was beginning to assume alarming proportions, gave the alarm there, and no people could have responded with greater alacrity and with fuller hands of benevolence than did the noble people of Louisa. Catlettsburg will never forget their noble generosity. To cap the climax of fraternal charity, the noble order of Odd Fellows in that place, although a small band, set to work among themselves and supplemented the public charity of the people by sending to their water-beleaguered brethren at the Gate a supply of roasted ham, home-made light bread, baked turkeys, and chickens, besides many delicacies, altogether making a *menu* that an epicure would envy. All of these creature comforts were speedily transported to the people of Catlettsburg by volunteers from Louisa. Catlettsburg will never forget Colonel Northup nor the noble people at the Forks. Catlettsburg Odd Fellows will remember their noble brethren up there with heartfelt fraternal love.

Secretary Lincoln, at the request of Congressman Culbertson, sent a draft for $1,000. The State of Kentucky did handsomely, and that prince among gentlemen, Secretary of State Colonel McKenzie, came up to the Gate to see that the stores were properly distributed, and to encourage the distressed people. Many of our own citizens deserve great praise for their noble deeds of love and charity. Colonel Laban T. Moore gave food and shelter to all destitute of the same as long as any space was available in his large mansion, helping the extreme poor as well as the rich. James Wellman, R. C. Burns, W. N. Lanham, Captain Dye, John C. Eastham, Rev. Hanford, John Henry

Ford, E. T. Spencer, D. W. Eba, Captain Hopkins, Thomas Brown, George N. Brown, C. S. Ulen, Mrs. Rebecca Patton, Mrs. Richardson, and Rev. Mr. Meek, editor of the *Central Methodist,* gave over six hundred meals away, and never received one cent in return, not even in the provisions purchased with Government funds. But he and all who opened their houses to the flood sufferers have a better reward.

Those whom we have named lived above the water-line. A thousand kind deeds were done by others whose premises were inundated, yet having a fellow-feeling in common with humanity were busy in attending to the wants of the aged, the sick, and helpless poor.

When the flood disappeared from the lower floors and lawns, one could have a faint glimmer of the appearance of things after the subsidence of the great Deluge of Noah:—plastering falling from walls and ceiling; paper entirely ruined; windows broken, and doors so swollen out of size that they would not close; floors covered with yellow sediment several inches thick. Inside all was dark and gloomy. Without all was chaos. Logs, old gates, fence-rails, broken jars, a dilapidated bench, a dead cat, an old day-book, a broken sieve, a rolling-pin, paper bag full of spoiled crackers, a dead chicken—the whole medley, and much more, covered with mud three inches thick—greeted you. But look farther on, and all of the smaller outbuildings are gone. The barn is turned upside-down, and is a total wreck inside. The fences are all washed away. The alley in the rear of your premises is choked up with logs and drift-wood, and you can't get any thing hauled from that quarter. You look further on, and you see all of your neighbors in the same wretched condition as yourself. You take a census, and it shows that forty dwellings, shops, and stores have been washed from their foundations by the great flood. Only two or three of them could be returned; six or seven of them were never more seen nor heard from. The remainder were sold for trifles, to parties near by where they had lodged, or were wrecked and used for something, or were abandoned to any one who chose to use them. The store-buildings, great and small, presented a woe-begone aspect—plate-glass windows broken in; goods wet and dripping; owners cross and crabbed; no doors to shut the cold out, they were so badly swollen; every thing confusion. Housewives were tired down with anxiety, watching, and hard work, and children were cross and fretful.

Plenty of laborers offered their services to work, but generally at high prices. One week was spent in washing out houses, putting down carpets, and placing furniture; the next was spent in repairing walls and ceilings, and fitting in windows and doors. In a week more came paper-hangers and decorators, followed by the painter. During all this time men were busy cleaning rubbish from yards and lawns, and building fences and outbuildings. Furniture, parlor and bedroom, was added to make up for what was ruined or swept away in the flood. Not only were the dwellings of nine-tenths of the people submerged by the waters, but, to add to their burden, their churches were not in a single instance spared. They were to be cleared of the rubbish left by the overflow. New floors, new seats, and in fact a general renovation, had to be made before they were fit to worship in. But every one had a will to work, and in three months after the great event, the town had put on its former appearance, save that it looked cleaner and fresher. The houses were clean and healthy, and the churches greatly improved by needed alterations and decorations.

When the people took a retrospective view of things, they calculated that, after deducting the donations from all sources which citizens had received, the net loss on the total was at the lowest figure seventy-five per cent on their property destroyed. The money donated was a great boon to many, enabling them to get their houses back on the foundations from which they had been washed, to buy a stove or bed to supply the place of the articles lost, and to make their houses inhabitable until they could, out of their resources, raise means to make more permanent repairs. It was a great help in time of much need, and the people of Catlettsburg will never cease to hold in kind remembrance all those who aided them in any way in this great calamity.

CATLETTSBURG CHURCHES.

THE Methodist Episcopal Church, Methodist Episcopal Church, South, and the Presbyterians have each a brick church edifice, built in the order named. The Methodist Episcopal Church, South, is the largest, the Presbyterian the most artistic, while the Methodist Episcopal Church stands between in size and appearance. The Methodist Episcopal Church, South, has also a neat frame church in the lower suburb. The Christians, or Reformers, have a good frame church, and at Hampton City a fine frame free church has lately been erected. The colored Methodists have a good frame church. The Regular Baptists have laid the stone foundation for a fine church, which they intend soon to complete. In all, Catlettsburg contains seven church-buildings, all finished, and one under way. The first church built at Catlettsburg, or the Mouth of Sandy, was a frame one for the use of Presbyterians and Southern Methodists, in 1849. It stood on the lot now occupied by the Presbyterian Church.

CATLETTSBURG SCHOOLS.

A COMMODIOUS two-story brick edifice, finished and furnished in the most superb manner, is the seat of the Catlettsburg graded school. At present four professors do the work. The tuition is free, the people of the town supplementing the State tax, to keep the school in operation ten months in the year. The school-buildings in both of the principal suburbs are first-class frame buildings. The colored children have the advantage of a five months' school.

The East Kentucky Normal School has become one of the most noted and popular institutions of learning in the State. Its beautiful grounds, laid off into walks, parks, flower-plats, as well as its fine buildings, make it the pride of Catlettsburgers, and of Big Sandians as well.

CATLETTSBURG'S BENEFACTORS.

D. W. EBA, an old-time Catlettsburg merchant, has reared, by his liberality, a magnificent monument, in the erection of the Alger House, a hotel-building every way adequate, in size, location, and artistic design, to meet the wants of the live, wide-awake metropolis at the Gate of the valley. While Mr. Eba may not be commended for financial sagacity in investing so heavily, all must praise him for the good taste and self-dependence displayed in adding so much to Catlettsburg enterprise.

A. F. Morse, another old-time merchant, supplied a long-felt want by the building of Morse Opera-house in Catlettsburg. It is one of the ornaments of the town. It is not only thrown open for dramatic performances, but is used for great meetings, religious, educational, and political. It makes a fine impression on distinguished strangers visiting the town.

CATLETTSBURG'S BANKS.

BEN. BURK, a typical old-time Sandian, was the first to open and conduct a bank on Sandy. In 1867 he went into the banking business at Catlettsburg, but continued in the business only a year. Not finding it profitable, he wound up the business, and was appointed postmaster. No one lost a cent by Mr. Burk's bank. He died many years ago, greatly respected by all who knew him. His widow still lives in the Burk homestead, greatly respected for her many noble qualities of head and heart.

Wilson & Andrews' Bank.

IN 1868 Daniel Wilson and James A. Andrews came from an interior county of the State, and started a private bank. They brought a large, strong safe, which was hauled up from the wharf on the Sunday after its arrival, requiring a string of oxen two hundred yards long. They placed the safe in an unpretending building, and soon opened business. Money was abundant at that time, and very soon the great vault groaned under the heavy deposits brought to the bank by business men and others, who felt that their money was safer locked up in a bank vault than it would be in a trunk, or bureau-drawer. The splendid opening seemed to daze the young bankers. The families of both were favorably known to Big Sandians as people of the highest respectability, and the young men, meanwhile, conducted themselves with propriety. But they engaged in building and running large saw-mills and planing-mills, in buying suburban real estate and wild lands, and laying out a town, in building houses, in keeping blooded stock, in patronizing livery stables, and in attending festivals and all charitable gatherings of the people. Most of the things were laudable; but it took money, and the draft on their bank was too great to stand the strain. In 1873 it closed its doors, and made an assignment, when it was found to owe about $90,000, with estimated assets a little less. The latter consisted largely in the saw-mills and planing-mills, in cheap lots in the vicinity of Catlettsburg, and disputed accounts against individuals, which required vexatious and expensive lawsuits to settle. As the personal and real property was sold at a great sacrifice, creditors only received about forty per cent on their claims. Mr. Wilson went to Texas, and engaged in stock-raising, while his partner, Mr. Andrews, went into the coal business in Ohio, but soon after took his own life.

The failure of this bank, it being the first that tumbled to the approaching financial panic—which rose into great fury in less than two weeks after by the collapse of the great banking-houses of Jay Cook, Henry Clews, and soon by scores of others in the great money centers—was waggishly looked upon as the starter of the great financial panic of 1873; an evidence that the valley was not only noted for having been at one time the center of the greatest ginseng trade on the continent, and for being now the greatest timber center in the Ohio Valley, but must ever after be celebrated as the starter of the great financial disasters of 1873 in the United States.

Witten & Davidson's Bank.

SOON after the suspension of Wilson & Andrews, Green M. Witten and Joseph Davidson, two well and favorably known business men of Prestonburg, commenced business in Catlettsburg as private bankers. Both gentlemen had the confidence of the entire people of the valley; and while so many of the people had lost heavily by the failure of its predecessor, the bank of Witten and Davidson and of G. M. Witten was always held in high esteem; for no one lost a cent by it, while it was a great convenience to the people. After two or three years' run, Mr. Davidson withdrew from the firm, after which time G. M. Witten alone conducted its affairs with the same satisfaction to the business people as when Mr. Davidson was a member of the firm. Mr. Witten, getting tired of the worry of the banking business, and his health declining, he wound up the affair, and retired from the field in 1882.

A National Bank Demanded.

THE opening up of the Chatterawha Railroad to Peach Orchard, forty miles up the Sandy Valley, and the building of the E. L. & Big Sandy Railroad, so stimulated trade and commerce in the great valley, that merchants, timber-traders, and business people generally, more than ever felt the great need of a well-endowed bank at Catlettsburg, the wholesale mercantile center of the valley, where they might find a safe place to make their deposits and get their mercantile paper discounted. Having had a checkered experience with private banks, the people turned away from them, but wanted a bank with plenty of capital to meet the wants of their growing business, and conducted by men who, by personal fitness and training in banking business, would afford them assurance of fair dealing; and over all the strong arm of the General Government to supervise the institution, and thus make doubly sure that no more failures would occur.

Catlettsburg National Bank.

THE field being so promising, and the demand for such a bank so imperative, Mr. A. C. Campbell, of Ashland, made a full investigation, and satisfied himself of the expediency of occupying it at once.

Mr. Campbell, John Russell, of Ashland; Columbus Prichard, Robert H. Prichard, and afterwards Wallace J. Williamson, of Catlettsburg, and perhaps others, became stock-holders, and organized the Catlettsburg National Bank. The bank opened for business on the first day of July, 1882, having for its officers John Russell, president; Robert H. Prichard, vice-president; A. C. Campbell, cashier; James Trimble, teller; and J. Lewis Prichard, collecting clerk and messenger. The first building occupied by the bank was a neat and tasteful structure on Center Street, fitted up in the best manner to accommodate both bankers and customers. That the stockholders and officers of the new bank at once inspired the greatest confidence in business circles was no wonder, when it is known that every one of them was noted for business capacity, strict integrity, with ample capital; and, in addition, the president was an old bank director, while the cashier had had many years of experience as cashier of one of the most successful national banks in the State. These gentlemen, being safe and conservative, started the bank on a

THE CATLETTSBURG NATIONAL BANK.

capital of $50,000, but some time after increased the capital stock to $100,000, all paid in.

The steady growth of the business of the bank was so great that the stock-holders in 1885 found it necessary to provide more extensive quarters for their prosperous business. They procured the lot on the north-east corner of Division and Center Streets, being the most eligible corner in town, on which they erected a bank building, which, for beauty of architectural design, substantiality of construction, convenience of internal and external arrangements, and general appearance, is equal to the finest buildings for similar purposes in the great cities of the country. It is altogether the handsomest building in Catlettsburg, a little city now noted for its many handsome structures for both private and public uses.

The walls of the basement are built of ashlered stones, trimmed with polished blue freestone. From the top of the basement the walls are of pressed brick, laid in diamond cement, covered in by an ornate roof of the best of Pennsylvania slate. The spacious sub-cellar, which extends under the entire building, is as light and dry as the great halls above. Part of the space is used for a coal-bin. The great vault, used for storing the money and other valuables of the bank, rests on the bed-rock of the basement. The remaining space can be used for confectionery, cigar-stands, barber-shops, or other light mechanical or mercantile business.

If you wish to go above and look around and take in the main parts, you will ascend the wide, spacious stone steps, which face both Division and Center Streets, guarded on either side by huge dragons in bronze, and you are in the lobby, a large, spacious hall, capable of holding one hundred or more persons in comfort. Immediately in front of you, separated by a carved wood counter, extending to the ceiling, you will see the large counting-room in which are engaged the officers and employés of the bank, busy at work at their desks or at their money-tables. From the lobby you get a glimpse of the great vault, the receptacle of the vast sums of money that all those men you see in the office are busily employed, day by day, in receiving, counting, paying out, and caring for. When in the lobby or hall, should you desire it, and Mr. Campbell is not too busy, and should he know you to be a gentleman of principle, he will take you by a side passage-way to the private office of the bank, where the officers and directors meet to transact the business of the bank. He will also lead the way, and show you other apartments which are needful in the conducting of a first-class bank on strict business principles.

The exterior of the building is as beautiful and tasteful as the interior is commodious and convenient. The stained glass windows, the dormers in sides and roof, the beautiful minarets and graceful spires, all combine to please the eye and satisfy the esthetic taste. Not only the citizens of Catlettsburg, but the people of the Sandy Valley in general, take pride in surveying this beautiful structure, feeling that it is a Sandy enterprise, the building being almost entirely constructed by Sandy Valley mechanics and artisans, and the bank officials and stockholders embracing a large number of native Sandians.

The description of the bank and its young life would not be complete without a short sketch of the officers and stockholders.

The president, John Russell, came to this section of country from Pennsylvania when a very young man, and obtained a position at Amanda Furnace, which he filled so faithfully that the late highly respected Hugh Means, then of Bellefont Furnace, took him into partnership. It has been said that, owing to Mr. Russell's superior management "Bellefont made money in good times and bad times;" and yet not at the expense of the hands, for he was always liked by them. He prospered in business as the years came and went, until to-day he is one of the most extensive real estate owners and manufacturers in the county. He is also engaged in large coal-mining operations, and is a heavy shareholder and president of the largest iron-works of the kind, save one, on the Continent. In a word, he is an honest, safe, and conservative business man, whose reputation for wealth, business qualifications, integrity, and moral worth has never been questioned.

A. C. Campbell, cashier, is a younger man, but has lived long enough to make his mark as a banker of unquestioned talent. He came of a family respected for their moral worth, who, by honest labor, strict attention to business, and financial ability, became wealthy. He has not only followed in their pathway, but has advanced on what they had so well begun. In his boyhood he was qualified as a book-keeper to enter the counting-house of a large iron manufacturing establishment, and was, about the close of the late war, elected by the directors of the Bank of Ashland as its teller. On the death of the late John N. Richardson, so favorably known to the elder people of the Sandy Valley, Mr. Campbell succeeded him as cashier. This change occurred in 1868. In 1872, the Bank of Ashland, doing business under a charter from the State of Kentucky, was organized under the laws of the United States, and became a national bank, with an increased capital in its vaults. Mr. Campbell continued his official position with the bank as its cashier until the year 1882, when he asked to be relieved to accept the same office in the Catlettsburg National Bank; making a continuous service now (1887) of four years as teller, and seventeen years as cashier. This makes him a veteran in the banking business. He owns large real estate interests in Ashland and elsewhere, and is one of Boyd County's solid men.

Robert H. Prichard, the vice-president, is also

a man of solid wealth, and of great financial ability. By industry and close application to business, commencing when a boy on his father's farm on the Big Sandy River, to trade in a small way, he now finds himself, before he has arrived at the zenith of manhood, a man of wealth. He is a member of the timber-trading firm of Vinson, Goble & Prichard, and has other large investments.

James Trimble, the teller, like Mr. Prichard, is a native Big Sandian, having been born and educated in Floyd County, the home of his maternal ancestors for four generations before him. His father dying while he was a little child, after he received his scholastic education he was trained in mercantile affairs by Major Morgan Lackey, his great-uncle, a noted merchant of Prestonburg, Kentucky. The directory of the bank chose him to count their money, owing to his exact business qualifications, strict integrity, and general fitness—all based on Christian principles. It is an open secret that he bids fair to reach a still higher plane in banking and financial circles.

Wallace J. Williamson and Columbus Prichard, of the directory, are both Sandians by birth and raising. The former is a native of Pike County, where he has, by inheritance and purchase, become a vast land-owner, his property being valuable in timber and minerals. He is an extensive timber-dealer, and member of the firm of Williamson & Hampton. He has other large business interests, and is among Catlettsburg's solid men. Mr. Prichard is a brother of Robert H. Prichard, the vice-president, and, as has been said of his brother, was born and raised on Sandy. He is the owner of a wholesale mercantile house in Catlettsburg, and has other investments.

Crate Brubaker entered the bank as chief book-keeper on its opening, but was compelled by declining health, though reluctantly, to give up his position, which for more than three years he filled so ably. His departure from the bank was lamented by every officer and employé, for he was a skillful accountant and a polished gentleman, admired for his many virtues and social qualities.

J. Lewis Prichard, the collecting clerk, on losing his health, was compelled to ask to be relieved, and sought relaxation in a business which called for more out-door exercise. He, too, was a faithful employé, and was greatly missed.

Young Mr. Davis, son of Mitch. Davis, of Tazewell County, Virginia, is now filling the place of Perly Brubaker, while Bascom Hatton, son of J. F. Hatton, of Rockville Station, is the successor of Mr. Prichard.

It will be seen that the Sandy Valley is largely in the ascendancy in the number of officers and employés of the bank—another evidence of the success of business tact and qualification possessed by the Sandy young men.

LOUISA,

THE county town of Lawrence County, is sometimes called the Gem of the Mountains. It is beautiful of situation, especially so when viewed from the town hill. Frederick Moore and others owned the land on which it was built. It was laid out in 1821, and made the county seat. It has the best court-house in Eastern Kentucky, and among the best in the State. It has three good church-buildings—a Methodist Episcopal, a Methodist Episcopal, South, and a Baptist—all brick. It has a Masonic Hall, built of brick, under which is the public school building. It is the seat of a large trade. The Chatterawha Railroad, passing through it, has greatly helped to start it off on the road to progress. It has a live Democratic paper, published and edited by the Messrs. Ferguson and Conly, both natives of the Sandy Valley. A roller process flour-mill, the only one on Sandy, is located in Louisa. Many eminent men of the Sandy Valley have been at some time, or are now, residents of Louisa. It was once the seat of a great ginseng and fur trade. It is now the head-quarters for many timber men.

Lawrence County has vast forests of oak timber, and it is a wonder, the land being good, it is not denuded of it. There is a fine opening for investments in land for cultivation in Lawrence County. The county is Democratic in politics, but the people often ignore politics and put into office men of the minority.

At Louisa the first attempt to settle in the valley was made by the erection of two forts in 1787, by Van Cover and others.

RICHARDSON,

THE present terminus of the Chatterawha Railroad, is a bustling little town, perched on the east bank of the Sandy River, fifty miles from Catlettsburg. M. C. D. Preston, a fine representative of the house of Preston, is the hotel-keeper there, and in the store has for a partner Patrick Henry Vaughan, who honors the name by his manly ways.

PAINTSVILLE,

THE county town of Johnson County, was laid out in 1842, on the lands of the Dixons, one-half mile from the Sandy River, on Paint Creek. It has an old-time court-house, built of brick, and of sufficient capacity to answer the purposes for which it was built at the formation of the county. The people year by year grow in morality; and four days, and often less, is sufficient time to keep the Criminal Court and grand jury in session; and three or four days finishes the docket of the Circuit Court. The people are, perhaps, the most law-abiding of any county in the State, and all seem to pay their debts and settle their disputes without recourse to law.

Paintsville and Johnson County have good schools and churches, dotting the whole country. Rev. William Jayne, an educated Baptist preacher, has done much to help along the education of school-teachers in his "Enterprise Academy," located at Flat Gap, in Johnson County.

Johnson County is the opposite of its neighbor Floyd in politics, the latter being as solidly Republican, though by a smaller majority, as the former is Democratic. Before the war Johnson had at one election but seven Whigs in its borders. All others were Democrats. But the war changed it all.

Paintsville has two frame school-houses and three church-buildings. The first, built in 1866, the Methodist Episcopal, is a frame; the next, built in about 1880, the Methodist Episcopal Church, South, is a beautiful brick; and the last, a neat brick structure, belongs to the Christian or Reform Church.

Near Paintsville, on Jennies' Creek, lived Jenny Wiley, whose three children were killed by the Indians, and she was carried away captive, but returned several years after. The name of the fertile stream is her monument, and will perpetuate her name. Her descendants live in Johnson County.

MARTINSBURG,

The county seat of Elliott County, is located on the waters of the Little Sandy River. It has fair public buildings. The town is small, but is growing. The county has much good corn and grazing land, and is very rich in timber and coal; and is noted for the great number of horses and mules its people raise for market.

The morals of the people are greatly improved, for it is well known that for some time in the past much disorder prevailed in Elliott. Churches and school-houses are being built throughout the county.

Elliott County is overwhelmingly Democratic.

EDEN,

The county seat of Martin County, is a bright little place, nestled on the banks of the Rock Castle, eight miles from the Chatterawha Railroad, at Peach Orchard. It has a good brick court-house and jail, a good church (Methodist Episcopal, South), and a school-house. The land is covered with fine oak and poplar timber, selling at low prices. The great Warfield Salt-works are located at Warfield, on the Tug River, ten miles from Eden. A salt-well of great flow and strength of water is found on the farm of Wells Ward, a few miles from Eden, which has force enough to run a mill. One of the most prodigious gas-wells found in the Union is at Warfield, in this county. The gas from the well would, if applied, run all the machinery of the industries of Cincinnati, besides illuminating the great city. General George Washington noted the appearance of the gas at Warfield in his field-notes, when he ran the line up Tug in 1767.

The county is largely Republican, although the county offices are generally divided.

SALYERSVILLE

Is the county town of Magoffin County, and was made the capital on the formation of the county in 1860. It has a good brick court-house and jail. A good frame Methodist Episcopal Church and a school-building are among its public edifices. It has several large stores, doing a large business. Two good flour-mills and saw-mills, a woolen-mill, a large tannery, and other industries, make it a live town. The town is on the east bank of the main Licking, just below the celebrated Burning Fork, the seat of a great gas deposit. Salyersville is eighteen miles from the Sandy River, at or near Paintsville. It is near the seat of Licking Station, an old fortification built to guard against Indian depredations. Magoffin is noted for the fertility of its bottom lands and its forests of valuable timber.

In politics the county is very close, giving,

however, a small Republican majority; yet the county offices are generally divided amongst both parties. Congressman Taulbee lives in Salyersville.

WEST LIBERTY,

THE county seat of Morgan County, is on the Licking, but part of Morgan County is in the Sandy Valley. It is a small but substantial town, and has a good reputation for the number of able public men who have brought honor to the place by living in it. The county is rich in lands, minerals, and timber. West Liberty has a newspaper, formerly the *Scorcher,* now the *Gem,* which is one of the brightest journals in the State. In politics the paper is Democratic. It is conducted by the Hazleriggs, father and son. A good academy of learning is located in West Liberty. Splendid deposits of cannel-coal are found in Morgan. The county is strongly Democratic.

PRESTONBURG,

COUNTY seat of Floyd County, is the oldest town in the valley, having been founded in 1799, and named after Colonel Preston, who was at the time assistant surveyor of the public lands in Kentucky. Being so long the seat of political empire, it is natural that many great and noted men should seek a home in its precincts, or for a time sojourn in its borders. In addition to the personal annals of citizens of the county of Floyd, found recorded in this book, many events of a general nature should be recorded, also, to make the history complete.

Stirring events occurred in Floyd County during the great Civil War. At Ivy Mountain, in the upper edge of the county, the battle of that name was fought, in the Fall of 1861, between the Confederate forces, commanded by Colonel A. J. May, and the Union forces, led by General William Nelson. The Confederates had for some weeks been recruiting their forces at Prestonburg; but on the approach of Nelson with near five thousand men, they hastily left their camp at that place and retreated up the Sandy River. On reaching the upper part of Ivy Mountain, and at the head of a long, narrow stretch in the road, on one side of which was the Sandy River and on the other a solid cliff of rock, so precipitous that a squirrel could scarce find a foothold, the Confederates arranged themselves in battle order, and waited the approach of the Union forces. The battle was sharply contested. While the Confederates had the advantage in the ground selected, the Union force was greatly superior in numbers and discipline. When the whole Union force came within musket range of the Southern army, the latter retired in good order. Several were wounded on both sides. The killed were but two or three on each side. Among the killed on the Confederate side was Hon. Henry M. Rust, of Greenup, Ky. Mr. Rust had just finished his term of service in the Kentucky Legislature as senator from his district. Being a native Virginian, and his State having declared for secession, he felt morally bound to follow her in the war. His death was not only lamented by his Confederate friends, but he was mourned by the people of Boyd and Greenup with the most bitter sorrow; for all knew him to be a man of superior talents, and possessing a most generous nature. What made his fate the more sad was the fact that he was betrothed to a beautiful young lady, whose father was a distinguished senator. Some time after the battle his remains were carried to Catlettsburg, and buried.

Early in the year of 1862 the battle of Middle Creek, in Floyd County, was fought, General Marshall commanding the Southern forces, and Colonel Garfield, with his regiment, the 42d Ohio, the 14th Kentucky, and other forces, commanding the Union army. For several hours a continuous rain of ball and shell was poured out. The Confederates retired when they saw that they were overcome with a superior force and were being outflanked, taking their dead and wounded with them. They marched to Pound Gap. The Union army lost one man killed, Nelson Boggs, of the 14th, and several slightly wounded. Ten years after the battle a person could have picked up hundreds of bullets, as they lay scattered in every direction. This battle gave to Colonel Garfield a general's star, and no doubt started him on the road leading to the Presidential chair.

THE SMALL-POX.

IN 1883 one John Neal, or, as he was generally called, "Uncle Jack," a wealthy, miserly merchant, high up on Beaver, went to Portsmouth, Ohio, to lay in a stock of goods. He there contracted that loathsome disease, small-pox. Not knowing that he had been exposed to the disease, he returned by way of Catlettsburg, putting his goods aboard a push-boat, and taking passage on the same craft himself. Before reaching home he was taken sick, but still continued his journey until he reached his home. His neighbors, in the kindness of their hearts, for several miles round, called to see him, under the impression that it was measles, as he had broken out. Soon the old man died, and many flocked to his funeral. In ten days nearly fourscore cases of small-pox had broken out in the neighborhood. As soon as it was known that the disease was small-pox, the county authorities set to work to meet the great emergency that was upon them.

A young doctor of Prestonburg, named A. H. Stewart, who had just returned from Cincinnati, where he had been attending his first lectures, came home to spend Christmas vacation, and hearing of the great scourge, applied himself to treating the sick and burying the dead. For weeks he was completely shut in from the outside world, and battled heroically with the great scourge. Dr. Turner, of Paintsville, was called to his assistance, and rendered valuable service. Local doctors were also brave. The gallant young disciple of Esculapius, Stewart, remained on the ground until the loathsome pestilence was completely stamped out, and, after burning the infected buildings by order of the civil authorities, and disinfecting furniture and fumigating his own clothes, returned to Prestonburg, his home, to receive the plaudits of the people.

The people of Prestonburg, while always noted for intellectual culture, and given to hospitality, devoted more of their time and means to public affairs, national, State, and county, than to developing the town materially. But a tide of material prosperity is now flowing in, which bids fair to continue until the old, decayed buildings, erected by the first settlers, give place to modern structures, more pretentious in appearance and convenient in arrangement. Walter S. Harkins, Frank Hopkins, and others of the younger leading citizens, stimulated by their young blood, have set the example in erecting buildings, both for residences and offices, of handsome architectural construction, that would do credit to towns much larger. Especially is this so of the well-arranged office of Mr. Harkins, an illustration of which embellishes this book.

The older men of the place are catching the infection, and the time is not far distant when *old* Prestonburg will be clad in *new* garments of modern progress, and the oldest town in the Sandy Valley will become the most modern in material, intellectual, and moral prosperity.

In early days, Prestonburg was somewhat given to dissipation; but no town on the Sandy ever had a stronger moral and religious element to combat the vices of the day. The homes of the people were always the earthly paradise of preachers, the people showing them and the cause they advocated great love and respect. The great Dr. Peter Akers, once the brilliant lawyer of Flemingsburg, delivered the first sermon of his life in Prestonburg while attending court there. This great divine died in 1886, aged ninety-two years.

HINDMAN,

THE county seat of Knott County, is located on Beaver, a tributary of the Big Sandy. The public buildings are in course of construction. Knott County is a rugged, hilly country, but has valuable deposits of coal and a great deal of valuable timber within its borders. It is Democratic in politics.

PIKEVILLE

WAS laid out as the county seat of Pike on the formation of the county, in 1821. Thomas Owens, a New Yorker, but of English descent, the grandfather of Jefferson Owens, of Catlettsburg, owned the land at the time. Mr. Owens was often called "Dad" Owens as a nickname. He was a good man, upright, honest, religious, and liked by all. For a time he was a partner of Frederick Moore in selling goods at Pikeville. Mr. Moore had a large store at the "Forks." One day "Dad" Owens went into the store, and was told by his partner that he would let him take up to the Pike store all the coffee he might want; "for," said Mr. Moore, "I have just received the largest invoice ever brought to Sandy, being a full barrel of the enchanting berry." In that early day coffee was only used on rare occasions. A very sick person, or the marriage of a favorite daughter, would bring it forth; and sometimes a cup for the preacher, and one for the grown folks on Sunday morning, was indulged. Children never drank it in early times, and their health would be better and the race would be improved if they did not drink it now.

The public buildings erected were sufficient for the times, and though sixty-six years have come and gone, the same court-house and jail are doing service for the county. A new court-house and jail are now being constructed, to take the place of the old buildings. The new ones will be not only a credit to the county of Pike, but to the State.

Pikeville improved but little until 1845, when she made a forward movement. A good frame Methodist Church was built, and many other evidences of progress appeared. Since the close of the Civil War in 1865, Pikeville has been built up with more solid and commodious brick and frame buildings than any town of its size in the valley. Two new churches have been built, one by the Methodist Episcopal Church, the other by the Church South; and a large Masonic temple graces the place. Some fine brick residences adorn the avenues. Among the handsomest are those of Colonel John Dils, Jr., and Richard Ferrell.

The trade of Pikeville is very large, coming, part of it, for fifty miles. Pike County is a very rich county in farming lands, as well as in timber and minerals. Pikeville is a picturesque little town. As it skirts the banks of the Sandy, it looks like a variegated ribbon unrolled from the block. Its people are full of enterprise, thrift, and progress.

The county is Democratic in politics; but the people pay but little regard to the dictation of their party leaders on either side, and elect to office men who suit them, regardless of political bearing.

Pictorial Embellishments in the Book.

Each picture is designed to represent a special subject. Judge Borders, Moses (Coby) Preston, Ben. Williamson, Fred. Moore, and General Hager stand for the early pioneers. Nat Auxier, Colonel John Dils, Jr., stand for the people of the second period of Big Sandy history. Dr. Kincaid represents the old doctors, and Dr. Banfield, the younger physicians. J. Frew Stewart stands for the old classical teachers, and John W. Langley for the literary young men of the valley. Judge John M. Burns represents the brilliant family whose name he bears—a family which was a potent factor in the law and politics of the early days, and grows no less with time. Hon. M. J. Ferguson represents an honored family, and his own great name and fame. General G. W. Gallup stands for having attained the highest military title of any Big Sandian in the War for the Union; Major Burchett, to show to what eminence a young man may reach, though living in obscurity and laden with toil, if he only has energy. John S. Patton represents the young man who is sure to reach the pinnacle of fame by a steady resolve to do right and persevere. S. S. Vinson represents the sturdy Sandian overcoming great difficulties, and gaining the front rank as a business man and upright public officer. Rev. Z. Meek, D. D., represents the youth who, in starting out in life, wrote "Excelsior" on his banner, and never stopped until he achieved success as editor, minister, and business man. Captain Marcum represents energy peculiar to the Sandy people, and is an example of the success which may be attained by trimming the midnight lamp to get an education. Felix A. Barbee represents the newspaper fraternity, as does Captain Marcum and others. Captain A. E. Adams represents the dashing cavalryman, politician, and business man. Walter S. Harkins represents the successful lawyer, who applies the laws of business to all business matters, and is not neglectful of cultivating the esthetic graces that beautify mind and person. His uncle, John Harkins, stands for a brilliant lawyer and noble man. R. M. Weddington represents journalism and the head of an old-time and honored family. Captain John B. Goff stands for the warm-hearted man and soldier of the Confederate army. William Crum represents the struggling boy, making a success in life by close application to business; while Arthur Preston is given as a specimen of the energy and thrift of the later generations of the old house of Preston. Colonel Jay H. Northup represents a leader in the broadening out of the timber-trade, and the liberal promoter of public improvements in the valley. George S. Richardson stands for the pioneer in the development of the mineral resources of the valley. Rev. William Hampton fitly represents energy in improving the valley, and the Christian minister. His wife stands for all the virtues of the noble wife, mother, and Christian lady, and as a representative of the honored house of Buchanan.

The pictorial illustrations of the buildings found in this book are singularly correct.

The residence of Colonel John Dils, Jr., at Pikeville, is both spacious and ornate, just such a home as a wealthy and cultured gentleman would be expected to provide for his family.

Walter S. Harkins, of Prestonburg, is not behind Colonel Dils in building architecture. His law office is far in advance of any law office in the valley, both in beauty of design and completeness of internal and external arrangements.

Captain Frank Preston's homestead, at Paintsville, is ornamental enough, but, like its owner, is more solid than showy. It is one of the most comfortable and convenient homesteads in the valley.

The residence of John Lockwood, of Lockwood Station, on the Chatterawha Railroad, is called the best farm homestead in the valley. When it is stated that it cost $11,000 to construct it, it will be plain that it has no superior in the great valley.

The illustrations of the buildings are given as specimens of the numerous buildings now found standing in every section of the valley, both on the Levisa and Tug.

Coal Industries.

As far back as 1845 companies were formed in the North, and came to the Sandy Valley to mine the coal found in such abundance as to attract the attention of geologists and capitalists. One of the first to operate the mines on Sandy was an Ohio company with a Mr. Miles, a relative of the now great showman of that name, and Captain Milton Freese, with Mr. Robert Crutcher accompanying them. The company opened a mine a few miles above Prestonburg. Another company opened a mine still further up the river. Richard Deering, however, had built a mill at Abbott, some time before these other enterprises were started. He intended to mine coal; but his enterprise was nipped in the bud, and was afterwards taken up by a Pennsylvania company, which spent considerable money, but after several years of struggling abandoned the undertaking. William A. Foster, so well and favorably known at Catlettsburg, where he resided many years, first made his appearance on Sandy as store-keeper for the company.

A company operated the mines at Hurricane, eighteen miles from the Mouth, and always had a good trade in its products. Many mines along the river have been worked for forty years to supply the local trade, and furnish steamers with the fuel to run them. Among these were McHenry's, six miles above Louisa; Daniel Wheeler's, just below Paintsville, and Judge Layne's noted field at Laynesville. None of the enterprises named ever brought a fortune to the owners or prosperity to the valley, though a few have furnished a living for the men working them. No doubt all of these men would have made money, but for lack of transportation and market.

PEACH ORCHARD.

THE Peach Orchard Company rises above all other companies combined in the magnitude of business, largeness of undertaking, and carrying forward of improvements necessary to convey their coal to market. About 1847, George Carlisle (father of John Carlisle), R. B. Bowler, and other capitalists of Cincinnati, formed a company, and purchased a large tract of land lying on the east side of the Sandy River, forty miles above its mouth. The company proceeded at once to make preparations to open the mines, known by the natives to be of vast magnitude and of the most superior quality. In 1850 Mr. William B. Mellen, an Eastern gentleman of extensive business experience and of great culture, came to Peach Orchard, and for eleven years had full superintendence of the works. The members of the company being liberal, and having full confidence in the judgment and ability of Mr. Mellen, gave him almost unlimited power to carry forward the business of the company. Cottages of a superior quality were erected out of lumber cut by a saw-mill first brought on the ground by the company. A gristmill of fine construction was erected to grind wheat and corn to furnish bread for the people and provender for the animals at the works. The farmers for twenty miles around availed themselves of the opportunity of taking their wheat to this mill for grinding, it being the first one erected in the Lower Sandy Valley that made better flour than a horse-mill. It also had a first-class carding-machine attached, which was extensively patronized. The mill was of the most advanced pattern of its day. Time and tide carried it away after it had so long served the threefold purpose for which it was built. The company had a large, well-constructed school-house put up, well provided with good seats and ventilation, and placed in charge an educated and Christian teacher, to train the children of the miners, and others on the ground, for useful lives. And, to crown all, a commodious house of worship was erected, where God's Word was expounded on the Sabbath.

While mechanics were busy erecting the houses on the grounds, miners were equally busy in opening the mines; and as soon as barges were made ready, the Peach Orchard coal was tipped into them, ready to be sent to market on the first rise of water in the Sandy sufficient to take them out.

At that time not a cent had been spent to improve the navigation of the river. While small steamers could plow their way to Pikeville and return for five or six months in the year, when it came to float down the obstructed stream great barges laden with black diamonds, it was a harder undertaking. But with this great drawback, the plucky company kept steadily persevering, Mr. Mellen so managing as to keep the company from sustaining serious loss.

In 1859 the company invited Governor Floyd, who then owned the Warfield property on Tug, to join them in an effort to slack-water both rivers. Mr. Ledbetter, an experinced engineer from the Muskingum River improvements, attended the meeting at Peach Orchard and Catlettsburg, and reported the practicability of the proposition. Governor Floyd could not be present, but sent word that his desire was to have the work pushed forward. Before any thing could well be done, the clouds portending the most gigantic civil strife known to history appeared in the political horizon, checking all efforts to arrange for the work proposed.

The last *barge-load* of coal was sent to market from Peach Orchard in the Spring of 1861. Soon after this, Mr. Mellen moved to Cincinnati with his family, and took a position in the Union army. It must have been with many regrets that he left his beautiful home at Peach Orchard, when it is remembered that his house was equal to many of the suburban mansions of the Queen City, while his lawns and gardens were full of the finest shrubs, plants, and flowers, which had been transplanted from foreign climes to please the eye and refine the taste for the beautiful. Not only these evidences of culture, but a beautiful park stocked with native deer, afforded pleasure to the eye, and furnished juicy venison for the table.

When Mr. Mellen went away, Henry Danby, an Englishman, who had come to the works when young, and faithfully performed the duties placed upon him in the subordinate positions he had filled under Mr. Mellen, was left in charge, to take care of the property, and run the mill and store, waiting the time when the works would again be started up.

Mr. Danby, soon after the close of the war, became restive, and severed his connection with the company, going away with five thousand dollars or more, accumulated while in the company's employ. He had failed to woo and marry when a young man, and soon after arriving in Cincinnati, he, like many other oldish men, married a girl less than half his own years. The match was unequal, and turned out badly. In about 1883 Mr. Danby, broken down in health and showing signs of premature old age, came to Catlettsburg

alone, and took passage on an up-going Sandy
River steamer for Peach Orchard. He was put off
at the landing of Gordon Burgess, whose daughter
had long before married Chris. Neal, a chosen
friend of his. On going up to Mr. Burgess's house
he asked that he might be permitted to enter, and
die. The family, with that kindness of heart for
which they are noted, bade him come in and his
wants should be supplied. For several weeks he
lay at death's door, during which time the Burgess
family, aided by Chris. Neal, his old-time friend,
George S. Richardson, and others of Peach Orchard,
furnished every thing necessary for his comfort
while his life was ebbing away; and when death
came to the poor man's relief, those kind friends,
who had so generously stood by him in sickness,
gave his remains a decent Christian burial. Henry
Danby's life was truly one of sunshine and shadows.

GEORGE S. RICHARDSON.

WHEN Henry Danby quit the position he had
held during the war, the company placed their affairs in the hands of George S. Richardson, a business man from Massachusetts. The great store of
the company was conducted on a large scale under
Mr. Richardson's superintendency, assisted by
Andrew Butler, the father of Bascom Butler. The
latter has risen to the honorable position of auditor
of the Chatterawha Railroad. The mills of the
company were kept in operation, grinding grain for

the farmers, and while nothing was done to start anew the mining of the coal, the members of the company were casting about and maturing plans to construct a railroad from their coal-fields to the Ohio River. Mr. Richardson, the company's efficient agent, carried out his employers' suggestions by creating a public sentiment in favor of the road. He often rode up and down the proposed line, talking with farmers on the route, telling them of the importance of a more speedy and certain transit to the outlaying country for themselves and for the products of their farms. At Catlettsburg some opposition was manifested against the right of way through the town. This arose from the fact that several old citizens of the place had, about 1850, subscribed liberally to the building of the E. L. and B. S. Road, on condition that the road should be built through the place, and had been compelled by the decisions of the courts to pay their subscriptions, although the road under the old company was never built.

GEO. S. RICHARDSON.

These subscriptions fell heavily on several parties of the Gate City, especially on the widow and heirs of John Culver, whose donation to the defunct company was about ten thousand dollars. But on a vote of the people, by a large majority, the right of way was granted the road to pass over the streets and alleys of the town.

Ashland, wishing to have the road come within her borders, reached out her hand with great liberality, giving the right of way, Mr. David D. Geiger, a large real estate owner giving free passage over his land. The wealthy capitalists of the city took stock in the road, and as the water in the Ohio River at Ashland is always of sufficient depth to afford a good pool for barges, Ashland became the Ohio terminus of the road. From Catlettsburg to Louisa there was but little opposition among the citizens against the road going over their farms.

Louisa was more than liberal to the road. With Colonel Jay H. Northup, Judge M. J. Ferguson, Judge John M. Rice, and other liberal men living there, it could not have been otherwise. But how to get beyond Louisa was the rub. From some mysterious cause a fearful opposition was manifested among the land-owners between *Three Mile and George's Creek*. They were opposed to letting the road pass by their doors, with depots and stations established at proper points, affording them so many conveniences. They cried, "Away with it! Away with it!" One wealthy gentleman went so far in his opposition as to give fifty dollars to have the road cross the Sandy three miles above Louisa, and take a roundabout course to the Peach Orchard coal-fields, the objective point of the road.

Mr. Richardson, the company's agent, labored day and night to convince the people living on the route of the strong opposition, that they were working against their own interests in putting the company to an immense additional outlay, and at the same time driving the road from the best part of Lawrence County, to traverse one of greater distance, with but little to feed the road when finished. It is true the company might have sent their corps of engineers, with Colonel Forbes at the head, and laid out the road through the lands of the opposers, and afterwards sent a jury along the route to assess damages; but their patience was gone, and they at once adopted the Griffith's Creek route, cutting off from advanced civilization the splendid country lying between Three Mile and George's Creek, the State road passing up from Louisa having fallen, since the building of the railroad, into a mere neighborhood passway, while all is life and activity on the route along Griffith's Creek, although the lands are poor.

The road was at first commenced as a narrow gauge; but before completion the standard gauge was adopted, and when it was completed from Ashland, on the Ohio River, to Peach Orchard, forty-five miles, in 1882, it was found to be one of the best constructed short-line roads in the country. The people living along the route of opposition now lament their short-sightedness in not welcoming the passage of the great civilizer by their doors, but feel that it is now too late to make amends for past errors.

Mr. Richardson has held the office of vice-president of the road, and filled other places of trust and honor in the company. At present he is superintendent of the coal-mines which belong to the company.

The Chatterawha Road is being extended from Richardson, named in honor of George S. Richardson, ten miles above Peach Orchard, on the Sandy River, to White House, where is found one of the best fields of pure cannel-coal known in the State. The road will doubtless soon become a link in the great through line from Chicago to Charleston, and make the Sandy Valley one of the most prosperous regions of country to be found in the State.

JOHN CARLISLE.

A GREAT many men from other States and countries have come to the Sandy, and by their coming have added wealth to the valley; and to those men who have brought their energy, experience, and capital, the people at large owe much. But to no one do they owe as large a debt of gratitude as to John Carlisle, of Cincinnati.

Mr. Carlisle, when a boy, had visited the Peach

Orchard Mines, in company with his father, who was in his life-time a principal owner. Young Carlisle, although an only son, with great expectations of wealth by inheritance from a rich parentage, insisted on receiving an education which would specially prepare him for engineering and mining. Having his wishes respected by such a course in college, the bent of his youthful mind has ripened into full fruition in mature manhood. While he has had, and still has, large investments in railroads centering in his native city, and great ventures in the city of his birth and rearing, he has from boyhood looked upon the possiblities of the Sandy Valley with a devotion almost unparalleled. For nearly a quarter of a century his time has been freely given in pushing the improvements undertaken by his father and associates in days before the great Civil War, and carried since by himself. He has given of his means as freely as he has of his time to promote the same cause. And should the Chatterawha become a link in the great North-west and South-east through line, of which there is little doubt, his host of friends in the Sandy Valley hope to see him at the front of the great enterprise.

CHATTERAWHA OR PEACH ORCHARD COAL.

As soon as the Chatterawha Road was open to Peach Orchard, it was taxed to its utmost to provide transportation for the Peach Orchard coal,

COAL INDUSTRIES. 319

which had already gained a high reputation as one of the best articles in the country.

ASHLAND, KENTUCKY,

THE Ohio terminus of the road, has been greatly quickened into fresh life by this new feeder of her great industries.

CATLETTSBURG, KENTUCKY,

THE natural Gate into the Sandy Valley, with the Sandy River pouring into her lap the trade of the Upper Sandy, would have quivered under the blow had the road passed some other way than through her borders. The Chatterawha Road has added greatly in increasing the sales of her wholesale stores and numerous industries.

LOUISA

IMMEDIATELY felt the quickening power, and put on city airs, with city business to back her up. The most ornate and well-aranged court-house and clerk's offices in Eastern Kentucky now grace Louisa, resulting from the building of the road. Two superb churches have been added, to lead her people heavenward, while a splendid flour-mill, on the roller principle, is added to her industries. Mechanical shops have increased, and, although stores have sprung into existence all over the county, the merchants of Louisa make larger sales than ever before. Every hamlet through which the road passes has quickened and started out on a more prosperous career, while small industries have sprung up all along the line, from Ashland to Richardson.

These are only a small part of what may be expected when the road is pushed on up the valley.

COLONEL JAY H. NORTHUP,

FROM the first, has been a director of the road, and few men did more to encourage, by his wise counsel, and by contributing his means to carry the enterprise to completion, and when it became necessary to appoint a receiver and general manager to conduct the affairs of the corporation, Colonel Northup was, of all others, called

COLONEL JAY H. NORTHUP.

upon to fill the place. The position was a delicate one, requiring great business talent, integrity, and moral principles to satisfy both the owners and creditors of the road. But the colonel has satisfied all parties of his ability and trustworthiness to fill this position, which was unsought by him. Captain Joseph Mitchell, who had much experience in procuring right of way for other roads, was a very forceful factor in drawing the line of the road on the Kentucky side of the Sandy River, having to contend against Hon. C. B. Hoard, an extensive real estate owner of Ceredo, West Virginia, who held out strong inducements to have the Ohio River terminus at that point. Colonel Hoard's efforts were ably seconded by Judge M. J. Ferguson, who preferred the West Virginia route to the Ohio. Mr. Mitchell did valuable service to the people of Ashland and Catlettsburg in battling for the Kentucky line.

It is proper to state that the owners of the Peach Orchard coal-fields did not build the road without other aid. Outside parties took a generous amount of stock in the enterprise. But, after all, the road would not have been constructed had not the coal company moved first in the matter. Colonel S. R. Forbes, the engineer, who laid out the road to the great tunnel, is back at the head of the corps, and is as proud of his work as a mother is of her first-born; yet the Chatterawha is by no means Mr. Forbes's first work in railroad engineering.

Sandy Valley Timber Trade.

Many old men still lingering on the shores of time claim the honor of cutting and conveying to market the first raft of saw-logs from the Sandy Valley. It can not be stated with any degree of accuracy who started the trade in timber which has grown to such gigantic proportions. The Ratcliffs, the Williamsons, the Weddingtons, the Meads, the Borderses, the Prestons, the Garreds, the Hamptons, the Leslies, the Auxiers, the Mayos, the Burgesses, the Justices, the Bevinses, and others, were at an early day engaged in the timber trade.

The trade in timber on the Sandy was a small affair until 1840, when it began to assume great magnitude, and continued to grow rapidly. By 1850 the number of logs cut and carried to market had annually quadrupled in number, and had considerably increased in price. In 1860, just preceding the commencement of the Civil War, the run in timber had increased fourfold since 1850. From 1861 to 1865, inclusive, the trade almost entirely ceased, save in furnishing timber for gunboats. In 1866 the cutting and running of timber to market received a wonderful impetus. This was owing to the greatly increased demand for lumber to supply the lack caused by four years devoted to destructive war. The timber trade in the valley was greatly pushed, and, in fact, boomed, by Samuel S. Vinson and Brothers.

Colonel Jay H. Northup, a wide-awake New Yorker, who came to Louisa on the wave of the oil excitement in the Sandy Valley, was wise enough to see the great possibilities in the timber traffic; he formed a partnership with M. B. Goble, and, like the firm of Vinson Brothers, prosecuted the business with great vigor.

Captain O. C. Bowles, an Ohio man of broad business views, had the sagacity, supposed to be possessed by all enlightened men of that great State, to see the great opening for enlargement in the timbering trade in the Upper Sandy Valley, and embarked with great energy in the enterprise. He subsequently laid down tramways to reach his forests, and brought the timber to the Sandy River on trucks drawn by a locomotive. An amusing incident occurred in running the locomotive, which is remarkable in not terminating in a tragedy. The captain came down to Catlettsburg, and hired an old railroad engineer to take charge of his locomotive. On reaching the road he placed him on the snorting horse. The owner hoped for good; but with lightning speed the train rolled on. The owner and all hands were in great fright. The captain remonstrated with the man of the valve; but the engineer said that it was none of the captain's business; that he was put in charge and held himself responsible for the loss of life and property. The train by force was stopped. The first impulse of Captain Bowles was to knock the man down; but he thought it undignified to engage in a fight with an employé, and instead discharged him from his service. The man wended his way to Catlettsburg, and by his eccentric ways was discovered to be *non compos mentis*, and was taken by his wife to the home of their people in an Eastern State, where the unfortunate lunatic, a year or so after, died of softening of the brain. It is thrilling to think of a lunatic in charge of an engine on a railroad track.

Besides the firms named, there were many other men, natives of Big Sandy, who rose to the occasion of the timber boom after the war, and entered with great spirit in the tempting traffic. Wallace J. Williamson, Mont. Lawson, Butler Ratliff, the Prestons of Paintsville, the Mayos, the Bevinses, the Leslies, Sam Keel, Levi Atkins, Bill David, Garred Ratliff, Captain William Bartram, and, before him, his father, James Bartram, James A. Abbott, and many others, became heavy handlers of timber.

From the earliest period of running timber, it was bought from the producer at Catlettsburg by individuals and firms formed for that purpose; yet meanwhile much, if not most, of it was run to the markets on the Ohio River by the first owners, and sold on their own account. Among the most noted of the pioneer timber buyers at the Mouth were William and Levi J. Hampton, David D. Geiger, Hansford H. Kinner, John Meek, John Creed Burks, and some others; in fact, Mordecai. M. Williams should be classed with the old-time buyers, although Mr. Williams is not an old-time man. He was a mere stripling of a boy when he entered the field as a dealer in the great product of the Sandy Valley.

By 1875 to 1880 the trade had grown so great that firms representing heavier capital began to be formed at Catlettsburg. The earliest of these firms to go into the business there was Vinson, Goble & Prichard, consisting of Sam'l S. Vinson, M. B. Goble, and Robert H. Prichard. They made a new departure in the manner of conducting the business. Formerly no system of book-keeping was used in recording the transactions of buying and selling, but each member or individual would keep a memorandum of the business done for the season, and then call on some one supposed to be competent to settle up, and strike the dividend due each member. This firm believed that whatever was worth doing was worth doing well. So the first thing they did was to erect a suitable building, and fix it up with every convenience for an office in which to transact their business. They procured all necessary books and stationery to record and journalize the business, over which they placed that model accountant and book-keeper, George B. Patton, an expert in the science, who, although interested with his two brothers in a large wholesale manufacturing and commercial business in town, knowing that his interest would continue safe in their hands, was induced by a large salary to accept the place. Williamson & Hampton immediately followed suit in the same line, and placed their books and office in charge of George J. Dickseid, an ubiquitous Ohio man, who left the management of a large dry-goods establishment to assume the responsibility of the new field of figures, and well sustains his reputation as a correct accountant and book-keeper.

All other firms now dealing in timber have an office, and a book-keeper to do the writing and make the calculations incident to the buying and selling of the timber and lumber passing through their hands. This new departure has been of untold benefit to both buyer and seller. Many a dollar has gone to its proper place, whereas before a settlement was only guess-work; and many an expensive lawsuit has been avoided by the new method of doing business inaugurated by Vinson, Goble & Prichard.

The amount of money paid out annually at Catlettsburg for timber and lumber has risen from an insignificant sum in 1840 to $1,500,000 in 1886, the quantity of timber run and its cash value increasing year by year.

The manner of running the logs to the markets below on the Ohio River has changed as greatly as have the methods of buying. Formerly about twenty rafts were strung together, called a fleet, and guided and pushed by men. Now most of the timber is towed down by means of tow-boats, some of the boats owned by Catlettsburg timber-dealers.

The timber supply seems to be as prolific as it was a quarter of a century ago. Then the owners of timber-land were constantly giving out that timber was getting very scarce; but, for all that, the supply grows greater and better as the years roll on.

Big Sandy Newspapers.

In 1852 a printer by the name of Smith came to Catlettsburg, and started the first newspaper ever published in the Sandy Valley. The editor was no less a personage than Rev. E. C. Thornton. The paper was neutral in politics, although Mr. Thornton was an unflinching Democrat. It was called the *Big Sandy News*. It was published less than two years, and suspended for lack of patronage. The *Sandy Valley Advocate* was the next venture in the newspaper business on Sandy. James J. Miller, who came to the Sandy country under the auspices of Governor Floyd, established the *Sandy Valley Advocate* at Catlettsburg in 1859. Mr. Miller was a bright man and a spicy writer, and made the *Advocate* a very readable paper. It was the pioneer in the line of newspapers in the valley in advocating the development of the hidden wealth of minerals known to exist in the Sandy country. The paper had a good circulation, and the largest advertising patronage ever held by any paper in the valley. It was said to be neutral in politics; but as the editor was a Whig politician, the paper leaned considerably that way.

Mr. Miller was employed by the Government soon after the Civil War commenced, and gave up the paper.

The *Herald* was the next paper to occupy the field. Charles D. Coiey, a very amiable and brilliant young man, a New Yorker, bought the outfit used by the *Advocate*, and ventured on the *Herald* in 1863. Mr. Cory was a Democrat, and made his paper at first mildly Democratic; but as it grew in age it also grew to be a stalwart Democratic organ, even in time of the war. Mr. Corey was a genius; he was a photographer, printer, poet, painter, and a good prose writer. He made a good paper. He married a beautiful young lady of Grayson—Miss Lucy Lewis, the daughter of Hon. Nelums Lewis. But the married life of the handsome pair was cut short by the death of the husband, whose physical nature was almost ethereal, so delicate was he. The young, loving wife would not be comforted after her "Charley's" death, and she soon joined him in the "land of pure delight." The connubial love of this beautiful couple for each other was more than human.

The *Herald*, after the death of its gifted founder, was continued by H. M. Bond. Soon after, the Rev. Z. Meek, who had meanwhile started the *Christian Observer*, which was several years later changed to the *Central Methodist*, joined him in the printing business under the name of the "Herald Printing Company." The combination thus formed by Meek and Bond ran on successfully until 1872, when the junior partner bought the entire outfit, abandoned the *Herald*, and gave all of his energy and talents to building up the *Central Methodist*, a religious paper second to none of its class in the State in circulation and in the ability with which it is edited.

Colonel Rees M. Thomas, in the latter part of the year 1865, commenced the publication of the Catlettsburg *Tribune*, an eight-column, four-page weekly. It was ably edited, and a bright, newsy sheet. It was intensely Republican in politics, but dignified in its utterances. It suspended in less than three years after it was launched on the sea of political journalism. The editor married Adie, daughter of Rev. E. C. Thornton, who started into life the first paper ever published in Catlettsburg. Colonel Thomas moved to Texas some time after the paper suspended, where he now is, engaged in the newspaper business. His wife has been dead several years.

After the *Herald* and *Tribune* ceased to live, several other papers were started, none, however, of more than ephemeral existence. Judge Lewis started one, and one George Swap, another; but as neither bloomed out into full life and usefulness, we pass them by, not forgetting the *Enquirer*, published for about six months in 1874 by Colonel Samuel Pike, the veteran newspaper man, who had founded, and for a time, successfully edited and published over thirty Democratic papers, alternating between four States. He advocated in the columns of the *Enquirer* the claims of George N. Brown against W. C. Ireland for judge. The *Enquirer* was the grand old veteran's last newspaper venture. Like a wagon long in use, he went down all at once. He returned to his home in Ohio to engage in mercantile pursuits; but, instead, the messenger of death suddenly summoned him from earth, and he ceased to work and live at once. He was a strong and bitter partisan writer; but, politics aside, no man had a kindlier heart or more lovable nature than Samuel Pike.

R. C. Burns, some time in the seventies, published the *Index*, a monthly, devoted to the sale of real estate. It was a bright little sheet of its class, but soon retired from the field.

In 1881 the *Monthly Progress* appeared; its purpose was to advocate the development of the great material wealth of the valley. The circulation ran up to three thousand copies monthly. The paper was owned and edited by the author of this book.

The *Weekly Progress* took the place of the monthly in 1882, and disappeared in 1884, under the same management until the latter six months of its existence, when R. C. Burns owned and conducted it. Having a large law practice, he gave up its publication, greatly to the regret of the Republican party, of whose principles it was a strong advocate.

We have overleaped ourself in not noticing the *Kentucky Democrat*, which was established by Captain T. D. Marcum in 1878. This paper at once took a high rank in Kentucky journalism, and soon attained to the largest subscription list ever carried by any political paper in the Sandy Valley; and perhaps few outside the valley surpass it in these particulars. It continues to grow in influence, and is still edited by its founder, who has shown great ability in conducting a weekly paper.

The *Advance* was founded by Howes & Borders at Paintsville in 1880, and after nine months was moved to Louisa, Howes dropping out as partner, and Borders, in 1881, establishing the *Chatterawha News*, a very bright and newsy sheet. Both papers were non-political.

In about 1882 or 1883 Messrs. C. M. Parsons and W. M. Conley founded the Pikeville *Enterprise*, and conducted it with ability for several years. It was a very decided Democratic paper. Mr. Pherigo succeeded them, and perhaps some one else had a hand in its publication. About 1886 J. Lee Ferguson, a bright young lawyer, bought out the material, and is now publishing the *Times*, a Republican paper there.

In 1883, R. M. Weddington and J. K. Leslie, two able lawyers started the *Banner* at Prestonburg, a Democratic paper of great ability. It did not exist two years, however. About a year after, Joe H. Borders' *Chatterawha News* suspended at Louisa.

Professor Lyttleton founded the *Lawrence Index*, a Democratic sheet, which he edited with ability until about 1885. He sold out to Ferguson and Conley, who changed the name, first to the *Times*, and afterwards to the *News*, still, however, continuing it as a Democratic organ. Mr. Ferguson is a gifted son of Hon. M. J. Ferguson, and his partner is the son of Asa Conley, a representative of an old-time Sandy house—on his mother's side was a Leslie, a family as noted as any in the valley.

War Meeting.

In the early part of the Winter of 1860 and '61, at the instance of Kellean Verplanck Whaley, or, as he was generally called, "Cal. Whaley," an invitation was sent out to the men of North-eastern Kentucky, North-western Virginia, and Middle Southern Ohio, to meet at Catlettsburg and compare notes respecting the great agitation, then already commenced, which led to the greatest war the world had ever witnessed.

When the day arrived for the assemblage of the men of three States, the town was overrun with delegates from the three States mentioned, and a gentleman from Indiana being present, he was invited to take a seat with his brethren who had come up to consult together about the threatened break-down of the Government of the fathers of 1776. Many able and distinguished men were in attendance, and they were the most earnest set of men that ever assembled in the town.

The meeting was held in the large frame Church; but so vast was the crowd that the lawn surrounding the building, as well as the streets near by, was one sea of people. Alonzo Cushing, of Gallipolis, Ohio, a brother of Dr. Z. Cushing, formerly of Lawrence County, Ky., was made chairman, and presided with great ability. He made an able speech on taking the chair; but it was entirely destitute of point, adroitly avoiding the main issue before the people of the whole country. Captain D. K. Weise, now postmaster at Ashland, was one of the secretaries.

The principal speakers at the gathering were D. K. Weise, of Kentucky; Dr. Patrick, of Kanawha Valley, Virginia; Judge Johnson, who recently died at Ironton; Dr. Jonathan Morris, of the same place; Kellean Verplanck Whaley, of Wayne County, Va., and Dr. J. D. Kincaid, of Catlettsburg.

All the speakers living south of the Ohio denounced both secession and coercion alike. Dr. Morris and Judge Johnson, both of Ironton, contended that the Government had the power and right to put down by force of arms all who rose against it, whether foreign or domestic foes. Mr. Whaley, of Wayne County, Va., made the most pointed speech of any. He said, in reply to Judge Johnson, that should the Northern hordes undertake to coerce their Southern brethren, the men of Wayne County, Virginia, would rally from every hill and valley with bayonets gleaming in the sunlight, to welcome them to inhospitable graves. Yet this same Kellean Verplanck Whaley told the author, in the Spring of 1864, that President Lincoln was too conservative to be trusted further, and that a radical, like Wade or Chase, should succeed to the Presidency in the coming Fall. Mr. Whaley was a politician living on the Virginia Point when the war came on. In politics he was one-third Whig, one-third Native American, and one-third Democrat, but more Whaley than all together.

In the Summer of 1861, under the management of that most shrewd of political managers and brainy men, Levi J. Hampton, of Catlettsburg, Cal. Whaley was elected to the United States Congress from the Wayne County (Virginia) District, receiving all the votes cast which were less than three hundred. He took his seat, and was, after two years, returned to Congress, serving, in all, four years. He made quite a good showing as a member. Mr. Whaley settled in Point Pleasant, West Virginia, after he retired from Congress, and published a newspaper. He has been dead many years.

The meeting at Catlettsburg, perhaps, did neither good nor harm; for every one engaged in its counsels was at sea, without chart or compass.

THRILLING INCIDENTS.

IN 1811 Ed. Osburn, a large farmer owning slaves, was in debt, and his negroes were levied on by the sheriff of Floyd County to satisfy an execution. The sheriff, David Morgan, and his son, a deputy, being near the residence of Samuel Davidson with the slaves, was overtaken by Osburn, who killed Morgan and his son in cold blood. Escaping, he was not heard from for over forty years, when an old Sandian, passing through South-eastern Ohio, saw and recognized the double murderer. Osburn denied his identity at first, but, when pressed, piteously begged the venerable Sandian never to divulge his whereabouts till after his death. During the whole time he had lived within two hundred and fifty miles, on a straight line, of the place where he had committed the atrocious crime.

THAT TELL-TALE COAT.

IN 1858 George P. Archer, of Mercer County, Va., came to the mouth of Bear Creek, now Rockville, Lawrence County, Ky., and obtained work as a farm-hand. He brought with him a jeans coat of unusual woof and make, which seemed never to grow older. Archer, by his economical habits, had saved up enough money to join Dr. J. F. Hatton in a partnership in a general store at Bear Creek, in about 1864. In 1867, in January, Archer married a beautiful sister of his partner. She is now the wife of Ralph Booton, Esq., of Prestonburg. In April of the same year Hatton, the senior partner, went to Cincinnati with bark, where he remained some time. While gone, late one night, a man called at Hatton's house, saying to Mrs. Hatton, who was awakened by his raps on the door, that three raftsmen had landed in to get some tobacco. She told them to go to the store, where Archer slept that night, his wife having gone over to Round Bottom to visit her relatives. They, in a patronizing voice, called Archer up, repeating what they had told Mrs. Hatton. The fated man came down stairs in his night-clothes and handed them the tobacco. The men then concluded to buy of every thing freely, and soon three large sacks were filled and tied up, when one of the robbers (for such they were) demanded money. Archer, on reaching under the counter for his pistol, was riddled by bullets fired by the men. One of the men ran up-stairs to search the victim's clothes for money, but hearing what he took to be the sound of footsteps approaching, he grabbed a coat hanging on the bed-post, and scampered away, followed by his cronies. As Archer failed to be at breakfast next morning, and the store was closed, the door was pushed open, and Archer was found cold in death.

Archer was a man every body liked, and his tragic death created intense excitement. Suspected parties were arrested, and turned loose, no evidence appearing against them. But soon Archer's wife remembered the jeans coat, and that it could nowhere be found. Hope revived that the tell-tale garment would lead to the apprehension of the murderers. Men went everywhere to spy out the coat. At this juncture an old woman living on Cat's Fork sent word to the people at the mouth of Bear Creek that on the evening of the tragic murder Bill Wright and Jim and John Lyons stopped at her house, and told her they were on their way to the mouth of Bear Creek to rob a store, and that early next morning they returned with a large amount of booty, and stopped and got breakfast, dividing much of the property with her. Almost simultaneously with the old woman's story the coat was seen on Jim Lyons's back. He was arrested with the fatal coat, and taken to Louisa. John Lyons was soon found in Greenup County, and brought to Louisa.

The governor had offered a reward for Bill Wright, who was believed to be skulking about in the Little Sandy country. In a few days he stepped into the store of Jack Allen, a brave mountaineer in Magoffin County, and Allen, seeing that he answered the published description, at once covered him with his pistol and brought him to Louisa.

The three were put in irons, and the jail was guarded to prevent escape. The mountains were full of desperadoes, engendered by the opportunities of the war, the courts and society not having fully resumed their normal condition. News went out that a lot of cut-throats, friends of the accused, were soon to move on Louisa, and liberate the villains. No reasonable person doubted the guilt of the men. At the preliminary trial the coat was a swift witness, and the old lady aforementioned brought into court the goods the robbers had given to her, which were proven to be the goods of Hatton and Archer. Archer's friends concluded that there was danger in delay, and one hundred and fifty of them, embracing the best men of the lower part of Lawrence County, Ky., and Wayne County, West Va., without any disguise, rode into Louisa, ordered a gallows erected, dispersed the guard at the jail, forced the jailer to surrender the keys, and brought out the prisoners, telling them to prepare for death, for that within a few hours they must die.

Judge M. J. Ferguson and Rev. J. F. Medley pleaded hard that the law be allowed to take its course. The mob listened, but went on with the preparations. The criminals spent most of their time in making sensational confessions, each one claiming to be less guilty than the other two, neither one denying the crime.

At about three o'clock P. M., every thing being ready, a road-wagon was driven under the gallows, and the criminals were made to ascend into it. They were then asked to say what they might desire; but as recriminating lies were being passed among the wretches, the men in charge of the execution, sickening at their profanity, ordered the wagon to move, and the murderers were quickly suspended between the heavens and the earth. When dead, the bodies were cut down and buried, and the mob left town in as orderly a manner as it had entered.

Bill Wright was forty-eight years old. He enlisted in the Confederate army, but soon deserted, and turned thief and robber. Jim Lyons was thirty-five years old, and served two years in the 5th Virginia, Union army, but deserted, and ever after colleagued with Bill Wright. John Lyons was only eighteen years old, but, according to his own confession, the world has lost nothing by his death. The men composing the mob were indicted, but the governor pardoned them all.

Mobs are illegal, and should be frowned down by all good citizens; but no one doubts the righteousness of the fate of Bill Wright and Jim and John Lyons.

Fires in Catlettsburg.

[CONTINUED.]

From the coming of Sawney Catlett, in 1808 or thereabout, down to July 22, 1878, no widespread conflagration had ever fallen on the place. Fires had at different times broken out, and single dwellings, shops, stables, or outhouses had been consumed, but had always been extinguished, or ceased further ravage for lack of adjoining buildings to spread the flames. The town authorities were both unable and unwilling to provide either a fire-engine or a ladder and bucket company, to buffet with the flames, should they be put in motion by some unforeseen cause.

In all alarms given of fire, no people could have responded to the call with greater unanimity or alacrity than did the population of Catlettsburg; for not only would stalwart men rush to the rescue, bucket, ladder, or ax in hand, but women and children were often first to appear on the scene of danger, to add a mite toward extinguishing the flames which threatened the destruction of the houses of the place, dearer to them than any spot on earth. For nearly a generation fires occurred, either at short or long intervals, doing, it is true, but slight damage to property, entailing but a small loss on some one only, who if not able to stand the loss alone, was helped by the charitably inclined.

As no one had badly suffered by a fire in the place, although the buildings generally were of wood, and many were mere fire-traps, the inhabitants had somehow fallen into a state of false security, and expected, or at least hoped, that the same good fortune would continue to fall to their lot. But the hope proved delusive in the end. A bitter day came when none expected it. A repose of many months, in which no fire-bug had kindled a flame in any building in the place, had led the inhabitants to believe their property was safe from the incendiary torch, or the accident that kindles a spark that burns up great cities, as well as small towns. This hope was scattered to the winds.

On the 22d of July, 1877, at just twelve o'clock, noon, the alarm was sounded that Peter Paul Schauer's bakery on South Front Street, was on "fire." Scores then repeated the fearful little monosylable. Dinner-bells continued ringing after their usual call for dinner, while the large church-bells pealed forth in louder tones, warning the people of approaching danger. Above the hoarse voices of the people and loud ringing of dinner and church bells, the whistle at every mill and factory screamed shrilly, like some wild monster raising his voice above the clamor of pandemonium. The noise was terrific, equaled only by the sight of the towering blaze from the burning building. Two minutes after the alarm was given, the streets and alleys approaching the ill-fated house were a surging mass of terror-stricken humanity. One look from even the least practiced was sufficiently convincing that no human aid, without the immediate help of a fire-engine, could quench the flames and save the building.

The fire had burst through the brick chimney or stack of the bakery, and had set the house to burning, inside and outside, near the roof. It was a two-story frame and as dry as powder. Before any one could form or express an opinion as to the best thing to do under the circumstances, seeing they had no fire-engine, the fire was spreading to other buildings. All hands, including young ladies and elderly matrons, the fairest of Catlettsburg's womanhood, almost instinctively betook themselves to saving the goods, merchandise, and household effects of the people whose houses lay in the range of the devouring element.

The day was not only intensely hot, but not a breath of air stirred sufficient to put in motion the down on a gossamer-plant; yet the flames and smoke caused an artificial motion that propelled the fire from the river backward. So rapid was the spread of the flames that in two hours from the first alarm, all the buildings, from the foot of Main Street to Center, thence to Louisa, and onward to Clay Street, were a mass of ruins, or were fiercely burning, save only the dwelling of Mrs. Alex. Botts; thence to South Front Street, on Sandy, and down to Main. A cordon of men, with blankets, carpets, quilts, etc., was formed on Main Street, opposite the burning houses, and all the way up to Clay Street, who, by keeping the cloths saturated with water, prevented the wild flames from reaching across the avenues named, and firing the buildings on the opposite side.

Within an hour and ten minutes after the fire had started on its wild career, farmers living two miles below Catlettsburg in Ohio had hurried over the river with their teams, to assist in hauling goods, merchandise, and household plunder to places of safety.

By three o'clock P. M. all was in ruins. The people, or all save a very few left on guard, retired to partake of refreshments, the first since breakfast, while many of them had no food, nor house in which to eat it if they had the food, having lost all, every thing but their lives and energy; yet God is the Father of all, and every man is a brother. No one returned to look again upon the awful wreck and ruin caused by the fire-fiend that had not partaken of food to his full satisfaction. Those who were not burned out fed their brethren in distress out of their larders with a heartiness so liberal as to show the true principles of benevolence and charity.

Great occasions bring out great deeds. Humanity was touched by the great stroke. The wail of distress from the sufferers affected all the family of man dwelling in the place. All felt stricken. All suffered directly or through the sympathetic touch. Catlettsburg people, who were not material losers by the fire, most nobly dispensed their charity in tokens the most substantial.

But Catlettsburg people were not alone in their deeds of charity at this period of sore distress; for before five o'clock P. M. had been measured by the sun's steady tread, Ashland, through a delegation of her generous citizens, had sent up large stores of food, clothing, bedding, and general household goods, and established a commissary near the burnt district, from which supplies were furnished to those who had lost all or had suffered by the great fire. The Ashland store was kept open night and day for more than a week, from which every one who asked was assisted, without money or price.

When gratitude is no longer held as a cardinal virtue as well as grace, Catlettsburg will forget the noble charity bestowed upon her stricken children by Ashland's generous sons and daughters, but not before.

A few days after the fire took place the board of trustees of the town passed an ordinance that no wooden houses should be erected on that part of the burnt district lying between Main, Center, Louisa, and Franklin Streets, and the Sandy and

Ohio Rivers, a space covering at least four-fifths of that burned over by the fire. Nine-tenths of the houses consumed were of wooden material, and the town board was morally bound to legislate as far as possible to provide against a future calamity like the one just passed. They provided, by solemn ordinance, that ever after no frame or other wooden building should be erected on the burnt district, except that part lying above Franklin Street. The ordinance, no doubt, worked hardships to a very few, but that it was a wise measure, calculated to advance the private interests of the many and redound to the great benefit of the general public at large, no one whose opinion is valuable has seriously doubted. The block upon block of palatial brick structures built since the fire, covering four-fifths of the ground burned over, is a standing proof that the Fire-line Ordinance, as it is called, was passed none too soon.

There was sadness in the hearts of the people as they viewed the ruins spread out in hot ashes and burning cinders before their smoke-swollen eyes. But they were buoyed up with the hope that a brighter day would dawn upon them. And with this hope to cheer them onward to activity, many had planned in their minds at least to build again as soon as the ashes could be cleared away. This determination was entertained by many before sleep came to their eyes after the great fire.

Where to obtain brick with which to lay the

walls, was the problem to be solved by every one. Home supply had never been good, nor even sufficient for ordinary demands. Now many were wanted, and few to supply the great demand. Captain Honshell, in three days after the conflagration, solved the problem to the satisfaction of nearly all who wanted to build. Representing his son, Gus. Honshell, and James W. Damron, doing business on Front Street as Damron & Honshell, he contracted with the Messrs. Blair, of Cincinnati, to furnish brick from that place, and to lay them in the walls at a less sum than had been thought possible by even home builders; and the material was greatly superior.

That stroke of Captain Honshell opened the way to all who wished to commence at once to build. In a very few days most of the spacious brick structures adorning Front and Division Streets were under contract. The merchants were permitted to erect temporary store-houses in which to transact business while their permanent houses were going up. Ten days after the fire all was life and bustle. Only during the timber-running season and in war times had Catlettsburg shown so much business life and activity as during the building period after the great fire. The great buildings went up as if by magic. By the 1st of January nearly all had moved into their new quarters, and were doing well. In fact, they had a splendid trade while in their temporary buildings.

The usual Winter trade being followed by an extra Spring and Summer boom placed Catlettsburg's merchants and business men in as good financial shape as before the fire; perhaps better. Especially was this true of those who had been prudent enough to carry even a minimum of insurance in proportion to their loss by the great fire. Thus in a year after this calamity, Catlettsburg was richer in all of the elements of substantial wealth than ever before. Of course there were cases where men, well stricken in years, or with broken health, or with some other draw-back, fell out of business line, and either disappeared from public view, or linger still in poverty's vale.

The losses by the fire were: two drug-stores, two hardware stores, two jewelry-stores, one fancy store, two shoe-stores, one clothing and custom-work store, five hotels, two saddle and harness shops, one leather and shoe finding store, two bakeries, one artist's gallery, two tin and stove stores, every grocery in town but one, six dry-goods stores, most of the lawyers' and other offices in the place, Masonic and Odd Fellows halls and regalia, and sixty dwellings.

NEW ENTERPRISES AFTER THE FIRE.

FROM the coming of Sawney Catlett near the birth of the nineteenth century, who was the first inn-keeper at the Mouth, good eating-houses were the rule, and not the exception. But when the great blaze swept from the earth every hotel in the place, D. W. Eba, an old Catlettsburg merchant, without asking co-operation from any one, employed an architect to draw plans and specifications for a hostelry commensurate with the progress of the times. Mr. Eba spared neither time nor expense in putting up and completing the building in the most substantial and artistic style, and, more still, desiring that the advanced house should not suffer for want of a fit person to run it, procured an old-time city caterer to take charge of and conduct it in a way to win the patronage of the most fastidious travelers on the road. As long as the "Alger House" stands, it will proclaim the public spirit and private enterprise of Daniel W. Eba.

The magnificent Opera-house is also a child of the fire-king, and a very stately song princess she is. Formerly all concerts and entertainments were given in the ill-adapted court-house, or found reluctant quarters in one of the churches; but now no city twice the size of the Gate City can boast of a finer structure devoted to the drama and song. The late Arthur F. Morse, like the builder of the Alger House, was an old-time merchant and business man of Catlettsburg, who possessed the New England pluck as well as taste peculiar to his section. Unaided from any quarter, he gave to Catlettsburg, in the noble structure bearing his name, an educator more potent, in a refined, cultivated sense, than can be found in any other part of East Kentucky. Mr. Morse needs no marble slab to commemorate his life. "Morse Opera-house" is a perpetual reminder of his good taste and noble deeds.

The reader will conclude with us that a worse misfortune may overtake a town than a fire—perceiving that, while nature made the Mouth of the Sandy the Gate opening up the valley above, it was not until after the building of the large business houses, but more especially the Alger House and Morse Opera-house, all consequents of the great fire, that *City* could properly be added to *Gate*, making Catlettsburg the "Gate *City*" of East Kentucky.

THE SECOND FIRE A HOLOCAUST.

ONE would have thought that no time would have passed, nor money have been withheld, in procuring an engine to guard against a future conflagration. But the people who controlled, to a great extent, the purse-strings of the corporation felt secure in their thick, well-laid brick walls, with metallic roofs, and regarded the possession of an engine and hose as unnecessary after the destruction of so many fire-traps; and then the cost was beyond the ability of taxation to justify the expense, they argued; and as one great fire had already baptized the town in flames, it was very unlikely, when so many causes to feed another had been removed, that a like calamity should invade the city. How delusive was that hope! A worse calamity was then knocking at the door, taunting the authorities for their indifference in not providing means to stay the flames when first they started on their furious round of death. The inhabitants, while resting in false security, suspecting no danger from the fire-fiend, were startled from their early slumber, soon after midnight, on Sunday morning, in August, 1884, by night-walkers, while on their busy rounds of sin and shame, and by one not polluted with the stain begotten of the social evil, who was going hurriedly for some son of Esculapius to administer a balm to a sick child, then lying in its crib, tossing to and fro upon its downy little bed, racked with pain and scorched with burning fever. The dismal cry of fire uttered by these was heard by others within their houses, who rushed frantically to the street and added their voices to the alarm. Soon the great church-bells pealed forth in loud, clanging tones, calling the people to the scene of danger.

When it was made known by sight or voice that Patton Brothers' great Drug Emporium was the place from whence the flames arose, a shudder ran through every breast, knowing that, in all large wholesale drug warehouses, combustible matter in great magnitude is ever piled up on shelves and platforms, and lying round loose, an inviting medium for a

THE SECOND FIRE A HOLOCAUST. 353

fire, once under way, to feed its fury on, and to extend its sway of destruction, and sometimes death. Then it was also the very center of the best blocks of brick buildings in the city. Must they all fall before the devouring flames? Yes, they were destined to fall a prey to the fury of the flames. In a few minutes after the bells were rung, the street in front, and the alley in rear of the burning house were packed with people, drawn thither to see the progress of the fire, or to assist in extinguishing it, if possible, and to give aid in removing the goods from the burning or adjoining buildings. All saw at once that no human effort could stay the fire, so far as the Patton building was concerned. Yet all realized that, were an engine at hand, the fire could be intercepted and the adjacent buildings saved. Scores rushed into the Patton house, and as the flames spread to Andrews's dry-goods store on one side, and Prichard & Wellman's wholesale grocery and the Carpenter Mammoth wholesale dry-goods house farther on, men were busy in carrying out goods from these busy marts of trade.

All was wild confusion, when suddenly the wall between the Patton and Andrews building fell in, with a loud crash. Soon a wail of anguish went up from the red-hot bricks and blazing rubbish—a wail that struck terror to every soul who heard the awful sound. The news passed through the surging crowd that James McKenzie had been caught beneath the falling wall, and that there were no possible means of rescuing him from the fiery furnace. Some prayed, while others cried aloud in agony! The cool-headed and more practical hastily procured long scantlings, and made a causeway on which to reach the point from which the shrieks arose, hoping to snatch him as a brand from the burning. Scores tried to make the point; but as often as they essayed, were driven back by the hot blazes and stifling smoke which met them from the first step to the last. Groans and sighs continued to arise continuously from the sufferer imprisoned in his fiery cell. Heroic men rushed forward at the great risk of life and limb, as if determined to save the suffering boy who called so piteously for help. More than half an hour had passed (some said a full hour) since first the terrible cry was heard. The father, mother, brothers, and sister of the wretched sufferer stood by and looked more dead than alive. After the long agony, a shout went up from hundreds of people when they saw several brave men bearing to the street the charred body of young McKenzie. When it was known that he still lived, their thankfulness to God was expressed with equal warmth. The poor young man, more dead than alive, was placed upon a mattress, and borne to his home, accompanied by Dr. Smiley, the family physician, who did all that it was possible for science and skill to do, in behalf of the sufferer; but science and skill,

THE SECOND FIRE A HOLOCAUST. 355

as well as the affectionate nursing of mother, father, and sisters, all combined were impotent to save his life. He was burned to a crisp from the crown of his head to the sole of his feet, and how he bore up under the terrible stroke is a mystery. He lingered, however, for ten days before death came to release him from his great suffering, which he bore with stoic fortitude.

Shortly after McKenzie was carried home daylight appeared, and the Huntington fire company, with engine and hose, arrived, having been summoned to Catlettsburg's relief. All danger from further spread of the fire was soon quelled, when the engine began to pour vast streams of water on the burning mass and on the adjoining buildings.

About this time the news spread that a young colored man, who had come but a short time before from Virginia, and had conducted himself so well as to gain the respect of all who knew him, had been taken from the fiery mass, so badly burned as to make his recovery impossible. To add to this horror, it was soon discovered that John Graham, a colored stone-mason, had perished in the flames.

Many of the people had gone to their homes to partake of food, as the great tax upon their bodies and minds had awakened a keen sense of hunger, when reports of a fresh horror startled them. A young man by the name of David Kinner, a son of David Kinner, Sen., and a cousin of S. G. Kinner, Commonwealth's attorney of the district, who was reared in Catlettsburg, but at that time had his home in Williamsburg, Ky., was visiting at Catlettsburg. Hearing the alarm of fire, he had rushed from his bed to the scene of danger, and was reported to be missing. Search was made at the home of all his relatives (for he had several uncles and aunts living in Catlettsburg), but he could not be found. The young man's relatives and the entire community were horrified to think that, in addition to the casualties already mentioned, another victim, under the most distressing circumstances, was to be added to the holocaust. The Huntington fire company had left as soon as all danger had passed of the further spread of the fire; and now men went to work with shovels, spades, and picks, to bring up from the ruins the remains of poor Kinner and the colored man, John Graham. The workmen were driven back by the pent-up heat whenever they essayed to ply their tools. To overcome this, a line was formed from the ruins to a cistern two hundred yards away, and water was passed for deadening the heat, in order to give the men a chance to proceed. The long strain upon the men of the town had well-nigh exhausted them; but others fresh from Ashland and the surrounding neighborhood, as well as a number of the more delicate sex, urged on by the instincts of humanity, took their places in the line, and passed the buckets of water for hours, or during the whole forenoon.

Among the men who stood the rays of the scorching sun was the venerable Harman Loar, of near Louisa, who was stopping at Catlettsburg at the time. Mr. Loar was not only an old man, but a cripple as well, and had to stand on one foot supported by his crutch; he proved himself a man of noble instincts. Patrick Moriarity, a popular Irish citizen of Ashland, not only labored, but his generous nature was all broken up with sympathy for the dead and their heart-broken friends.

At noon the charred remains of the young man Kinner were exhumed, only recognizable by some metal substances impervious to fire. They made such a ghastly appearance that none of his relatives dared look upon them. John Graham's mutilated body was found about the same time. The people sat down in silence, and wept. It was Sunday; but few of the people were found in the churches that day. They remained away to mingle their tears with the relatives of the dead and suffering.

A dispatch was sent to Williamsburg, Ky., notifying the parents of Mr. Kinner of the sad taking away of their noble son. They could not reach Catlettsburg before Tuesday, and on that day the funeral took place from the Presbyterian Church, the Methodist Episcopal Church, South, of which the young man's family were members, being closed for repairs. The beautiful edifice was most handsomely draped in weeds of mourning, and the auditorium was packed to its utmost capacity.

Rev. J. H. Jackson was equal to the occasion, and delivered a sermon of great power and pathos.

John Graham, the colored man, was buried almost as soon as his remains were exhumed, his people hurrying up the funeral. The other colored man who was injured by the flames, and died next day after the fire, had been but a short time in Catlettsburg, but had conducted himself so well as to win the esteem of all who knew him, both white and colored. The trustees of the Methodist Episcopal Church opened the doors of their Church for the funeral ceremonies. The ladies of the place festooned the Church in the most appropriate style, although the man was nothing but a negro. The house was packed with an audience composed, not only of black people, who were the chief mourners in front, but the wealth and heart of the white people were out. Humanity was touched as never before in Catlettsburg. Rev. Thomas Hanford, the pastor of the Church, delivered a grand oration, and Rev. Mr. Jolly, of the Baptist Church, offered the most sublime and eloquent prayer that the author ever listened to.

Ten days after the fire poor McKenzie ceased to live. How he survived so long is a mystery past finding out. His remains were taken to the Methodist Episcopal Church, where the family worshiped. An immense audience was present, showing great sympathy. The pastor, Rev. Thomas Hanford, delivered a grand eulogy on the deceased.

McKenzie, like Kinner, had just come to manhood, and was the stay of his father's family. He was a tinner by trade.

The death of young Kinner was doubly sad for his relatives and friends to bear, from the fact that as his father, by reverses in business, had fallen somewhat into decay financially, the son was the stay of the family. Under the guidance of that clear-headed and kind-hearted business man of Lawrence, Colonel Jay H. Northup, in whose employ he had been for some time, he had grown to be an expert in measuring and judging the quality of timber, and was called down into the southeastern part of the State to take charge of one of the largest timber interests of Kentucky, at a handsome salary. Perceiving that the condition of the whole family could be financially improved by joining him at his new quarters, young Kinner induced his father to move to Williamsburg, his head-quarters in business, where the family are still living. He was spending a few days at Catlettsburg with friends, and had arranged to leave for home the day before the fire occurred, but yielded to the entreaties of a fond aunt to defer his departure for another day, by which his valuable life was brought to an awful termination.

The incineration of so many Catlettsburg people caused a reaction, and the authorities immediately procured a first-class fire-engine, with hose, and put up a substantial engine-house, at a cost altogether of over twelve thousand dollars. The machine is first-class, and will throw a double stream with force on the roof of a six-story house. The people now have no fear of a wide-spread fire, although no number of fire-extinguishers can be expected to prevent single houses from burning. Another lesson taught is, that it is not necessary for people to rush into a burning building to save property, regardless of their own safety, in order to prove their good citizenship, as every prudent business man has it in his power to protect his interests by insurance. Mr. N. P. Andrews, in whose house the men lost their lives, warned all of the danger; but they failed to heed his advice.

Bright Young Men.

James W. Reily, the first clerk of the Boyd courts, was intellectually as bright as a diamond. He could quote whole pages from Tom Hood, Burns, and Edgar A. Poe. He was finely educated. The milk of human kindness bubbled over from his great, loving heart. If a little child stubbed its toe, no matter what the surroundings, Jimmy Reily ran to its relief. He died unmarried in 1865. He had his little besetments, yet was a noble man.

Judge William Sands was a gifted personage. He studied law with Hon. G. N. Brown soon after coming home from service in the Confederate army. He went to Greenup, and was soon made county attorney; then he was elected district attorney, and followed right on as circuit judge. He had dazzling talents; but the sunshine of public favor fell too heavily upon his ethereal make-up, and, like a tender flower, he was cut down in early morn. He died trusting in the Redeemer.

W. Mate Strong, of Paintsville, possessed rare talents. His mind fairly glistened with bright thoughts. He was an educated young lawyer. He fought against pulmonary trouble; but it conquered his frail nature. He was all mind. He died young.

THE TURMANS

CAME down from Floyd County, and settled near Round Bottom at a very early day, about the time of the War of 1812. The father of James Turman had other sons besides James, who intermarried with the leading families of the neighborhood. The Turmans are thus well connected.

James was not the only prominent one of the family; but, by force of character and circumstances, he was properly the leader of the house of Turman in the valley. He married Margaret, a daughter of James Rouse, father of Esquire Samuel Rouse, who is, and has been many years, a magistrate in Boyd County. James Turman paid great deference to his wife, always addressing her as Miss Margaret. When a young married man he bought land on the Kentucky shore of the Sandy River, opposite the Bloomer Bar. He opened a farm, established a ferry across the Sandy, and entertained travelers at his inn. In the early days of Kentucky history a ferry carried with it the privilege to retail spirits, and Mr. Turman, with his keen· scent after money, was not slow in availing himself of the privilege. When the privilege was taken away by legislative enactment, he procured license from the County Court, and continued selling as a hotel-keeper until the war, in 1861. By farming, hotel-keeping, ferrying, and retailing ardent spirits he became well-off. Few men on Lower Sandy were better known than was James Turman, not only to the people of his own section, but to those throughout the valley.

One outcome in the life of James Turman differs from that of most men similarly situated, which it is not out of place to mention. Statistics prove that ninety per cent of all retailers of ardent spirits not only become hard drinkers, but lose their property, and are sooner or later reduced to poverty. The statistics referred to proved only half true in Mr. Turman's case; for while he drank his dram continuously, he continued to prosper in business to the end of his life. This is accounted for by the fact that he strictly adhered to the laws of trade, saving every day something above his outgo. He was a very joyous, sunshiny man, and was friendly to all; but his hilarity never carried him so far as to cause him to lose his balance, and give to relative or friend one glass of liquor. Every body who drank his grog was compelled to pay down before he got the beverage. As whisky in those days only cost about twelve cents per gallon, the owner could afford to partake of all he chose, and still have immense profits to place to his credit.

Turman's Ferry, for twenty-five years previous to 1864, was the most prominent point on the Sandy River between Louisa and the Mouth. Rockville, a short distance above, on the Sandy, and Railroad, and White's Creek, and Lockwood Station below, get most of the trade that used to center at and near Turman's Ferry. Mr. James Prichard, also in the Round Bottom, divides patronage with the places mentioned.

There is but very little crossing now at the old landmark of Turman's Ferry. Mr. Turman died some years after the close of the great war. He left several sons and a daughter. One of the sons, Samuel, lives on and owns part of the old homestead, and is a prominent citizen in the neighborhood and county, while others are in the far West. The daughter married Philip Fannin, an official of Boyd County, and one of the most prosperous and wealthy farmers and stock-traders in the Sandy Valley. Mrs. Fannin is a worthy helpmeet to her husband, being possessed of all the characteristics of a noble wife, mother, and neighbor.

Mrs. Turman, or Miss Margaret, as her husband fondly called her, still lives in contentment at the old homestead.

An incident well illustrating Mr. Turman's social nature, but more especially his love of gain, happened in the Summer of 1860, which is historic enough to be recorded in this sketch. The county of Boyd had been formed during the session of the Legislature of 1859 and 1860. The new county, with Lawrence, was made a legislative district. The Whig-American combination in politics appointed a day to hold their convention, to bring out a candidate to represent the district in the lower branch of the Legislature. Turman's Ferry, being centrally located, was selected as the place where the first convention of the people of the two counties should assemble to make a nomination. The day on which the meeting of the clans occurred was lovely in the extreme. The Sandy River had, from recent rains, swelled sufficiently to enable a Sandy steamer to take the delegation from Catlettsburg to the meeting. The people of the Gate City, as the county seat had been fixed at their place, were in a mood to love every body, and felt that it would be courteous to go *en masse* to the gathering of the people from Lawrence and their own proud little county, and thus show by their presence that they wished to bind in the bonds of indissoluble friendship the people of the two counties. When the boat left Catlettsburg it was alive with people, including many ladies, all bent on a day of pleasure. Many of the people had baskets well filled with viands, of which to make their dinner. A few, however, had not taken their lunch along with them; but they cared nothing for that, as Mr. Turman was prepared to feed all who might apply for dinner. Those who had lunch were very liberal in sharing it with those who were not so fortunate Vast crowds came down from Louisa and vicinity, and as most of them came on horseback, it was inconvenient to cumber themselves with a lunchbasket, especially when they knew that they could be supplied at the Turman Hotel.

The great meeting was held in Mr. Turman's

new barn, just erected, as if for the occasion. Captain William Vinson, Daniel Johns, Laban T. Moore, together with many other noted citizens of Lawrence County, were present.

Daniel Johns was nominated, and, at the ensuing election, elected to the Legislature, being the first to fill that honorable position in the new district. Mr. Johns served faithfully and received the plaudits of his constituency; but soon after his term expired he removed to Minnesota, where he has ever since resided. The removal of Mr. Johns created a vacuum in the affairs of Lawrence County, which has been hard to fill by another. He was a very kind, genial man, and sensible as well. He has filled official positions in his North-western home with credit to himself and profit to his constituents.

But to the incident. After the nomination was made, many of those who had brought no lunch rushed to the hotel, where Mr. and Mrs. Turman had made ample preparation to feed all who might call for dinner. The tables were filled with rich viands, that were devoured with a keen relish by the hungry crowd who filled up the tables; all, however, in the best of spirits, praising the dinner, and heaping encomiums on both host and hostess for the great labor they had undergone to feed the hungry delegates. Mr. Turman's business tact never forsook him—no, not under the most trying circumstances. From the many praises his big dinner was receiving from almost every one partaking of his food, he must have been led to believe that the feasters thought it was a free-to-all meal, and as he dignifiedly passed up and down the hall, talking pleasantly to all, he remarked that he had plenty to eat, and it was free to all; "but," said he, "if you see proper to give a quarter a piece, old Jim [as he called himself] will not be offended." If any one had had previously supposed that his dinner was free, he was now undeceived, and all planked down the quarter. It was not meanness in him, it was a very soft way to manage business with a promiscuous crowd.

THE GOBLES, OF LAWRENCE.

GREENVILLE GOBLE and his wife were originally of what is now Carter County; but were early in Lawrence, and may be styled old settlers there. Mr. Goble was a man of talent, and possessed of great energy. He was a lawyer of more than average capacity, and successfully practiced his profession, not only in his own county of Lawrence, but in adjoining counties. He filled the office of prosecuting attorney for one term. Like many lawyers possessing energy and a taste in that direction, he was also an extensive farmer and trader. He was the owner of one of the best farms in Lawrence County, outlying from the river. The Goble place, four miles from Louisa, on the West-Liberty road, not only had many broad acres of land under a high state of cultivation in grains and grass, but the excellent dwelling, barns, and large, well-kept orchards gave evidence that a master was at the head.

Mr. Goble was not only a busy man, attending strictly to money-getting, but was also a man of great public spirit, and devoted much time in studying the interests of his county and section. Along in the forties he was convinced that tobacco could be raised to great profit by the small farmers of the county, and yield greater returns than any other crop they might raise on the space of ground taken in its cultivation; and he further argued that it was a crop which every little boy could assist in raising, thus inducing the boys not only to learn industrious habits, but adding something to the family purse also. So anxious was the philanthropist to have the people engage in tobacco culture, that, in many instances, he obligated himself to buy their tobacco, or at least market it for them. Quite a number availed themselves of the generous offer of Mr. Goble, and raised their first crop of the weed. But having had no experience, and being careless in its handling, their tobacco made a shabby appearance when offered for sale in market. Mr. Goble kept his word with all, and lost money by his neighbors' bad handling of their first and last crop of tobacco. Had the farmers done their work as scientifically as did Mr. Goble, his expectations would have been realized, and they would have received better returns for their labor.

In the prime of life Mr. Goble died, leaving a widow, several daughters, and one son, none of his children having reached mature age. The widow and mother was in every way qualified to take up the burden of conducting the large farm, with the skill of one who had been trained to such a life, even buying and selling horses, mules, and cattle, with the clear business judgment of the best farmers and stock-traders. The Widow Goble's farm was one of the best-kept in the county, affording a good profit by the superior skill and good management with which it was conducted. The daughters, as they grew up to womanhood, married, settling with their husbands in Lawrence County, where they were raised.

The son, Montraville B. Goble, studied law, but was elected to and filled the office of Circuit clerk when quite a young man, which no doubt caused him to give up the practice of the law, and ultimately to engage in other pursuits. When quite a young man he married Miss Burgess, a daughter of George Burgess, a wealthy and honorable citizen of Lawrence County. Mr. Goble's wife was a noble Christian lady. They lived in Louisa, where he engaged in timber-trading on the Sandy. He was not only one of the leading business men of his county, but took rank as a leader, a public man, and a politician. Mr. Goble had the misfortune to lose his wife by death early in the seventies. She left two sons, George and Greenville, and four daughters. George, the elder son, died suddenly in 1885 or 1886. Greenville, the younger, is now just grown to manhood, and is employed as clerk in one of the many industries his father is interested in. One of the daughters is the wife of Mr. Magann, son of banker Magann, of Grayson, Ky. He is a gentleman of fine business tact, and is doing well. Another daughter is the wife of Maguffey Wellman, a young business man of Catlettsburg. Another daughter died on the verge of young womanhood. Miss Lilian, the only one at home, adds a charm to the home circle and to society by her lady-like manner and graces.

Mr. Goble, after the death of his wife, married for his second wife, Miss Northup, of New York, a sister of Colonel Jay H. Northup, of Louisa. It was a match well worthy to be made, she being a lady of education, refinement, and great suavity of manner. One child, a son, now ten or twelve years old, blesses this marriage. Some short time after Mr. Goble's second marriage, he moved from Louisa to Catlettsburg, where he still continues to reside. He is largely engaged in timber-trading, saw and planing milling, and holding real estate, all together giving him as much to do in looking after his many ventures as can be crowded on one man.

Mr. Goble is a member of no Church, but leans strongly toward the Methodists, and, when possible, he attends Methodist revival meetings, taking in the hearty singing and testimonies with a keen relish of religious delight. He contributes of his means to support the Gospel. His first wife was a leading Southern Methodist. The present Mrs. Goble is a Presbyterian, and so are the daughters.

Mr. Goble was at one time not only a Democrat of Democrats, but would go any reasonable length to see his man elected, whether the man was right or wrong. He is still in principle as strong a Democrat as ever, but by no means so zealous a worker in the party traces, and would be apt to kick if a really bad man were put up for his support. He is a strict temperance man, casting his vote against the sale of liquor whenever the subject comes up.

The widow of Greenville Goble and mother of M. B. Goble is still living, at a good old age. She makes her home with one of her daughters, near Louisa, Kentucky. She is a ripe Christian lady, having been most of her life a professed Christian, in communion with the Methodist Church. She is loved by her children and grandchildren and esteemed by her neighbors, and is waiting on the shores of time to "go up higher" when the Master calls.

TWO HISTORIC SISTERS.

HENRY SOVAIN was a scion of the house of that name, in Alsace-Lorraine, a former province of France, but now of Germany. Some of the Sovains came to America as early as 1755, and settled in Philadelphia, where, by industry and thrift, they accumulated property, but lost it in the War of the Revolution and in that of 1812. The Sovains are referred to in sketching the history of a family of note in Catlettsburg, who are at the head of one of Catlettsburg's most useful industries, and noted for their education and knowledge. But it is needless to refer to the branch at Catlettsburg, who, by the maternal side of their house, have the blood of the Sovains.

Henry Sovain, wishing to seek a location farther south, and hoping to improve his worldly prospects, when a young man went south into Virginia, where he married the daughter of one of the first families of Central Virginia. The young husband and wife settled on a farm at the foot of the Alleghany Mountains, where they intended to live the remainder of their days. But shortly before Louisa became a town, which was in 1821, many people in the neighborhood of the Sovains sold out, and moved to the Sandy Valley, then the "promised land" of that section in the "Old Dominion." Among the emigrants some of the relatives of Mrs. Sovain were found. This, no doubt, hastened the removal of Henry Sovain and his wife to the Sandy Valley, which took place a little before or soon after the new county of Lawrence was formed.

While living in Central Virginia a little daughter was born to Mr. and Mrs. Sovain, to gladden their hearts. They named her Mary Jane. When they moved to Sandy she was four or five years old. They at first settled in Wayne County, Va., near Louisa, Ky. When, not long after, another daughter came to add to their cup of joy, they gave her the name borne by the wife and mother, Millie. Mary Jane looked upon her baby sister as a little angel, sent down from above by the Good Father, to be her companion, for it must be recorded that Mrs. Sovain was a warm-hearted Christian of the Methodist faith from early childhood, and it was no trouble, with the pious mother's teachings, for little Mary Jane to believe every thing that she thought was good to be a gift from God.

The two sisters, Mary Jane and Millie, were destined, in God's providence, to be great actors in life's drama in the rôle of sister, daughter, wife; the former, as mother, step-mother, both being Christian workers and merchants. The girls, as they grew up, received the best moral and mental training possible from a Christian mother, with the aid of the best schools of the new settlement. The Sovains, not being possessed of a large share of worldly wealth, could not afford to send their daughters to boarding-schools to have them trained, which they would have gladly done had they been able. With all of these drawbacks, so well was the education of the daughters managed by parents and teachers that, on arriving at young womanhood, each had a fairly good education.

Mary, the elder, in young womanhood, married

Mitchell Stewart, a young farmer. It proved to be a happy match, the union, however, only lasting a few brief years, when it was terminated by the death of the husband. Mr. Stewart left behind him a widow, with the care of two little children, a son and daughter. The son, Henry R. Stewart, was a precocious child, and gave promise in early youth of great intellectual attainment, which was realized, although a promising career was cut short by his early decline, and by his death at the age of twenty-eight years. Henry R. Stewart was fairly well educated, and had a retentive memory; he was a great reader, and possessed an analytical mind, capable of properly applying what he had read, which made him one of the best informed young men of his time in Louisa, where he lived and died. He never married.

The sister of Henry R. received the name of her aunt and grandmother, "Millie," or Amelia; but the child's uncle, John Cook, fondly called the winsome child "Did," and to this day she is addressed by that appellation by her intimate friends. She grew up to womanhood, the idol of mother, brother, and associates. She was trained in the principles of religion, and her mind was cultivated in the best schools in her native little city, thus qualifying her, though unseen at the time, to fill the place with credit as the wife of a public man. At fifteen years of age, or, perhaps, a little before, she was a bride, marrying Kenas F. Prichard.

He was at the time, a rising young lawyer, practicing his profession in the town of Louisa, and is now the Hon. Mr. Prichard, a prominent citizen, lawyer, and political leader, living at Catlettsburg.

Mr. Prichard and family, about 1870, moved from Louisa, Lawrence County, where he had filled several important offices and where he was regarded as a man of great intellectual ability. Since his residence in Boyd, he has been State senator, but is more noted as a great lawyer and pleader at the bar than a seeker of promotion in official life. Mr. Prichard and family occupy a high position in the social circle of Catlettsburg, and live in fine style at their magnificent home on Broadway.

To the union of Keen F. Prichard and Amelia Stewart have been born four children, three daughters and one son. The oldest daughter married a scion of one of the old aristocratic houses of Fleming County. They live in Omaha, Nebraska, where the husband is engaged in commercial pursuits. The young wife, although the distance is great, comes back often to the home of her childhood, to bring sunshine to the hearts of her father and mother and former associates, not forgetting to cover her Aunt Shearer with kisses of love. The second daughter wedded a prosperous young manufacturer of Omaha, and, of course, lives there. The youngest daughter, an uncommonly bright and winsome miss, just approaching young womanhood, was carried to the tomb by a sudden stroke of heart disease. Her untimely taking away crushed the heart of father, mother, sisters, brother, and Aunt Shearer, and brought sadness to all of her young associates and the older people who had become acquainted with the bright little lady. Henry, the son, deserves a medal of the Red-Cross Legion of America as a reward for the performance of an heroic act, which saved from death by drowning two valuable lives.

When the great flood of 1884 was at its highest, Mrs. Judge C. L. McConnell and her little maid were precipitated into the swirling waters at a depth of seven feet, and would have perished but for young Henry Prichard. Being near by in a joe-boat, he heard the plunge, as well as the screams of distress uttered by the lady and little girl, and with lightning speed flew to the scene of danger. He caught the little miss by her hair, and pulled her into the boat; the lady, fortunately seizing the craft, was assisted in by the brave lad, and landed on the stairway out of danger.

We now leave the house of the Stewart branch of the Sovains, and ask the reader to turn back to Mrs. Stewart, the mother of Henry R. and his sister, Mrs. K. F. Prichard, and follow us while we trace her eventful life. Some years after the death of her husband, Mitchell Stewart, she for the second time became a wife; Milton Ferguson winning her heart and hand in holy wedlock. Mr. Ferguson was a well-to-do merchant at Wayne C. H.,

Virginia, now West Virginia, and was a man of honor and strict integrity. He was a widower, with three sons. C. W. Ferguson, for many years a well-off farmer and store-keeper, near Wayne C. H., is one of the sons. We have already, under another head, given a short sketch of the life of another of the sons, the late Hon. M. J. Ferguson, of Louisa; and Captain Joseph M. Ferguson, of near Ashland, Ky., who, like his brothers, has always sustained the highest reputation as a man of honor, is the third brother. It is not historically amiss to state that Captain Ferguson fought bravely on the Confederate side during the Civil War. That he was conscientious and brave is proven, although not alone, by the fact that when the war was over, and he returned to his home, he set himself bravely to work to rebuild his own personal fortune, making himself useful to the people of his section in straightening out the difficulties the war had brought on his country, never abusing either the Government or those brave men who met him on the field of battle in the great contest.

But we bid adieu to the three full brothers Ferguson, and again retrace our steps to Mrs. Ferguson, formerly Stewart, *née* Sovain.

To the union of Milton Ferguson and Mary Jane Stewart were born two children, a son and a daughter. The son, John Ferguson, first studied law, but having no taste for it, turned his attention to steamboating and river-trading. He is almost a recluse so far as society is concerned, but when he does emerge from his chosen obscurity, few men make a better impression upon acquaintances and friends. Laura, the daughter, was trained from infancy by her doting mother with all the care that it is possible for a Christian parent to bestow on her offspring. The father died when the child was very young, and the entire responsibility of her training in life consequently devolved upon her mother. As the daughter, from her youth, gave every indication of strength of character and vigor of intellect, the mother was encouraged to bestow extra labor and expense in training at home, and had her educated in the best schools, fitting her to fill with credit and usefulness in life the responsibilities which awaited her, at least in expectancy, as a woman of high position in society.

When Laura Ferguson grew up to young woman's estate, she was not only the idol of her relatives, but was regarded by all who knew her as a young lady of rare excellence, being beautiful in person, graceful in manners, cultured in mind, and, to crown all, a Christian believer. After the death of Milton Ferguson, Laura's father, her mother opened and carried on a store in Louisa, not giving up the business until early in the sixties, and although living some time after she gave up business, she died before her daughter was fully grown.

It is necessary to go back many years, and more fully sketch the history of Millie, the younger sister of Laura's mother. John Cook came from Marietta, Ohio, prior to 1840, and established the tailoring business in Louisa, adding ready-made clothing to his calling. It is well to state in this place that at that period of time the sewing-machine had not been invented, and all the clothing men and women wore was made by hand. As the tailoring business was one of great utility and profit, the sons of the rich, as well as the poor, in many instances, learned that trade. Such a thing as a store which kept only men's garments on sale, prior to the coming of the sewing-machine, the invention of Elias Howe, a good Quaker of Long Island, New York, was regarded as an innovation and a profitless financial venture. Many German tailors had come to the United States, who, as a class, were not so well skilled in the art as the American, English, or Irish tailors, and were compelled to work at their trade for almost what boss tailors chose to give them. This, no doubt, had something to do in starting up clothing-stores in the large cities of the land. But John Cook's starting such a business in the then small town of Louisa looked, to conservative old store-keepers, as a doubtful experiment, indeed. Mr. Cook was a typical Ohio man, having the pluck of the New Englanders who founded the great State of Ohio by establishing a colony of hardy pioneers at the mouth of the Muskingum. He thought that, by attention to the laws of trade, any legitimate business could be made successful. His was the first clothing-store established in the Sandy Valley; and it proved a success. He afterwards added a general store to his business, doing a prosperous trade up to the time of his death in 1856.

In 1840 Mr. Cook married Millie Sovain, sister of Mary Jane Sovain. The union was a very happy one. While Mrs. Cook paused to weep for her dead husband, she was supported by the sublime truths of the Christian religion. Though no children were born to her, who might by their very dependence have mitigated her grief, she felt that as her husband, who was all the world to her, had finished his course on earth, and had been transplanted to the celestial world, that she would not be honoring his memory by sitting down in idle lamentation for her loss. Besides, were there not helpless ones to think of? She had no children to receive the warmer love bestowed by a stricken wife and mother, to be sure; but there were her aged parents and her sister's children, who needed her counsel and aid. While generous to all of her relatives, more especially did her yearning heart go out after her niece, Laura. She took upon herself the privilege of sharing with the mother the training of the young, sprightly niece, hoping to see her in after years occupying a high sphere in the moral, intellectual, and social walks of life; and she was not disappointed. Seven or eight years after the death of her first husband, John Cook, Mrs. Cook married Samuel Wellman, a wealthy and very prominent citizen of Wayne County, West Va.

Mr. Wellman, as perhaps has already been said, was a brother of the late Judge Wellman, of Catlettsburg; also the uncle of James, Calvin, and Noah Wellman, of the same place—all prominent people. He was also the father-in-law of the late Hon. M. J. Ferguson, a short sketch of whose eventful life is given in another place. Mr. Wellman, of course, was a widower when he married the Widow Cook. The union proved to be a very peaceful and happy one, but was terminated in a brief space of time by the sudden death of Mr. Wellman.

We failed to state before, that after the death of John Cook, her first husband, the widow continued the business of merchandising in her own name from Mr. Cook's death till 1861 or 1862; and it is proper to say that she was regarded during her whole mercantile life as a lady of fine business capacity. Few *men* could have excelled her as a first-class merchant. But whether merchandising or not, she was always busy in useful labor, although much of her time—indeed all of the time since her first marriage until the present—she could, with her sufficient means, have lived without it. But she believed that no drones nor idlers could be good Christians, and as her whole life from childhood had been under the control of a strict religious influence, if she found nothing else to do, she busied herself in doing acts of kindness to the distressed, and helping with her means and by her works to build up the cause of sound morality and Christian love and charity. She and her sister, as well as parents before her, were strictly religious, all being of the Methodist faith and order; and after the division in 1844, herself and all of her relatives have been and are now active leaders in every good work undertaken by the Methodist Episcopal Church, South. Not many years after the death of Mr. Wellman, she married, as her third husband, the Rev. Walter Shearer, a noted and able traveling minister of the Methodist Episcopal Church, South. This marriage, like the two former, proved a happy one, but was in several years terminated by the death of the husband.

Along in the last half of the seventies Laura Ferguson, Mrs. Shearer's niece, who, we have already stated, received so much love and affection from her Aunt Millie, was married, with the aunt's approbation and blessing, to Dr. J. M. Sweatnum, a very talented and promising young physician. The hopeful young doctor took his beautiful bride to the West, settling in a live, progressive town in Northern Missouri, where the young physician and able business man went to work with a vim, which could not fail to lead to success, adding to his extensive practice, dealing largely in real estate, publishing a newspaper, etc.; and, in a material point of view, gaining almost daily in worldly wealth.

But he had been settled in his Missouri home little over a year when his mind was filled with forebodings; for it burst upon him that his Laura was not long for this world. Never rugged in health, yet never complaining, her removal from the more genial clime of the Sandy Valley to the higher latitude of Northern Missouri—an almost treeless region, the bitter cold winds coming down from the frozen north—was more than the Southland flower could stand. A decline set in so alarming, that her husband, with the strong solicitations of sister, brothers, and aunt, brought her back to her Big Sandy home, stopping with her sister, Mrs. Prichard, where husband, sister, aunt, and other relatives and friends did all that human love and skill could do to fan back to her pale cheek the roses of health peculiar to her girlhood. But the Great Shepherd above called her to his own fold, and she left her friends with the assurance that a bright flower, nipped by some untimely blast, was transplanted in the Garden of Delight, to flourish while eternity rolls on. She left one child, a daughter, a little wee thing, whose prattling innocence won the hearts of grand-aunt, aunt, uncles, and cousins; in fact, every one who saw the sweet little child was carried away with its loveliness.

Soon after the death of Rev. Mr. Shearer, his widow, although having ample means to keep up a separate establishment, but not wishing to be alone, sold her possessions in Louisa and took up her residence with her nephew and niece, Mr. and Mrs. Prichard, at Catlettsburg, feeling that her chief duty to remain at Louisa was at an end. Her father dying there late in the fifties, and her mother ten years later, giving them, in their declining years, all the care and attention which was possible for a Christian daughter to bestow upon her aged parents, she yielded to the loving solicitude of her friends at Catlettsburg, to take up her residence with them. While the affections of Mrs. Shearer were strong for all of her friends, her heart went out after the little daughter of her niece, Laura, with a tenfold cord binding her to "Little Nellie" with more than a mother's love. From the day of the death of little Nellie Sweatnum's mother, the main object of the great-aunt's life has been to guard the little treasure with as much care, and of course more sacredness, than the miser watches his golden treasures. Although the father of Nellie was amply able and willing to take the child back to his Western home, and there carry on an establishment with hired, skillful nurses, who would do as much as hired help could be expected to do, and while it was painful to him to leave his little pet behind him so many miles, and return to his desolate home in Missouri, he felt that it would be cruel to take her away, at that time at least, from the fond embrace of the child's doting friends; especially would it have been more cruel, he saw, to snatch her from the arms of her great-aunt, so plain was it to the father that her love for his child was pure and unselfish.

After consigning the loved form of his wife to the tomb, interring her in the Ashland cemetery, a beautiful resting-place for the ashes of the dead, Dr. Sweatnum left his little baby girl in good hands, and, as duty called, went back to resume the routine of a busy life. Some two or more years after the death of his first wife, the doctor married again. Not long after the second marriage, like all affectionate fathers, he thought it his duty to have his child brought home and reared in the precincts of his own family. He made a trip to Catlettsburg, and carried away his little daughter, who day by day had, if possible, grown more lovely. The taking away of the child was a sad blow to the great-aunt, aunt, and cousins, but they were reconciled by the fact that she was in good hands. Mrs. Dr. Sweatnum the second must have been a remarkably good woman, for little Nellie always speaks of her in the most loving manner. But the step-mother of little Nellie, however good, was destined to fill her place as wife and step-mother for a very brief space of time; not much over a year had gone when she was called to the spirit land.

Not long after the death of his second wife, Nellie was brought back to her old home, greatly to the delight of the little miss's relatives. After Nellie had been trained by her aunts, and had been sent to the best primary schools in Catlettsburg, her father thought it best to have her with him, she being at the time about twelve years old. But unwilling to separate her again from her aunt Shearer, he provided in the city of Omaha, Nebraska, a house furnished in the most luxuriant style, over which he invited Mrs. Shearer to come and preside, thus enabling the young miss to be with both father and aunt. Nellie was placed in a preparatory school, to qualify her to enter a ladies' seminary further along in life, when she should be old enough to be separated from the restraints of home life. After two or more years' stay in the great, bustling, giant, Western city, it was agreed by both father and aunt that it was time that their charge should be placed in a ladies' boarding-school, as Miss Nellie was now verging on to young womanhood. A noted school in the suburbs of the Queen City was selected by the father, with the approval of the aunt.

How eventful have been the lives of most of the persons sketched in this article! The full history can not now be finished. Dr. J. M. Sweatnum intends, when his daughter's five years' course is finished at the female school, to take her to Europe, where she may have access to the great universities, art galleries, and other centers of knowledge, thus rounding up her already well-begun education. While in the old country he will be able to visit the home of the Crosses in England, from which house Mildred Cross Sweatnum, his great-grandmother, sprang; and in northern Ireland he will hunt up some of the Jemisons, a daughter of that house capturing a young Ferguson, who had come down from his highland home in Scotland to capture cattle, but instead was himself noosed by a handsome maiden, from which union came the family of the Fergusons on Sandy. Of course Alsace-Lorraine will receive the visit of the party, so that the daughter may trace back one of her ancestral lines who first came into note in that historic country.

Providence shapes the destiny of all who, if faithful to duty, are led, if not to wealth and fame, to honest respectability.

THE DELONGS.

AT an early day in Sandy history the father of James Delong, Samuel Delong, and George Delong, and others of the family, came from the Muskingum country at or near Zanesville, Ohio, and falling in love with a bright-eyed Sandy maiden, courted and married her, and became a good loyal Big Sandian. The Delongs are of French extraction, and the house of Delong in America has become a noted one. The Sandy Valley house of that name has the same ancestral beginning as had the great Arctic navigator of that name, and the great editor at the Golden Gate.

The marriage of the elder Delong to a member

of one of the most prominent families in the valley connects them not only with the Auxiers, but numerous families of note in the valley. James Delong owns and lives on a very fine farm not far from its mouth on John's Creek. His wife was a Ward, a kinswoman of Rev. Z. Meek, D. D. One or more of James's sons served in the Federal army during the war. Several of the sons of Mr. Delong went to Texas, and are prosperous citizens of that giant State.

James Delong and family are adherents of the Christian Church, and in politics Republican. Samuel and George Delong live in Martin County, on the Middle Fork of Rock Castle. They both own large boundaries of land, and, like their brother James, are well supplied with money. Samuel and George adhere to the Methodist persuasion, Samuel being a member of the Methodist Episcopal Church, South, at Eden, Ky. They, like their brother, are Republicans. All are people of great respectability.

A CLOSE CALL.

IN the latter part of the Summer of 1862, the Ohio and Sandy Rivers at Catlettsburg were extremely low. The Sandy at the ford at the Mouth was not over nine or ten inches deep, with a well-beaten track, over which teams, horsemen, and even footmen, by stepping from rock to rock, could cross with perfect ease and safety. Catlettsburg at the time was the depot of vast quantities of Government stores, as well as having located a corral, where many government horses and mules were kept to supply sudden demands for horses used by the army of occupation in the Sandy above. At the time the general stores of the place carried large stocks of goods, especially in the line of ready-made clothing. Not a soldier was on hand to guard the Government stores, much less to protect the private property of the town. Ten armed men could have come in and captured the place, including the rich Government treasures.

At about eleven o'clock A. M., on the day indicated, the few persons who happened to be passing up Front Street were attracted by a dense cloud of dust a mile or two distant on the road leading to Ceredo, West Va. By the time the first observers had called to others to come and look, it was discovered that the great cloud of dust was put in motion by the feet of several hundred horses, whose riders carried the colors of the Southern Confederacy, and wore the gray, the emblematical uniform of that party. From the time the flying dust was first noticed, not more than five minutes had elapsed when it was apparent to all beholders on the banks that a large force of Confederate cavalry in a few minutes would be in Catlettsburg, capturing rich government stores and private booty, and, perhaps, would not stop at carrying away as much stores as they might choose, but would burn the town as well. But when the troopers had come within three hundred yards of the ford over Sandy, all stopped as suddenly as if a thunder-bolt had struck both horse and rider dead. The soldiers remained sitting on their reined-in steeds as if in a short consultation. Their halt or check-up added consternation to the few denizens of the anticipated ill-fated town at the Mouth. The consultation of the troopers was at an end in less than two minutes, when the whole regiment turned about and rode away in the direction from which they came. Both joy and wonder filled the hearts and minds of every beholder who viewed the maneuvers of the troops.

Why they came so near the town with no obstacle to their coming or staying, and why, when within two minutes' ride of all that would gladden the hearts of men half fed and clothed, was a profound mystery, but was made plain within less than twenty-four hours. On the morning in question Solomon McBrayer, a citizen of the East Fork country, who had moved into town for a temporary purpose, was living with his family in the old Catlett house, since torn down. McBrayer had persuaded two young men, refugees from Virginia, to accompany him that morning on a squirrel-hunt in the dense forest lying between the Sandy River and Ceredo. Having no guns, they by some device procured each a government Enfield rifle. The trio walked to Hampton City, an upper suburb of Catlettsburg, crossed the Sandy, and went up to near the upper end of the woods near Ceredo. They were in sight of the troopers as they passed down the road, and the men believing capture, and, perhaps, death would be their fate if they returned to town before the Confederate soldiers had left, and fearful that their lurking-place might be discovered on the return of the troops, concluded to seek a safer retreat, and also one from which they could view the force on its return from sacking Catlettsburg, discovering thereby the result of the raid. They hastened toward Twelve Pole Creek, keeping near the hill which reached from the Sandy to almost Twelve Pole, so they might not be observed. Coming to the Creek, they easily crossed over, and ran up the hill by the residence of Fred. Holden, who was a brother-in-law of Congressman Eli Thayer, who founded Ceredo. Immediately on the top of the hill, or rather cliff, a dense growth of trees and underwood were interlocked, making it impossible for any passer-by on the road, which lay at the foot of the cliff, to see any one within two hundred feet of him.

A soldier living nearly opposite Ceredo, in Ohio, was at home on a furlough, and had his Enfield with him. Seeing the troops passing down in the direction of Catlettsburg, and expecting their return after they had sacked the town, he took up his gun and walked down near the edge of the water in the

Ohio River, a dense willow thicket having grown up, and a large pile of drift accumulated in the preceding Spring freshet. Behind the drift-pile he placed himself, and, concealed by the willows, awaited the return of the raiders. They returned much sooner than he had anticipated. When the man took his position in the willow thicket, he intended to fire into the ranks of the soldiers as they passed back on the highway. But when the cavalrymen reached a point where at that time stood a large mill, and perceived a road leading down the river bank (just below Ceredo), they turned in that direction, and kept on to the river for the purpose of watering their horses. The man in the thicket took aim and slew one of the troopers, who fell into the river. Two of his comrades jumped from their horses, hastily raised the dead man from the water, and, placing him before another soldier, the whole party, carrying their comrade with them, scampered away. Ten minutes brought them to the place where Sol. McBrayer and his companions were lying in ambush. Riding in haste, and greatly chagrined at their ill-undertaken expedition, they were not looking for any more danger ahead, as they were beyond the range of a ball from a gun fired from the Ohio shore. But how often is it that the very moment we feel most secure is the one we are in most danger! When the troops were immediately opposite the ambush, the three concealed hunters all fired at once, yelling at the top of their voices to an imaginary main body of troops to come to the front and fire in companies, leaving the impression on the minds of the surprised raiders that a large Union force had collected to cut off their retreat. The men in ambush discovered that two of the fleeing raiders had been wounded by their shots, and news reached Catlettsburg afterwards that they had both died.

The Confederates hastened on to Guyandotte, to meet the frown and receive the rebuke of the colonel of the regiment, who had given strict orders to his men to keep away from Catlettsburg. Many of the men had been recruited in the neighborhood of Guyandotte, and the colonel had permission to go with them there, that the men might visit their families, and procure, if possible, a better outfit of clothing and camp equipage. On the morning of the attempted raid some of the officers and men told the colonel that it would be a good thing to go down to Catlettsburg and sack the town. But the commander forbade it in the most positive terms; "for," said he "I have many friends in Catlettsburg, some of whom are Union people, and I can't find it in my heart to inflict an injury on them, especially so when it is probable that if we should go down there and raid the government stores, a greater calamity would be visited on us than we might scourge them with." But, the colonel being absent from his command for an hour or so, the restive subordinate officers resolved to go, in disobedience to the order of their chief. On returning to head-quarters, the colonel was overwhelmed with anger to find the men away, and, on learning where they had gone, hastily wrote an order, and put it in the hands of a safe courier, mounted on a fleet charger, commanding the messenger to travel with all speed, and, if possible, overtake the men before they reached Catlettsburg; but if not so successful, to go into the town and bring the men away, and to tell them to leave their plunder behind.

Sol. McBrayer, two or three days after these stirring events, went to Louisa and volunteered in the 39th Kentucky Infantry, and a day or two after, while sitting on a dry-goods box, a rusty nail projecting through the wood scratched his thigh, causing a slight abrasion of the skin, producing gangrene, which terminated in his death within twenty-four hours. His widow's pension runs back to the day of his death.

MORE ABOUT MAGOFFIN.

That part of Magoffin County west of the main Licking was, up to 1860, a part of Floyd County, and the people living in there were not only bound together in county relations with Floyd, but their social and commercial relations were identical. Hence, in sketching the history of the people of the Sandy Valley, the citizens of the territory named come under the same head as those of the

Sandy Valley proper, though not in the Sandy Valley.

The Patrick family was well known from the settlement of the ancestors of Reuben, Elijah, Wiley, and other sons, and of Mrs. Neri Sweatnum, daughter of the ancestral Patrick, who founded the house in the Sandy and Licking country in an early period of Sandy history, settling on the Burning Fork of Licking, about twenty miles from Prestonburg. From the day of the coming of the elder Patrick to the present time, the family has held a high rank in social, intellectual, material, and Church progress in the affairs in the country.

Captain Wiley Patrick married a daughter of German Huff, of Paintsville, Ky. This brave Union officer was killed while gallantly leading his men in battle in one of the hotly contested fields of Georgia. Reuben married, as has already been said, a daughter of General Hager, while Elijah also married into an old house of Sandy—a Miss Rule. The Patricks were old-time Whigs, and are now Republicans. They are members of the Methodist Episcopal Church, and are an aggressive, forceful people.

The Praters, like the Patricks, were early comers to the same locality, and have run on the same line with the Patricks. They are a solid people, and many of them have intermarried with the prominent people of the valley.

The Powers, too, from their early settlement in

the same section of country, have ever maintained a high place in the affairs of honor and respectability in their section. They are Democrats in politics. John Powers was a captain in the Union army.

ADAMS FAMILY.

NO FAMILY in the section of the three last named were more forceful in the material affairs of the country round about Licking Station, now Salyersville, than the Adams family. William Adams, the second in descent from the early pioneer of his house, during his long and useful life (which terminated in about 1879), was to his section what Judge Archibald Borders, of Peach Orchard, was to his. He was not only a large farmer, but a merchant, manufacturer, and hotel-keeper. He carried on a large tannery, shoe-shop, saddlery, flour-mill, etc., with great profit to himself, giving employment to a multitude of men. The energy of William Adams took such deep root that Salyersville has to this day maintained a reputation as being the chief manufacturing center in East Kentucky, east of the Licking. This has been stimulated by the push and pluck of the Adkinson brothers (Ohio men), aided in no little degree by D. Milt. Hager, a brother of John F. Hager, who was educated on the Sandy. William Adams's brother settled on Burning Fork, and, like his brother William, maintained a lofty position as an excellent citizen.

William Adams's children and grandchildren have come to honor. One son, Smith, was captain in the Union army during the great civil conflict, and sustained himself nobly in that position. All are prominent people.

Austin Litteral was on Little Paint, in Magoffin County, in early times, where he obtained an immense boundary of land, giving a large farm to each of his numerous children. He was an old-time, zealous, Methodist layman, and a man of high character. He still lives, well up in eighty, to bless the world with his many virtues. He had a brother living near Greasy, on Big Sandy, who was equally distinguished in his day. He was one of the leading old-time Sandy timber-traders. He died before the great war, leaving a large and respectable family behind, still prominent on Sandy.

James Turner, near Paintsville, was an old settler, and was one of the well-known men of the valley. He reared a large and respectable family, who are connected by matrimonial alliances with many of Big Sandy's noted people. One of his daughters married a Stambaugh, whose children are a bright, thrifty group in Johnson. Dr. Turner, a physician of mark in Paintsville, is James Turner's son. "Sud" Turner, another, though erratic, is a brainy fellow. The other children are notable.

The Salyers family is very numerous, and mostly found in Magoffin and Johnson Counties. The county seat of Magoffin was named after the representative of that name, who was in the Legislature when the new county was formed. Hon. John Salyers is a lawyer and an intellectual man. He has held official position in a governmental department at Washington. Ben. F. Salyers has for a generation been hotel-keeper at Flat Gap. He has a son living there, who is a lawyer. Many more of the Salyers family might be named as prominent people.

WALTER FAMILY.

The father of Robert and Calvin Walter and their sisters—Mrs. James Graham and Mrs. Winfrey Holbrook, both of Blaine—was a noted Baptist preacher in Russell County, Virginia, where he died in about 1818. The widow and her children moved to Blaine soon after, where Robert married the daughter of Neri Sweatnum, and settled on a large farm. Here he lived until his death, in 1878 or '79, his wife having died two years before.

Mr. Walter left three sons and four daughters. E. L. Walter is a wealthy old bachelor, living on one of his farms on Blaine. M. M. Walter, the youngest son, is an extensive farmer in the vicinity, owning and living on the old homestead of his father. The other son is a wealthy farmer and county officer in Kansas. The oldest daughter is the wife of Judge J. R. Dean, of Lawrence; the next is the wife of the author of this book; while the youngest daughter and child is the wife of Wm. Wood, a prominent farmer and stock-trader in the western part of Lawrence County. The remaining daughter is the wife of John Sturgill, a farmer in Kansas.

Robert's brother, Calvin, married a sister of William Jefferson Ward, of Johnson, who was an aunt of Rev. Z. Meek, D. D. Calvin raised three sons, who are numbered among the good citizens of Johnson County. The father has been dead several years.

THE WHEELERS

ARE scattered all over the Sandy Valley. A very numerous family of them are citizens of the Blaine country. The ancestors of this branch arrived in Blaine at an early day, from North Carolina and South-west Virginia. The family are nearly all Baptists, and several preachers of that faith have gone out from the house of Wheeler. Lawyers and doctors have also added to the importance of the family.

Another branch of the numerous house is found near Paintsville. Daniel Wheeler is a prominent old citizen, and having married a Miss Hager, a niece of the General, brings him into relationship with many of the strong families of the valley. His son, Samuel Wheeler, married Miss Van Horn, a daughter of John Van Horn, late of Boyd, and a well-known, old-time Sandian. A daughter of Daniel Wheeler is the wife of Dr. J. F. Hatton, of Rockville, and another daughter is the wife of George Sick, of the noted house of that name in Pike. While George's family name is a burden to carry through life, he is one of the healthiest men in the valley.

Daniel Wheeler, like his namesakes over on Blaine, is a Baptist; but while they are "united" in the faith, he is equally emphatic in his "Free-Will" Baptist principles. He is a large farmer, and has coal mined from his rich deposits of the black diamonds.

SAMUEL PORTER

Was an early settler on the Sandy, only a little later in coming than the Hagers, Laynes, etc. He married into the prominent family of the Damrons, who are found living in the valley from Pike County, Ky., to Twelve Pole, Wayne County, W. Va. Mr. Porter was a sharp business man, and in his day was one of the largest land-owners in the Sandy Valley. He owned the entire valley of Miller's Creek, now Johnson County, and many broad acres on the waters of Little Paint, in Floyd County, besides a great boundary on the Sandy River, where his daughter, Mrs. Bird Preston, and family reside. Mr. Porter was of a jovial turn of mind, and delighted in fast horses and other sources of amusement. He raised a large family of children, who became and those now living still are, prominent people of the valley.

Walker Porter, a son of Samuel Porter, was, during his life, one of the bright men of Prestonburg. A daughter of Walker's is the wife of Dick Mayo, a bright scion of the old famous house of Mayo.

John Porter was a large farmer on the Sandy River, above the mouth of Miller's Creek, but sold his farm, moved to Catlettsburg, and went into the hotel business. But, owing to the heavy loss sustained by him in the two great floods, and other unforeseen disasters, he has been reduced from affluence, but, with a heroic courage peculiar to the Porters, is battling to gain the summit of the hill of prosperity. He married a daughter of Judge Thomas Brown, of Paintsville, and has a family noted for grace and sprightliness of mind. Henry Porter, the oldest son, a very bright and promising young man, met with a frightful accident in 1885, by the accidental discharge of the pistol of a guest who was passing the weapon to his care while he remained a guest at his father's hotel. This sad affair caused the amputation of one of his lower limbs. But in due time he was restored to strength, and on procuring an artificial limb, obtained a lucrative position suitable to his condition in Cincinnati, where for some time he has been engaged. John Porter's oldest daughter married Glen Ford, an only child, and son of James R.

Ford and Sally, his wife. Glen has the largest material expectations of any young man in Catlettsburg.

Hon. James Porter, another son of Samuel Porter, has represented Floyd and Johnson Counties in the Kentucky Legislature. Logan, another son, is a merchant and farmer on John's Creek.

Another daughter of Samuel Porter is the wife of Mr. Burgess, a son of the late Edward Burgess, of Lawrence. He lives on Miller's Creek, being a well-to-do farmer. Samuel Porter and wife have been dead several years, both living to a good old age.

Mr. Porter was able to give all of his children a large, productive farm, and then have plenty left for himself to use as long as he lived.

THE BOOTENS,

WHILE not a numerous Sandy family, have always occupied a good place in the moral, intellectual, and material affairs of the Lower Sandy Valley. The wife of the late Major Bolt, who was the father of Montraville Bolt, the latter well advanced in years, was a Booten. This lady was noted for the vigor of her mind, and for her great kindness of heart, showing every mark of an old-time cultured Virginian. This venerable woman died in either 1885 or '86, near ninety years of age. Her mental powers were clear up to the last, and she did not give down in physical strength till over eighty. Major Bolt and wife reared a family of great respectability.

Captain J. M. Ferguson's wife is of another branch of the same family of Bootens.

Ralph Booten, a prominent lawyer of Prestonburg, is of the near Louisa branch of Bootens. Ralph Booten, in addition to his law practice and the time heretofore given to the duties of county official life, has lately, with another, started into life an industry which, though small, is destined to add more wealth to Prestonburg than the carrying on of the largest store in the valley. Stores are great conveniences to a community, and the occupation is an honorable one, but they add no wealth to a country, while a manufactory adds wealth in proportion to the amount of material found in nature in its raw state, which is taken up by skillful workmen, and transformed into useful articles, to add to the comfort and happiness of man. The difference between the price of the raw wood and iron of which a common road-wagon is made and the worth of the wagon when completed is the amount of wealth added to the community at large, the capitalist, of course, gaining his profits out of the things produced; but as he is a component part of the community, the whole county is benefited as well as himself. The little outcropping at Prestonburg in mechanical life is a forerunner of the time not far distant when the town that was asleep in material life for sixty years will become a manufacturing center on Sandy, as it is the geographical center in the valley. The boy who shaves out a shingle, and stops a leak in the roof of a house, adds to the world's wealth the price of the shingle, while the boy who cuts off a yard of calico for a customer, adds no wealth to any one, and yet the latter feels himself above the former. But he is not.

THE McGUIRES, OF LAWRENCE.

NICHOLAS McGUIRE is of Irish descent, and married a Miss Rogers, of the same nationality. They settled near Louisa, in Lawrence County, about sixty years ago (now 1887). Mr. McGuire opened up a fine farm two miles below Louisa, where the family still reside. The wife of Nicholas McGuire came of one of the most substantial families in Cincinnati. The Rogerses, for more than half a century, have been amongst the notable business men of the Queen City, and intermarrying into prominent families, still increases their high social and business standing. The McGuires are devout Catholics, as are also the Rogerses; but while holding tenaciously to every tenet of the Catholic creed, so careful are they to avoid giving their Protestant neighbors offense that no friction has ever been manifest in their intercourse with the people in religious, social, or business life. It can be said that, instead of repelling from the

McGuire household, it has attracted to themselves the love of many and the respect of all their Protestant neighbors.

A large family of both sons and daughters blessed the union of Nicholas McGuire and wife. The sons, on coming to man's estate, developed into keen business men, some going into railroading, others into the steamboat business and general trading, while others still are farmers. The daughters are ladies of uncommon sprightliness. Nearly, or quite all, of the large household of daughters, in addition to the good domestic training given to them by their well-qualified mother, received a finished education at one of the best convent schools of the Catholic Church, giving them a polish of manners pleasing to all intelligent observers. Louisa, and, indeed, Lawrence County and the valley at large, is much better by the McGuires having lived there.

The old gentleman, Nicholas McGuire, is high up in eighty—indeed, can almost reach over to the ninetieth yearly mile-stone, set on life's highway; but, with all these years upon him, he is as hale and hearty as a man of sixty. His devoted wife, while some years younger than her liege lord, is not so robust in health as he, yet is able to move around, cheering the household with the sunshine peculiar to one who has all along life's journey honored the great Father by doing deeds of kindness to her children and neighbors.

THE PETERS FAMILY.

JACOB PETERS came to Lawrence County from Virginia about 1836 or 1837, and married a Miss See, who was a Garred on her mother's side. Jacob Peters and wife have raised a large family of children. The sons are good citizens and prosperous men. James, one of the sons, is a merchant and trader. He married the eldest daughter of Captain William Bartram, a highly educated lady. The Peterses are Democrats in politics. They set a good example for their countrymen to follow by their industry and economy.

THE CLARKS,

OF Pigeon, Logan County, West Virginia, are from farther over in Virginia, and while not among the oldest settlers, the family of Ira Clark, brothers and sisters, have always held a high rank in the business affairs of their locality. The ancestor of the present old generation of Clarks laid a good foundation for future prosperity when he settled in the valley, by opening up a large, productive farm and erecting a dwelling and other buildings, not only commensurate with the good farm, but in advance of any other settler in the neighborhood. Dr. Waldron's wife is a Clark, the doctor being one of the progressive doctors on Tug.

It not unfrequently happens that a family pre-eminent for their good social and moral position has some member in it that brings distress upon the rest of the family by some wicked or unmanly act. One unfortunate brother thus troubled the peace of the Clarks. Guy was an awful drunkard (unusual with the house of the Clarks), and lost all reason and restraint. He became so vindictive toward his wife and children that it brought him to a most tragic death, four miles above Catlettsburg, Boyd County, Ky., several years after the close of the Civil War. The wife and children had the sympathy of the community, which, to the great honor of the Clarks, was shared by them.

JAMES STAIRS.

NOT far from the home of the Clarks, on Pigeon, lives James Stairs, a very old man, who has been living where he now lives many, many years. He is somewhat peculiar. He is a great economist, though by no means a miser. He never had any children to share his joys and sorrows, but he and his wife have been useful members of society. Mr. Stairs, by his industry and economy, has been a constant reminder to his neighbors of the value of time and the importance of improving every moment of it in doing good, by laboring for the bread that perishes and for that which never is lost.

Mr. Stairs is one of the most noted of the old-time Methodist laymen found in the valley. While very methodical and exact in his dealings, saving, and sharp in material matters, many years ago he built, without aid, a good stone church, and presented it, free of incumbrance, to his Church (the Methodist Episcopal). The good old man had never studied architecture, and never traveled much to enable him to take up models of handsome church buildings; consequently the appearance of the church is a little out of modern style, yet, nevertheless, it stands on the roadside on Pigeon as a reminder to the passer-by that God is venerated and worshiped in that locality, and that Uncle Jimmy Stairs is his humble servant.

Were the President of the United States to stop with this old servant of God, he would not be permitted to sleep at night nor eat in the morning until he joined the family in humble praise and thanksgiving to the Supreme Being for his goodness and mercies to the children of men.

THE LAWSONS,

Of the Tug region, are of Virginia origin, and not many families in the valley exceed them in industry and personal enterprise, in devising honorable means to increase their individual wealth.

Captain Mont. B. Lawson, who died in 1885, down South, where he had gone to recuperate his failing health, was a man of great force of character. As farmer, trader, and public citizen, he was for many years one of Pike County's most honored citizens. He was a great friend of common-school education, and favored all honorable methods to promote progress and advancement in the material wealth and betterment of his State and county. Dr. Lawson and his other brother are, like Montraville, men of energy, and rank high as useful, solid citizens in the Tug Valley.

THE SMITHS, OF TUG.

THE father of Jacob Smith, the wealthy Pond merchant, and John Smith, a business man, now of Sandy City, came to the county when a boy, from Virginia. Jacob Smith, his son, is now, by a long course of work and saving, and by his keen business talent, employed in the accumulation of material wealth, properly set down as among the four or five very wealthy men of Pike County, as wealth is compared on Sandy. John Smith has erected an imposing dwelling in Hampton City, and also a long string of small tenement-houses, which, of course, have added to the prosperity of the place.

THE RUTHERFORDS,

ON Tug, came from Virginia. Dr. Rutherford has for more than thirty years been known as one of the leading practitioners of medicine in the Tug Valley. Many other members of the family are prominent people in the doctor's neighborhood. They are farmers and timbermen.

THE SLATERS,

OF Tug, are of an old Virginia family, having emigrated to the Sandy country at an early day. The daughters became the wives of some of the leading men of the county. The family is an influential one on Tug.

THE TAYLORS

WERE from Virginia, also, in an early day. Green Taylor, of Tug, is a very forceful man, and has had much experience in mercantile life. He is now a farmer. Mitchell Runyon's wife is one of the same branch of Taylors.

"OLD TOM HACKNEY"

WAS a noted character of Sandy almost from time immemorial.

In all mountain regions there are places found where the natural make-up of the locality seems to defy Nature in her diversity of uniformity, ignores all laws governing topography, geology, mineralogy, and almost challenges geography itself. Such a place is seen as one passes along the banks of the Levisa Fork, as it plows through the mountain pass from Wise County, Virginia, into Pike County, Kentucky. Here for a long time lived Tom Hackney. To say that he partook of the wild and slipshod appearance of the view spread out before you, would hardly be true; but, rather, Mr. Hackney was part of the wild scene himself. He did not drink in the rugged views surrounding him, that being impossible; but, rather, he was a part of the wildest crags of the partially torn-down glomerate, an unseemly, misshapen limb of one of the scraggy pines that had hard work to reach downward and find soil and moisture sufficient to retain the size and strength it had already attained before it was diverted to other little sproutlet pines striving to assume tree manhood. He was as uncomely in person and dress as the half-starved, stunted timber of the place. In speech he was not only uncouth, but vulgar. But he was a fair liver, and many noted men have, in times gone by, partaken of his hospitality. General John C. Breckinridge has been his guest. Mr. Hackney must have had a good wife, for his descendants are by no means wild, like their ancestor.

Captain O. C. Bowles, an Ohio man, who married a Sandy lady belonging to one of the proud families of Pike (a daughter of Judge William Cecil), in addition to farmer, merchant, timber-trader, lawyer, and law-maker, concluded, some fifteen years ago, to add steamboating to his other branches of business, and built a craft to ply on the waters of the Big Sandy from Pike to Catlettsburg. He gave to his craft the name of *Tom Hackney*, and, as the boat, or monster, came plowing through the water toward you, you instinctively felt like getting away, so hideous did it appear. When she made her landing you were made nervous by the threatening aspect of the paddle-wheels, raising their arms high up the sides of the boat, as if defying you to come near at the peril of great danger. Should you be brave enough to go aboard, you would be amazed and almost horrified at the wild construction of the machinery used to propel the craft. And when the great cog-wheels met your gaze, you felt that all mechanical rules had been ignored in their construction. Captain Bowles being a man of learning, and not wishing to disregard all rules of steamboat construction, for a time tied the *Tom Hackney* to the bank, and set to work and built a real first-class Sandy steamer. But Captain Bowles had either a strength or weakness for naming his boats after some noted citizen of the county of his adoption. For his second venture, while constructing it, he chose the name of another dweller at the foot of the Cumberland Mountains. This fortunate man was *Jerry Osburn*.

On going up the Sandy, a good half-day's ride or more above Pikeville, you come to Elk Horn, a branch of the Russell Fork of Sandy. Near the mouth of Elk Horn, in a wild and romantic spot, in about 1883 or '84, the celebrated "mountain evangelist," Rev. George O. Barnes, held a camp-meeting. When appointed, it was thought by many of his friends that thousands would flock to hear him expound the Word of Life; but, instead, comparatively a few attended the gathering of the Christian people who came in spite of hindrances. The population for miles around was but sparse, and the great inconveniences in reaching the camp were many. Therefore, with all the eloquence of Mr. Barnes, and the charming music of his gifted daughter, the camp-meeting was a failure. Near this spot a post-office has been established, named to commemorate one of Mr. Barnes's hourly expressions, "Praise," with the last words left off.

Passing up Elk Horn, you come across more Potters than can be found anywhere else in Eastern Kentucky. But they are only Potters by name, and not jug and crock makers. They are peaceable tillers of the narrow bottoms skirting the creek. After a few hours' ride you reach the home of Jerry Osburn, quite close to the celebrated Pound Gap, an opening in the huge mountain through which is a pass-way between Virginia and Kentucky. Mr. Osburn is an old-time citizen, and has lived nearly all his life in this, his romantic home. He is honored by his neighbors, and respected for his good citizenship. The people of Pike, a few years ago, elected him judge of their county, and it is due to the people of Pike, and to Hon. Mr. Osburn as well, to say that they made no mistake in clothing him in judicial robes. He was a good officer. He is a warm-hearted gentleman, and for a long time in the past, as now, has ranked as one of Pike's solid men.

Before the war, Mr. Osburn's place was noted in a commercial point of view. A great and prosperous trade was kept, until destroyed by the Civil War. This trade reached from Saltville, Virginia, to the iron-works in Bath County, Ky., and on the Red River in the same State. Salt was hauled in wagons from the salt-works in Washington County, Va., to supply much of the demand in the counties of Pike, Letcher, Floyd, and Perry, and iron was taken back from the iron-works in Kentucky, and distributed as the great huge teams returned back to Virginia.

Judge Osburn's hotel was one of the most important on the entire route. In addition to the calling of innkeeper, he kept on sale salt, iron, and other needful articles of merchandise, for the convenience of his neighbors and to add to his own wealth. The Osburn place was a busy place until the traffic which kept it up was turned into other channels and other directions. But still the old judge is well provided for by the cultivation of a large farm.

Captain Bowles's steamer, *Jerry Osburn*, proved to be a great success, and was a source of great profit; not owing, however, to the fact that she wore the honored name *Jerry Osburn*, but because the brainy captain had learned by experience how to build a boat, and what kind of a boat to build, to make a success. Tom Hackney was the image of the wild nature surrounding him, and the steamer named to publish his name was an image of him.

THEN AND NOW.

THE best means to find out what progress the Sandy Valley has made in the last quarter of a century is by taking into consideration the amount of mail matter taken up the valley, say in 1861, and the amount going up now (1887). In 1861 old Stephen Bartram was the mail contractor and carrier between Catlettsburg and Pikeville, Kentucky. Many of the older people may call to mind "Uncle Steve's" little white pacing-horse, on which the mails were conveyed, making two trips a week, if it did not rain too hard. All the mail matter could then be put into a good large pair of saddle-bags, such as travelers on horseback used to carry. In fact, the mail-bag was full to repletion not more than once a week on going up, and on coming down the postmaster had to shake carefully the bag to find any thing in it, on many occasions. Money was never sent through the mails before the Civil War, but the owner either brought it down to the Ohio River, and procured a draft at the nearest bank to the Mouth, or, if it was going to Cincinnati, sent it by the Honshell line of steamers.

The mails were so uncertain and slow in their movements in those days that few people in the Sandy gave them much attention. But now (1887), how changed!

Stephen Bartram appeared like an old man when he was carrying the mails up Sandy in 1861, but still lives, hearty although venerable.

The bag that held all the mail matter then going up the valley would not hold all the letters and papers now stopping between Catlettsburg and Catalpa. The amount has increased more than one-hundred-fold in twenty-five years. It would take two mail hacks, such as Green Meek uses in conveying the mails from Richardson to Paintsville, to convey the Ashland mails up the valley. The increase is simply wonderful, and proves that the Sandy people have progressed in gaining knowledge and worldly wealth, according to the number of letters they send away and receive, and the number of papers taken and read by them.

In 1861 but few post-offices were found outside of the county towns; now a post-office is established at almost every store in the valley. Not only the man of business looks anxiously for the approach of mail-day, but women and children are on the alert for the arrival of the mail-man, who brings letters and magazines and papers for mental food, as well as kind greetings and messages of love from dear ones afar; sometimes messages of sadness are conveyed by the mails, too, but it is as necessary to hear bad news, when it must be communicated, by rapid transit through the mail as by a slower process.

THE GREAT FLIGHT.

MANY exciting events occurred on the Sandy during the progress of the great civil conflict. The battle of Ivy Mountain was attended with great excitement and, of course, alarm, as men fell dead or wounded from the rain of shot and shell, pouring forth death and carnage. It was a serious day on Middle Creek when General Marshall, at the head of his Confederate band, and Colonel Garfield, in chief command of the Federal forces, measured military strength with each other, and grape-shot and musket-balls rained down like hail-stones. It was fearful to think of.

But, excepting the human slaughter, the excitement attending those battles sink into insignificance compared with the great scare and hegira which came off at the metropolis of the valley on the day of the Presidential election of 1864. Nearly a quarter of a century has been rolled up in the curtain of time, and but comparatively few of the old, or even middle-aged, residents of Catlettsburg are now living who witnessed the awful scenes through which the people were called to pass on that eventful day at Catlettsburg.

Wishing that events so stirring in their nature as those hinted at might be preserved from dying with the oldest man or woman at the Mouth, the author feels that he would not be a faithful chronicler of events if he failed to give them a place in the history of the Big Sandy country. As the author was an eye-witness to the principal acts of that occasion, and, indeed, was a partial actor himself in the great rout, he is enabled to describe with accuracy and faithfulness the whole wonderful affair.

As already stated, the Presidential election was being held in all of the *United* States, but the inhabitants living in the States *not united* paid no attention to the election for President of the United States. But in Kentucky, while not a very strongly *united* State, all who chose voted either for Abraham Lincoln or George B. McClellan. A number of soldiers had come home to Catlettsburg to vote. Some availed themselves of the privilege, and some did not. The election at the Mouth created no excitement whatever. The author was acting as sheriff at the polls, while W. O. Hampton, then a prominent young lawyer, was the clerk. Who the judges were, the author fails to remember; but as long as memory lingers he will never fail to remember the awful scare and suspense which came over him and many of his fellow-citizens at the hour of half-past three o'clock P. M., on that day, which will ever be noted in Catlettsburg annals, not as the day of the great national election, but as the day of the great scare.

THE GREAT FLIGHT. 419

At the hour named a hideous noise was heard. The sound came from the upper end of Louisa Street. The author rushed to the door, when a sight met his eyes which beggars description, and the sounds heard were equally indescribable. Men, women, and children were rushing pell-mell down the street, screaming at the top of their voices, "*The rebels are coming! The rebels are coming!*" At every jump the affrighted runners made, they would look back over their shoulders to see what headway the gray-coats were making. In the din of noise made by their yells they roused a lazy dog of Alex. Botts's from his slumber in the yard, and he joined in the chase. The agonizing yells of the hurrying mob and Alec's dog stirred up an old cow that had been reposing in a dog-fennel bed, and she took to her heels and ran down the street, giving out a bawl as she plowed through the excited crowd, that added largely to the pandemonium of noises. The event here narrated as being witnessed by me did not occupy over a fourth of a minute. I turned to the judges and the amiable clerk, and said that, if they did not object, as sheriff I would for the present declare the polls closed. There being no objection, I announced the close, in a monosyllable, saying to my brother officers that I wished to go to my store and lock the door. I walked away with great dignity, as I was at the time the town deputy sheriff, and it would have seemed bad for the sheriff of Boyd to appear excited on such an occasion, when it was his duty to lend, by his noble bearing, confidence to those not clothed in official robes. As I stepped along Louisa Street, I did not increase the frequency of my steps, but I measured out the length of each step *more* than usual in distance. In a minute I was at the corner now known as the Opera-house corner, and, on looking down the street, I saw my hopeful son Charles, then a lad of fourteen Summers, or rather Winters, pacing backwards and forwards, with a gun raised sentinel-like, acting precisely like a trained veteran. I hurried on down to the store—at that time the only building on that side of the street after the old frame was passed where the great temple of song now stands, save the old Catlett House, which stood back from the street—and took the gun from the brave lad and pushed it under the platform in front of the store-door, and told Charley he had better go home. I should not fail to mention that Pleasant Savage, Esq., father of Judge Savage, had given the gun in my charge, to keep for him until he called for it. Finding that the musket was more dangerous in the muzzle than in the breech, I carefully set it in an out-of-the-way corner, as a silent sentinel. Never till then had it been called into use, except on dress parade.

On looking up I heard the clatter of horses' hoofs, as if coming down Louisa Street; but whether the number was fifty or five hundred, in my desperate state I could not divine. A half-minute had not passed before the great cavalcade came in sight, when, lo and behold! instead of the stars and bars, with soldiers dressed in gray, the riders were my own friends and townsmen, not wearing any uniform, but very independent in the cut, make-up, and color of their clothes. How much one, on great occasions, can take in and digest in the mind! As the flying troopers turned into Division Street, and whirled round on Center, I could but notice the contrast in the horses of the braves, and the variety of suits in which they were clad. But more especially did my eyes take in the picturesque display of garments. Some were clad in the blue and trappings of the Union officer, and others in the dress of the private soldier. Some, again, wore long-tail coats, and some had on short-tail coats; but one at least had no coat of any pattern to impede the progress of his march. He had neither coat nor vest, and his pants were held up by the aid of one suspender. This great scene was all taken in in less than thirty seconds of time.

As the scared host appeared at the entrance to Division Street, the tall, commanding figure of some great military hero met my gaze; it proved to be that great old veteran, Colonel John L. Zeigler. While the main body pushed down Center Street, he kept on down Division, at the risk of death or capture, while all others were intent on personal safety.

As he drew nearer I thought the grandest

sight that I had ever beheld met my vision. He was dressed in the uniform of a colonel, with military cap and spurs, the same he had worn on many a hotly contested skirmish and battle in the Virginias, while commanding the 5th Virginia Infantry, which command, after two years of hard and honorable service, he had resigned, being succeeded by A. A. Tomlinson, a Catlettsburg boy, now one of the wealthy men of Kansas City, Mo. The brave old colonel was riding his old war-horse, which had carried its master oftentimes into the thickest of the fight, and on this solemn occasion seemed to be clothed in all its former glory.

As the colonel approached me, under a swift lope, his right hand clutching the bridle-reins and also resting on the horn of the saddle, and his left hand waving high in air as he dashed along, exclaiming in tones of thunder that the people must get out of their houses, his body sitting erect in the saddle, his long gray hair streaming out from under his cap, caused by the swift motion of his steed, and his eyes apparently emitting fire in the excitement of the hour, it was a sight that few are permitted to see more than once in a generation.

Walking swiftly to Andrews' corner, and looking down the grade, I saw that the wharf-boat and a consort of barges had been cut from their moorings at the wharf, and were floating out into the current of the Ohio. The boats were laden with Government stores. Hastening on down to Main

Street and out to the intersection with Center, but looking up Center to make sure no enemy was in sight or hearing, I turned down Center to reconnoiter. Before going many steps, I saw men pouring out of North Street, some riding tall mules, some on the backs of poor mules, some on mules with sore backs, and some perched on mules with very sharp backs. Many of the riders—most of them, indeed—were employés in the Government stables, and the mules they rode were Government animals; John Vannata, the chief hostler, was anxious to have the men ride the poor beasts out of danger. The last I saw of this tail-end delegation, moving forward to join their comrades, they were turning into the street, or road, below John Falkner's present residence, each one looking back over his shoulder to see if the enemy was upon him.

The observer went back up-town, and, seeing Judge Rice sitting on his porch, called to him to know what his opinion was in regard to the Confederates being near town. The judge said he did not believe that an armed Confederate was within fifty miles of the town. I agreed with him; yet he believed what he said, while I only hoped that it might prove correct. Walking on up to the voting-place, Mr. Hampton, the clerk, told me that the whole thing was a false alarm; indeed, was a farce.

The children of Hampton City went to school out at the Murphy place, and the school was dismissed at three o'clock, as most of the pupils were of tender years. On leaving the school-house on that day, a little boy said to his friends that they must play soldier by forming in line, and marching into town. He procured a breakfast-shawl from one of the little girls, tied the garment to the end of a hoop-pole found near by, and was joined by another boy, who procured two sticks by the road-side, and with these drummed on his tin dinner-bucket. With banner flying and drum beating, the young soldiers were soon filing round what is now known as Cemetery Hill, in sight of Hampton City.

A woman, whose husband was engaged in the war, owned a little brindle cow, which had lain out the night before, but when it came up, though at an unseasonable hour, she concluded to go out with her pail and extract the lacteal fluid from the bovine's udder. When she was about half done milking, the little cow made a lunge, upset the bucket, spilling contents on the ground, and started off in great affright. The woman, on raising up, happened to cast her eyes in the direction of the Cemetery Hill, and caught a glimpse of the soldiers mentioned. She imagined them to be Confederate soldiers, coming in for pillage, and cried out in alarm at the top of her voice. The cry was taken up by men several hundred yards nearer Catlettsburg, that the rebels were coming, which brought out all the inhabitants of the hamlet of Hampton City, who, on a running jump, entered the town with a loud outcry: "The rebels are coming! the rebels are coming!"

After the excitement had somewhat subsided, the election went on as before, and all, when assured of the cause of the scare, laughed heartily, and resumed their usual vocations, but expressed some interest as to the whereabouts of their fleeing brethren, who had started toward the setting sun. The people who had not been able to get away were anxious to hear whether the great crowd of men who had ridden so hurriedly away had made a stand at Ashland, five miles below; or had they crossed over into Ohio and pushed on to the alum-cliffs on the Scioto, where they could easily throw up fortifications, and hold the fort against all the Confederates in Kentucky? Or, on reaching Ashland, had they turned to the left, hurried on to Carter Caves, and taken refuge in those subterranean recesses of mother earth, blocking the entrance to their retreat by rolling the great stones found in the caves across the entrance?

But the anxiety of the home folks was soon relieved by the arrival of one of Ashland's citizens, who had come up to let the friends of the absentees know that they had fallen into the hands of kind friends, who were willing to protect them to the last extremity. The messenger found many evidences of rapid flight on the road the braves had passed over, such as overcoats, saddle-girths, broken horseshoes, pint bottles. The bottles were empty, however. The owners were cool-headed enough to know that bottles filled with fire-water, falling into the hands of the Confederates, would only stimulate them to greater speed. When Night had drawn the curtain of darkness over the earth, the men returned to their homes, coming, however, in ones and twos, and were not seen very much in public for several days, when the matter had grown somewhat stale by the intervention of other exciting scenes.

While the author witnessed almost all that took place, he has no remembrance of any one of the excited men who left the place, save alone the late brave Colonel John L. Zeigler, who certainly manifested great bravery in delaying his exit from town to warn his townsmen of what he thought to be immediate danger, and all at the risk of his own life, or liberty at least.

TWO CHURCHES.

In writing the history of the Big Sandy Valley, it would be a dereliction of duty to pass over the two divisions of Methodism in the Sandy Valley; that is to say, to give a history of the Methodist Church in the valley immediately following the great separation at the General Conference of the Methodist Episcopal Church in 1844, soon after which the Methodist Episcopal Church, South, was organized.

In the Sandy Valley, or that part of it lying exclusively in the State of Kentucky (for of that territory alone will we now write), the members of the Church, either by their votes or by acquiescence, adhered to the fortunes of the Methodist Episcopal Church, South. This was true of the Methodist Church from Catlettsburg to Pikeville, Kentucky, save only at Louisa, and a country Church or two in the west part of Lawrence County, and, several years later (1854), one at Catlettsburg. At Louisa Robert D. Callihan, a wealthy local preacher, and Mrs. Jones, widow of Daniel Jones, Mrs. Sarah Savage, mother of Judge Savage— both ladies of the highest religious and social position—with Rev. George Hutchison, the father of Rev. I. B. Hutchison, and a few others, organized a Methodist Episcopal Church soon after the separation, and built a small brick church, which is still used as such by the denomination that built it. A log church was built on the lands of Rev. George Hutchison, five miles west of Louisa, soon after the Louisa church was constructed, and perhaps a church, or at least a preaching place, still farther from Louisa. At Catlettsburg, in 1854, a Methodist Episcopal Church was organized with about a dozen members; and in 1857 the Catlettsburg Church built their excellent house of worship, which still well serves the purpose for whom and for which it was built.

Save these places named, the Methodist Episcopal Church, South, was the only branch of Methodism in the valley until 1864. The great Civil War affected the Methodist Episcopal Church, South, in the valley to a great extent, and for a time (three or four years), in many localities on Sandy, its places of worship were closed, and its altars had fallen into decay.

In 1864 ministers were sent into the valley from the West Virginia Conference, Methodist Episcopal Church, to preach and organize Churches, and as the people were hungry for preaching, many joined the Methodist Episcopal Church, and considerable progress was made in organizing charges.

In the year 1866 the Methodist Episcopal Church, South, held its first General Conference after the war, and made some fundamental changes in the polity and rules of that Church, such as providing for Church and district conferences, thus bringing the laymen to the front in Church affairs, and abolishing the probationary system. These enactments by the General Conference touched the hearts and minds of the laymen, who immediately, with the preachers leading, set about the restoration of the Church of their choice in the valley. That was twenty years ago. At that time all was chaos. From the Minutes of the Western Virginia Conference, which has a presiding elder's district in Kentucky, mostly in the Sandy Valley, it is recorded that the Church had, in 1886, 4,757 members, 42 churches, and raised for Church purposes, in one year, $5,405.56. The statistics of the Methodist Episcopal Church, embracing the same topics for the same year, as taken from the Minutes of that Church, are as follows: Members, including probationers, 2,412; churches, 32; raised for ministerial support and Church benevolences, $4,358.17. The presiding elders' districts do not precisely cover the same territory, but are not far from equal; for where one is found in a separate field alone, the other is occupying a small territory not occupied by the other.

The reflections to be made are, that instead of either branch of the Church being in the other's way, each stimulates the other to greater activity in noble Christian endeavor. Sometimes a slight friction may arise, to mar the harmony of God's host; but it is not more discernible in the workings of the two Methodist Churches in the valley than in other denominations in their religious intercourse with each other.

TWO NEW CHURCHES.

THE history of the Sandy Valley would be incomplete did we not briefly mention the two churches named below, though we have no definite data to enable us to particularize. But the main facts are given.

UNITED BAPTISTS.

Some years ago, the date not remembered, those ministers belonging to the old regular Baptists, sometimes called Hard Shells, who did not indorse what was known as the "Hard Doctrine" of that Church, organized the United Baptist Church, and nearly all the Baptists in the Big Sandy Valley belong to that Church.

FREE-WILL BAPTISTS.

The Free-will Baptists organized a Church in Johnson, the second of the denomination in the State. Rev. Thomas Williams became their pastor, and several of the most influential people of the vicinity of Paintsville joined the Church, among them Daniel Wheeler, Wiley Williams, John Richmond, and other noted people.

SANDY VALLEY PROGRESS.

The early school-teachers in the Sandy Valley, as a class, had but little education, and, what was still more to their discredit, they drank whisky, sometimes taking their bottles with them to school, getting drunk in the morning, and remaining in that condition all day. A teacher who could read, write, and cipher to the single rule of three in Pike's Arithmetic, was thought qualified to teach a school. Now how changed! Not only does the State law require a teacher to prove a good moral character, but the people at large refuse to employ one who drinks liquor. Not only do they require the teacher to possess a good character and be of temperate habits, but he must have education as well. Prior to 1861 no private schools, or but few, of high grade were to be found in the Sandy Valley. Now no part of Kentucky has private schools and seminaries of learning surpassing those in the Sandy Valley in all the essentials going to make up first-class institutions of learning.

The Normal at Catlettsburg is fully equal to the high-schools of the largest cities in the State, both in its curriculum and its beautiful grounds and buildings. Louisa, Eden, Flat Gap, Paintsville, Prestonburg, Pikeville, Medina, Blaineville, and some other places, have good high-schools, where a good classical or scientific education can be obtained by both sexes at a reasonable expense.

All over the valley good common schools may be found, supplementing the five months' free schools, or public schools kept in motion by State taxation. And all of these schools are well patronized.

Previous to 1861 but few Sandy Valley young men were sent to college. Now many are receiving collegiate training in the best colleges and universities in the country. A few wealthy men in the valley had their daughters educated away from home in young ladies' seminaries; but even this was rare, and almost created a sensation. But now how changed! As many as four or five young ladies of Louisa alone are now studying, or have graduated, from the Wesleyan Female College at Cincinnati, one of the best and most expensive ladies' colleges in all the land. Quite a number of other young ladies of Louisa have been, or are now, attending female schools or colleges at other places. This state of affairs exists from Catlettsburg to Pikeville, and extends from Pond, on the Tug River, to Salyersville, in Magoffin County.

THE EARLY PREACHERS

WERE not whisky-drinkers, like many of the first teachers, yet no doubt some of the men of the cloth in the early days of Sandy Valley have taken their cups, as that was not an unusual thing, even in staid New England. The morals of the good, old-time preachers were commendable, and those servants of God who labored hard to win souls to Christ, and received but little or nothing for their toil and anxiety, are worthy the gratitude of the present generation. All honor to the early fathers! They did well, according to their knowledge, and many of them knew more than some people now are willing to concede.

More opportunities to obtain a good training for the ministry are offered to the present generation of young men in the ministry than the old-time preachers were blessed with. And the facts prove, when stated, that the Sandy Valley ministers of the

SANDY VALLEY PROGRESS. 433

present have advanced beyond their fathers by applying themselves to a higher course of reading and study. It would be offensive to name the old-time preachers, and then compare the younger men, or rather the men of to-day, with them, and strike a contrast made up by the difference of the lack of education of the old preachers, who have passed to their reward, and their successors, who are still on the walls of Zion. But it is essential to historic facts to name, at least, some of the natives of the Sandy Valley who are now filling pulpits or are engaged in other ministerial work at home and abroad, thus enabling all to judge whether progress is being made in the superior culture and ability of the present preachers beyond those who preceded.

Rev. James Harvey Burns, nephew of Jerry Burns, the founder of the house of Burns in the valley, and son of Lewis Burns, born and reared on Sandy, is an able minister of the Methodist Episcopal Church, South, in the Western Virginia Conference of his Church.

Rev. J. H. Hager, son of Harmon Hager, will compare with the ministers anywhere in logic, choice, strong language, and general ability. He is of the Methodist Episcopal Church, South.

Rev. Z. Meek, D. D., who has represented his Church in the General Conference, is not only an able minister, but for twenty years has proven himself one of the ablest editors of his Church, the Methodist Episcopal Church, South. His paper, the *Central Methodist*, at Catlettsburg, is recognized as one of the ablest in the connection.

Rev. Charles J. Howes, whose father and grandfather were both preachers, is an able preacher, standing among the leaders of the Kentucky Conference, Methodist Episcopal Church. Mr. Howes not only represented his Church in a General Conference, but was made one of the secretaries of that august body.

Mr. Howes's younger brother, Rev. G. Winn Howes, although prepared for and having practiced law for a few years, is now, though young in the ministry, an able expounder of the Word in the Methodist Episcopal Church.

Rev. John W. Hampton, though not leaving the practice of the law until over forty, is regarded as a strong preacher in his Church, the Methodist Episcopal, South.

Rev. William Jayne, the founder and conductor of Flat Gap Enterprise Academy, received a college training, as others named did, and is an able minister of the Missionary Baptist Church.

Rev. Coleman, of the Pike family of Coleman, is now an able preacher of the Methodist Episcopal Church in Iowa.

All these named were and are native Big Sandians.

Rev. T. F. Garrett, a native of Prestonburg, is an able and leading minister in the Kentucky Methodist Episcopal Conference.

THE LAWYERS.

McConnell, the elder Rice, Robert Walker, Henry C. Harris, R. T. Burns the first, Green Goble, Hon. John P. Martin, Hon. John M. Elliott, Hon. Harvey Burns, and others of their generation, were good lawyers, and most of them eloquent, some having a national reputation. In the days of those whom we have named education was not diffused among the masses as now. The people at large received their political information from lawyers, who were generally good stump-speakers. But few books and no papers were read by the common people; hence a man who is deemed of fair ability to-day would have appeared great indeed in the early days of Sandy history. Now nearly every one reads books and papers, and forms his opinions without consulting those who would have been guides forty years ago. The people, being better informed, have lifted themselves on a level with those who stood far above them in bygone days, owing to the fact that the public men of that day possessed educational advantages above the masses.

The science of law, like every other science, has advanced both in its pleadings and in its practice. Much of the old-day glamour has been dissipated. The lawyer of the olden time was expected to make an eloquent speech to a jury, though the speech might be mostly sound. If he did not, he fell in the estimation of the hangers-on at courts, who went there to hear grandiloquent speeches delivered to judges and juries by some visiting attorney. Most of the verdicts of juries were influenced, too, at that time, by the eloquence of the lawyer. But now more depends on the instructions of the court, predicated on the law as expounded by the attorney. The bar of the Sandy Valley is much abler to-day than ever before. A court of common pleas may dispose of trials on its docket for a whole month, with scarcely three speeches. The law and evidence is closely applied, and the case is submitted with a mere statement by the attorney to an intelligent jury, the judge supervising the action of both attorneys and juries.

Many old-time Sandians complain that the courts have fallen into decay! They fail to see that, instead of having fallen into decay, the forms of justice have progressed with the times.

Formerly a circuit court resembled a convention, over which a solemn man, called "the judge," presided, supported by a number of bright men called lawyers, bringing into the court-house each a green satchel filled with books, which almost struck terror to many of the lookers-on. Now a a circuit court resembles a body of learned men, sitting in solemn conclave, examining and determining the truth as the object of research, and applying that truth to the protection of the innocent and the punishment of the guilty, for the general welfare of society at large. Sandy courts, as well as Sandy lawyers, have certainly advanced in the progress of time.

THE DOCTORS

OF the early period of Sandy deserve great praise for the good they accomplished in behalf of suffering humanity. It is, however, no disparagement to them to say that the poverty incident to a new country forbade them to expect fees sufficient to buy suitable medical books or prepared medicines. Hence the most of them were "root and herb" doctors. They had never read a book on botany, but being born and reared in the woods, were practical botanists, and, familiar with nature, they knew the medicinal virtue of every plant and root found growing in the Sandy Valley. Sometimes the earlier doctor of Sandy history would gather his medicine while on the way to visit his patient, and prepare it after he had arrived at the house of sickness. All is changed now. Doctors with diplomas from colleges of medicine are found practicing in every part of the valley. Nearly all are native Sandians.

THE OFFICE-BEARERS

OF the Sandy Valley will compare in ability with those of other parts of the State or the United States. Hons. Mr. May, John. P. Martin, and John M. Elliott (the first and last Sandy born), were able members of Congress, and each had a national reputation. They lived in Prestonburg. Hon. Laban T. Moore and Hon. John M. Rice sustained the reputation of their predecessors for ability. These gentlemen were also Sandians, born and bred.

THE SANDY JUDICIARY

Has been, and still is, an able one. Judges James M. Rice, William Harvey Burns, M. J. Ferguson, James E. Stewart, George N. Brown, John M. Rice, and John M. Burns will compare, in legal knowledge and ability to expound the law, and in clean-cut records, with the judges in other parts of the State; and all are native Big Sandians.

THE PROSECUTING ATTORNEYS

Of the Sandy Valley courts, like the judges, including A. J. Auxier, James E. Stewart, and S. G. Kinner, all native Sandians, in the able discharge of official duty, are not surpassed by prosecuting attorneys in other sections of the State.

THE SANDIANS

Who have filled State offices have not only been fully up to the standard of ability displayed by their predecessors filling the same positions, but many think the Big Sandians have surpassed them in official work. Thomas D. Marcum had not long been acting as register of the land-office when it was said, by all who knew the duties of the position, that he was not only equal to the task, but before his official term expired it was proven by his work that the office of register was never filled by a more competent man.

The lamented John George Cecil, son of Samuel Cecil, of Pike, gave great promise of distinguished work in the same office; but disease and death overtook him before he had been in the office a year. The short time he served, however, gave assurance that, had he lived, he would have been equal to any preceding him in upholding the Sandy official banner.

UNITED STATES GOVERNMENT OFFICES

HAVE been held by Sandy men, who have shown as much talent and ability in discharge of their official duties as the occupants filling similar places from any other part of the State or United States.

A. J. Auxier, as the United States marshal, left a record for integrity and ability in managing the intricate affairs of the marshalship second to none who has ever filled the same position.

Captain A. E. Adams, of Pike, was commissioned to go as consulate to a distant country, but failed to go. Judging from the past official life of Mr. Adams, neither Sandy's reputation nor the government would have lost any thing, but would have gained much had he gone on his mission.

John W. Langley, of Prestonburg, received many promotions in a Government department at Washington for intelligent and faithful service.

Other Sandians have received commendation for competency and faithfulness in national official duty. In the highest official positions of the district, State, or nation, to the lowest, Big Sandians have been fully equal to the tasks assigned them. These positions they have filled with an ability which can not be denied them. Comparing their official labors with others in similar places elsewhere, they stand with the best.

HARD TO GET OLD-TIME INCIDENTS.

MANY families who settled early in the Sandy Valley, and assisted in making an honorable history, left no record or annals which the historian can gather up and prepare for printing. A great many families whose names are familiar to the people of the valley, and most of whom have descendants still living there, come under this difficulty. On inquiring of one whom the author thought well informed in the matter, for an early history of the Stratton family, the person applied to said that one thing was true about them—for every body said so who remembered the ancestors of the Stratton house on Sandy (head-quarters at Prestonburg)—and that was that they were the most intensely religious people that ever lived in the valley. They were Methodists.

The Colemans, of Pike, were an old-time family, with a good historic record, if it could be had. So is the Belcher family, and the Hoffman family, of which Archibald Hoffman, the store-keeper of that name at Pike, is a member.

The Goble family, of Floyd, is an old-time house, and quite prominent. Lawyer Goble, of Prestonburg, is a son of William Goble, who was a son of Isaac Goble, one of the early settlers of the county. Dr. Isaac Goble, of the mouth of John's Creek, is a cousin of lawyer Goble. The doctor was a soldier in the 39th Kentucky Volunteer Infantry during the war, and served in the hospital department. He is farmer, doctor, and merchant.

The Conleys came early into the valley, and have become a numerous host. Many of the Conleys have risen to places of rank and official honor. Lawyer Wince Conley, of Pike, but a native of Johnson, is a leading man. His brother, who was at one time county judge of Johnson immediately after the close of the war, almost created a sensation at the time by his zeal in making good roads in his county. A doctor of ability was a brother of the lawyer and judge, and the same house furnished a good magistrate to Johnson County. Another branch of the family live at Flat Gap, one of whom is a lawyer there.

The Pickelsimers are a large family of the Sandy Valley. The father of Dr. Pickelsimer, the druggist, and a prominent physician at Paintsville, died at a great age since the writing of this book was undertaken. His farm is not far from Flat Gap. The old gentleman was a man of high honor and great respectability.

The Robinsons are found scattered all over the Sandy Valley. Many came in an early day, and were foremost in opening the forests for the cultivation of food for man. The gentleman who is now chief magistrate at Piketon bears that name. He came but recently from Virginia.

Samuel Keel, on Shelby, has added wealth to the valley, as well as being a promoter of morality.

The Hurts, the Honakers, the Sicks, the Reynoldses, the Greers in Floyd, must not be neglected; but especially should the name of Rev. Joseph Langley, of Middle Creek, be mentioned, to show that a young man born in poverty may, in this country, by industry and economy, with moral integrity to guide him, though not permitted to stand before kings, come to the front, at least, as a man of wealth and influence, leading his family in paths of usefulness and honor.

The Vaughans, of Prestonburg; the Smiths, of the same place; the old Widow Ford, who was, before marriage, a Mayo, were noted for their religious zeal in early days. The only member of the first Fords living at this writing is Thomas, who still sticks to the early capital of the Sandy Valley, his children having married into prominent families round about.

George Peck, of Lawrence, is a very old-time

Sandian, related to the McClures. He owns a large boundary of land commencing on the Sandy River at the mouth of Griffith's Creek, and running back. Peck's Chapel, on the line of the Chatterawha Railroad, is named for him. The Pecks, like the McClures, are staunch Methodists, in communion with the Methodist Episcopal Church.

The Shannons are of an old-time family of the Lower Valley, and are connected by marriage and consanguinity with many strong houses of the county.

While Walter Osburn, of Lawrence, has been referred to already, it is not out of place to state that he still lives on Blaine, at a very advanced age. After he was eighty years old he would walk from his home (twenty odd miles) to Louisa on business. He has filled many official stations.

German Huff, of Paintsville, has also been an educator, if not a benefactor, by his example in the practice of economy. By following the laws of trade from the time he made salt on Middle Creek to the present, he has never wasted any thing worth saving, whereby he has lived well and at the same time accumulated a competency. It was said by one who knew of his current savings, that he could take twenty dollars, have a basket of provisions prepared, the product of his garden and farm, take a canoe and push it to Portsmouth, Ohio, and back home to Paintsville, and, in the sale of goods bought with the twenty dollars, make a snug profit.

The Parsleys, on Lower Tug, are descendants of

an old family. Jesse has not only been a large land-holder from young manhood, and he is now growing old, but a large store-keeper and timber-dealer. His brother Moses lives on Emily Creek, but has retired from saw-logging and gone to farming.

Captain Kirk, one of the members of that numerous family in the Lower Tug country, served in the Union army during the Civil War. His son James is a lawyer, but was for many years clerk of the county court of Martin. The office is now held, however, by George W. Hale, son-in-law of Moses Parsley.

Mark Dempsey was a very prominent citizen before the war, and in good circumstances. One of his sons, Lewis, is a merchant at Eden.

The Maynards, an old-time family in the valley, are settled from the Cumberland to the mouth of Tug. Many of them are prominent people. John B. Maynard, of John's Creek, is a large timber-dealer. Dr. Maynard, also of the John's Creek country, is a well-to-do farmer and physician. He married a daughter of the Widow Jones, of Louisa. A large family of the Maynards live on the Rock Castle at its mouth and near by. Some of them have filled official stations.

The Cline family have their seat high up Tug, although one of them lives in Martin, who has been county judge, and had many good roads built in his county. Perry Cline has for many years lived in Pikeville. He has been sheriff and school commissioner of his county, and represented his district in the Legislature.

The Bentleys, the Dotsons, and many others in the eastern part of Pike County, not named, have helped make up the history of that rugged section.

In going back to the Levisa, one is almost sure to find a Justice at every turn in the road, yet they have not *all* staid near by their ancestral home; for Timothy Justice lives down on Rock Castle, and Fleming Justice makes brick in Hampton City.

Of old-time physicians, we may here mention Dr. H. S. Sweatnum, who has practiced his profession since the forties; first at West Liberty, next at Paintsville, and now at Louisa. Dr. A. E. Gray, of Pike, has for twenty years been practicing at Pike, and Dr. Callihan has practiced at Prestonburg about the same length of time.

Many of the children of the old-time people of Prestonburg have come to honor. Among the number, Dr. Steel's son, John, is now not only a good physician and a large land-owner, but is a man of standing in Carter County. One of his brothers, Samuel, still lives at Prestonburg, a fixture of the town.

The Ferrells live along the Tug in different sections. Richard Ferrell, the wealthy capitalist, came to Pike after the war, from Virginia, and has grown rich and influential.

The Yorks are a Sandy people, dating back but one generation, however, having their seat on Griffith's Creek and Donathon. Dr. Joshua was killed near the close of the Civil War by some one who had taken him away as a prisoner for loyalty, as his friends say, to the flag of his country.

The Carters, of Lawrence, are a noted family. They came from South-western Virginia. They were of a wealthy family. G. W. Carter has represented his district in the Legislature. His first wife was a daughter of Rev. George Hutchison, and sister of Rev. I. B. Hutchison, who is a brother-in-law of James A. Abbott, the prominent timber merchant of Louisa.

The Burtons, of Lawrence, are of the old-time stock. Samuel Burton is now judge of Lawrence.

The Sparkses, of Lawrence, are of the old-time people, and are held in high repute, as are the Ramys, Gambrells, Rices, and many others of the same section.

HUGH BOGGS, OF BLAINE,

The Nestor of the Boggses on Cane's Creek, a branch of the Blaine, has been a man of remarkable energy. Hugh Boggs opened a large farm on his creek, and, by chopping wood and bossing other wood-choppers at the old-time furnaces, made money enough to build a steam saw and grain mill and a carding machine at quite an early day. Had Hugh Boggs lived at a place more get-at-able, he would have been to Cane's Creek what Judge Borders was to his section, and what William Adams was to Licking Station.

The country around Mr. Boggs was too sparsely settled to expand his business, yet nevertheless he was always a good liver. Cane's Creek, in Lawrence County, is a stream of wide and rich bottom land, almost all of which is owned by the Boggses, descendants of either Hugh Boggs or his kinsmen. He nears the end of his earthly race, being quite feeble in body but smart in mind. He has been a benefactor, an educator, and a philanthropist, although in his unselfishness he might himself never have suspected it.

OFFICERS OF THE ARMY.

Sandy Valley Men who were Commissioned Officers in the Union Army during the Civil War.

COLONELS.

Laban T. Moore, . . . 14th Kentucky, . Lawrence Co.
G. W. Gallup, ... 14th   "   .   "
John Dils, Jr., ... 39th   "   . Pike Co.
D. A. Mims, ... 39th   "   . Boyd Co.
J. L. Zeigler, ... 5th Virginia, . .   "
A. A. Tomlinson, . . . 5th   "   . . "

LIEUTENANT-COLONELS.

Joseph Brown, ... 14th Kentucky, . Boyd Co.
R. M. Thomas, ... 14th   "   .   "
Dr. S. M. Ferguson, . . 39th   "   . Pike Co.

MAJORS.

Bentley Burk, ... 14th Kentucky, . Boyd Co.
D. J. Burchett, ... 14th   "   . Lawrence Co.

448 THE BIG SANDY VALLEY.

MAJORS—Continued.

Ralph Ormsted,	5th Virginia,	Boyd Co.
John B. Auxier,	39th Kentucky,	Johnson Co.
Frank Mott,	45th "	Boyd Co.
John Henderson,	45th	

CAPTAINS.

Archie Means,	14th Kentucky,	Boyd Co.
Dwight Leffingwell,	14th	
James Whitten,	14th "	"
D. W. Steel,	22d "	"
Sol. Davis,	14th "	"
R. B. McCall,	5th Virginia,	
T. J. Ewing,	5th "	"
A. C. Hailey,	39th Kentucky,	"
T. D. Marcum,	14th "	Cassville, Va.
Wm. Bartram,	14th "	Lawrence Co.
Oliver Botner,	14th "	"
—. McKinster,	14th "	"
Watt Wood,	14th "	"
George Green,	14th "	"
Allen P. Hawes,	39th "	"
Thomas Russell,	45th "	"
Harry Ford,	39th "	"
William Ford,	39th "	"
Joe Kirk,	39th "	Wayne Co., W. Va.
Wiley Patrick,	14th "	Magoffin Co.

LIEUTENANTS.

George B. Patton,	14th Kentucky,	Boyd Co.
D. H. McGee,	14th "	"
—. Sperry,	14th "	"
George R. Chapman,	14th "	Lawrence Co.
Henry Borders,	14th "	"
—. Preston,	39th "	"
—. Burgess,	14th "	"
Martin Thornsberry,	39th "	Pike Co.

OFFICERS OF THE ARMY.

LIEUTENANTS—Continued.

James Foster,	14th Kentucky,	Boyd Co.
James C. Ely,	14th "	"
James Seaton,	45th "	"
Lindsey Layne,	39th "	Floyd Co.
L. J. Hampton,	39th "	Boyd Co.
J. Frew Stewart,	39th "	Lawrence Co.

No distinction is made between first and second lieutenants.

Col. G. W. Gallup came out of the army with the rank of brigadier-general by brevet.

James C. Ely was not made a lieutenant until after he became a veteran.

Captain T. D. Marcum was frequently a staff officer before he became a captain.

Lieutenant George B. Patton acted as adjutant, and was often on the staff of the general in command.

Major John Henderson was much of the time detailed as a mustering officer.

Lieutenant James Foster was quartermaster of the 14th Kentucky.

Lieutenant Layne was the quartermaster in the 39th Kentucky.

Lieutenant James Seaton was adjutant of his regiment.

Lieutenant L. J. Hampton was adjutant of the 39th Kentucky until killed in a skirmish at Weirman's Shoals.

J. Frew Stewart was adjutant in the 39th Kentucky after the death of Lieutenant Hampton.

JENNY WILEY.

The most romantic history, in the early settlement of the Big Sandy Valley, is that of Jenny Wiley. This history we proceed to give from the most reliable sources at our command, drawing our facts mainly from Hardesty's "Historical and Biographical Encyclopedia."

There is hardly a man or woman in Eastern Kentucky who is not familiar with the story of the life of this remarkable woman. The facts of her capture by the Indians, escape from them, and return to her home, have been handed down from parent to child, and they are well remembered. Her maiden name was Jenny Sellards. She married Thomas Wiley, a native of Ireland, who had emigrated and settled on Walker's Creek, in Wythe, now Tazewell County, Va., where they were living at the time of the capture by the Indians. She had a sister living near by, the wife of John Borders, who was the father of the Rev. John Borders, a noted Baptist preacher, Hezekiah Borders, Michael Borders, Judge Archibald Borders, and several daughters. Several families named Harmon lived in the same neighborhood, some of whom were noted Indian scouts.

At the time of the capture of Jenny, Thomas Wiley, her husband, was out in the woods digging ginseng. This was in the year 1790. The destruction of the Wiley family, as hereafter recorded, was the result of a mistake on the part of the savages. Some time previously, in an engagement with a party of Cherokees, one of the Harmons had shot and killed two or three of their number, and a party of five returned to seek vengeance on the Harmons, but ignorant of the location of their cabin, fell upon Wiley's instead.

John Borders warned Mrs. Wiley that he feared Indians were in the neighborhood, and urged her to go to his house and remain until Wiley's return, but as she had a piece of cloth in the loom, she said she would finish it and then go. The delay on the part of Mrs. Wiley was a fatal one. Darkness came on, and with it came the attack upon the defenseless family. The Indians rushed into the house, and after tomahawking and scalping a younger brother and three of the children, and taking Mrs. Wiley, her infant (a year and a half old), and Mr. Wiley's hunting dog, started towards the Ohio River. At the time the Indian trail led down what is now known as Jennie's Creek, and along it they proceeded until they reached the mouth of that stream, then down Tug and Big Sandy Rivers to the Ohio.

No sooner had the news of the horrid butchery spread among the inhabitants of the Walker's Creek settlement than a party, among whom were Lazarus Damron and Matthias Harmon, started in pursuit. They followed on for several days, but failing to come up with the perpetrators of the terrible outrage, the pursuit was abandoned, and all returned to their homes. The Indians expected that they would be followed, and the infant of Mrs. Wiley proving an incumbrance to their flight, they dashed out its brains against a beech-tree when a short distance below where Mr. William C. Crum now resides, and two miles from Jennie's Creek. This tree was standing and well known to the inhabitants of this section during the first quarter of the present century.

When the savages, with their captive, reached the Ohio, it was very much swollen; with a shout of O-high-o, they turned down that stream, and continued their journey to the mouth of the Little Sandy. Up that stream they went to the mouth of Dry Fork, and up the same to its head, when they crossed the dividing ridge and proceeded down what is now called Cherokee Fork of Big Blaine Creek, to a point within two miles of its mouth, where they halted and took shelter between a ledge of rocks. Here they remained for several months, and during the time Mrs. Wiley was delivered of a child. At this time the Indians were very kind to her; but when the child was three weeks old they decided to test him, to see whether he would make a brave warrior. Having tied him to a flat piece of wood, they slipped him into the water to see if he would cry. He screamed furiously, and they took him by the heels and dashed his brains out against an oak-tree.

When they left this encampment they proceeded down to the mouth of Cherokee Creek, then up Big Blaine to the mouth of Hood's Fork, thence up that stream to its source; from here they crossed over the dividing ridge to the waters of Mud Lick, and down the same to its mouth, where they once more formed an encampment.

About this time several settlements were made on the head-waters of the Big Sandy, and the Indians decided to kill their captive, and accordingly prepared for the execution; but just when the awful hour was come, an old Cherokee chief, who in the meantime had joined the party, proposed to buy her from the others on condition that she would teach his squaws to make cloth like the gown she wore. Thus was her life saved, but she was reduced to the most abject slavery, and was made to carry water, wood, and build fires. For some time they bound her when they were out hunting; but as time wore away they relaxed their vigilance, and at last permitted her to remain unbound.

On one occasion, when all were out from camp, they were belated, and at night-fall did not return, and Mrs. Wiley now resolved to carry into effect a long-cherished object, that of making her escape and returning to her friends. The rain was falling fast, and the night was intensely dark, but she glided away from the camp-fire and set out on her lonely and perilous journey. Her dog, the same that had followed the party through all their wanderings, started to follow her, but she drove him back, lest by his barking he might betray her into the hands of her pursuers. She followed the course of Mud Lick Creek to its mouth, and then crossing Main Paint Creek, journeyed up a stream (ever since known as Jennie's Creek) a distance of some miles, thence over a ridge and down a stream, now called Little Paint Creek, which empties into the Levisa Fork of Big Sandy River. When she reached its mouth it was day-dawn, and on the opposite side of the river, a short distance below the mouth of John's Creek, she could hear and see men at work erecting a block-house. To them she called, and informed them that she was a captive escaping from the Indians, and urged them to hasten to her rescue, as she believed her pursuers to be close upon her. The men had no boat, but hastily rolling some logs into the river and lashing them together with grape-vines, they pushed over the stream and carried her back with them. As they were ascending the bank, the old chief who had claimed Jenny as his property, preceded by the dog, appeared upon the opposite bank, and striking his hands upon his breast, exclaimed in broken English, "Honor, Jenny, honor!" and then disappeared into the forest.

That was the last she ever saw of the old chief or her dog. She remained here a day or two to rest from her fatigue, and then with a guide made her way back to her home, having been in captivity more than eleven months. Here she rejoined her husband, who had long supposed her dead, and together, nine years after—in the year 1800—they abandoned their home in the Old Dominion, and found another near the mouth of Tom's Creek, on the banks of the Levisa Fork of Big Sandy. Here her husband died in the year 1810. She survived him twenty-one years, and died of paralysis in the year 1831.

The Indians had killed her brother and five of her children, but after her return from captivity five others were born, namely: Hezekiah, Jane, Sally, Adam, and William.

Hezekiah married Miss Christine Nelson, of George's Creek, Kentucky, and settled on Twelve Pole Creek, where he lived for many years; he died in 1832, while on a visit to friends in Kentucky. Jane married Richard Williamson, who also settled on Twelve Pole. Sally first married Christian Yost, of Kentucky, and after his death was united in marriage with Samuel Murray. She died March 10, 1871. William raised a large family, and after the sale of the Wiley farm moved to Tom's Creek, about two miles from the mouth, where he lived until his death.

Of the children of Jenny Wiley, Adam P. was the most noted. In physique he was scarcely excelled by any man in the Sandy Valley. Tall, straight as an arrow, brown of skin, slow of movement and speech, he was an attractive figure to look upon. He was known far and wide as "Vard" Wiley, sometimes called "Adam Pre Vard." Why thus designated the writer is unable to say. In his early life "Vard" was a great fiddler, and carried his violin far and near, to make music for the young people to dance by. But uniting himself with the Baptist Church, he for a time gave up the fiddle and went to preaching. His sermons were, like himself, very long, and he was very zealous and earnest. After some years in the ministry—the number we do not remember—he gave up his calling, and was often seen making his old violin ring out charming music for the young people at the log-rolling, house-raising, or cornhusking. He lived to a ripe old age, and died only a few years ago, at his home in Johnson County. Before his death he visited the writer, for the purpose of having us write out the life of his mother, as he would detail it from memory, but our business engagements were such that it was impossible to comply with his request.

The Wiley family, descendants of Jenny, are quite numerous in Johnson; they are a hard-working set of men, and retain in their memory the heroic life of Jenny Wiley as a heritage of priceless value.

The farm upon which Mr. Wiley settled, just below the mouth of Tom's Creek, was known to all the old people, far and near, as the "Wiley Farm." About forty years ago it was sold to

James Nibert, who lived upon it until some ten years ago, when he sold it to Samuel Spears, who is the present owner and occupant.

As the writer was born and reared almost in sight of the "Wiley Farm," he is perfectly familiar with all the leading facts in the life of Jenny Wiley, during her stay with the Indians, and after her escape.

While they were camping on Mud Lick, some six miles above where Paintsville now stands, she said they frequently run short of lead, and when they wanted to replenish their stock they had no trouble to do so, and in a very short time. They would go out in the forenoon, and after three or four hours' absence return loaded with something which looked like stones. Then they would build a large fire out of logs, on sideling ground, throw the ore on, and it would melt and run off into trenches prepared for it; afterward, as needed, it was molded into bullets. But, notwithstanding the ease with which the Indians procured their lead, the whites have never been able to find the mines from which it was taken. Years have been spent in its search, and long pilgrimages have been made, by those claiming to be able to point out the place, but thus far to no purpose.

Were we to repeat all the legends that have been handed down from the days of Jenny Wiley, they would seem too incredible for belief in this age, when romance and hardships are not so intimately associated as they were then. So, in the preparation of this chapter we have confined ourselves to facts, leaving out the fanciful, which the imagination of the reader can supply.

That there are vast lead-mines in the valley of Paint Creek, perhaps on Mud Lick, there is little room to doubt. That they have never been found, in view of the universal belief of their existence, is likely due to the fact that the people in that section do not know lead ore when they see it. The story of Jenny Wiley was abundantly confirmed by Indians, friendly to the whites, in later days, but they would give no intimation as to the location. We are very sorry we can not tell our readers where to find these mines!

INDIAN GRAVE-YARDS.

From many indications, still existing, it seems evident that the aborigines of this section of country had their great cemetery at and near the mouth of the Sandy River. It is likely that their dead were brought from great distances and buried there. Evidences of this are found in the fact that for miles the skeletons of human bodies are found on digging wells, cellars, and vaults, not only immediately at the Mouth of the Sandy, but for miles up and down that stream. Bones of human beings are found buried even on the top of the high bluffs back of Catlettsburg, as though all the bottom land had been taken up. It is hard to find a place on the Ohio River where more of the remains of the Indian, or prehistoric race of man, have been and are still being found than at the Mouth of the Sandy River. Mr. Frank Fairbairn, a very intelligent gentleman, living as a recluse two miles back of Catlettsburg, who is well informed in antiquarian lore, has collected vast quantities of these relics, by which many a private museum of the country has been enriched, as well as adding to Mr. Fairbairn's exchequer.

THE WELLS FAMILY,

OF Johnson and Floyd Counties, is an old house in the valley. Rev. William A. Wells was for many years a local preacher in the Methodist Episcopal Church, South, an extensive farmer and land-owner, and an old-time physician, who did much to relieve the suffering of the people. He died only one year ago, leaving a large family of bright children. One son, Hon. John P. Wells, has been a member of the Kentucky Legislature, and is a prominent lawyer at Paintsville. Another son, Aaron, is a local preacher in the Methodist Episcopal Church, South; while M. L. K. Wells is postmaster at Boone's Camp. William is a prominent farmer and merchant, and Moses is a prominent farmer and trader.

George Wells is still living, though he is ninety-four years of age. His health is fair, and he is able to go from place to place with the steady step of one much his junior in years. He was a powerful man in his day, a great hunter, and raised a large family of children.

There is not in the valley a more honorable, upright, or generous family than the descendants of the old house of Wells. They are true men and women, honorable in every relation of life, and have impressed themselves upon the people for good.

Rev. William Wells, also a preacher in the Methodist Episcopal Church, South, is quite a prominent man in the ministry, and is also a physician. He is well known in the Upper Valley, and his talent is highly appreciated, both at home and abroad.

THE BRUNINGS.

FRANK BRUNING went to Catlettsburg when it was laid out as a town, taking his wife and several children with him. He was a German, from Prussia. He was at first a landscape and general gardener, and worked and prospered. When the war commenced in 1861, he had a large rectifying establishment in Catlettsburg, which he gave up when the tax was placed upon spirits by the General Government. He became a dry-goods merchant, but finally retired to a suburban home, and died in about 1880. He and his wife, who is still living, were people of wonderful politeness and courtesy. In social life none could surpass them in extending the nice little courtesies which go to make up a sunshiny social atmosphere.

His children grew to maturity, receiving a good education. The oldest son, who bears his father's name, is a lawyer, and has served four years as prosecuting attorney of Boyd County. Another son is a steamboatman. The others are engaged in lucrative mercantile pursuits in Cincinnati and New York. Of the two daughters living, one is married and lives in Ohio; the other remains at home to cheer her venerable mother in her declining years.

ALECK BOTTS

WAS a bright mulatto, who came to Catlettsburg amongst its first arrivals. He was born a slave, but was from birth nominally free, and was made legally so by his master afterwards. He was born at Olympia Springs, Bath County, Ky. He claimed to be a close relative of the celebrated John Minor Botts, of Virginia. He bought his wife, who is nearly white, although a slave at the time. When he settled at the Mouth, the now venerable M. L. Williams took a liking to him, and procured a horse and dray for the young and bright fellow, and waited till Botts could pay him out of his earnings. He soon paid his benefactor. Aleck never forgot the kindness of Mr. Williams, but took many opportunities to do him little acts of kindness in return for the confidence the generous man put in him when he was but a poor, free negro.

Few people of Catlettsburg were better known to Upper Sandians than Aleck Botts in his day. From draying he went to barbering, and also ale-selling. He was a keen trader, and accumulated much property. In fact, at his death, which occurred about 1870, he was called wealthy. His desire to please every one made him popular with all. He was the first to attempt to introduce modern fine horses into the Sandy Valley. He was not only a great lover of good horses, but a great trader in them. His zeal in this line brought him in contact with the large stock-raisers of the Blue Grass region of Kentucky, and some of the wealthiest of them have dined at the house of Aleck Botts. His judgment was acceded to by all, not only as to the value and blood of horses, but also in financial ventures in general. He left a widow and a number of children. The children, like the father, all died of consumption, except three sons, and one of these is a wanderer from home.

Aleck was a tyrant over his children. He was remonstrated with by some one for chaining his eldest boy to an iron block, and making him sit for hours on the public street, the jeer of every passer. He replied that white people did not know that it was harder to control negro boys than white ones. He provided well, however, for his household, and wished them to come to honor. He was, like the Kentucky branch of the Botts family, a Democrat, though he had the policy to keep it well to himself, for fear it might lose him the goodwill of those not of that political faith.

When he died, many of the first people of Catlettsburg and vicinity regretted his death, and attended his funeral and wept over his grave. They felt that he had been useful in the town during life, and had done much to promote its prosperity.

TWO SANDY COUSINS.

ALONG in the thirties two brothers from Virginia came into Pike County, Kentucky. The elder of the brothers, with his family, passed on to the Tygart Valley, in Greenup County. The younger married a young lady of a prominent family in the upper part of Pike County, and settled quietly down in life. The brother who went to Tygart died in middle life in 1852, at Portsmouth, Ohio, to which place he had moved in 1848. Seven children had been born to them in Kentucky, two sons and five daughters. The daughters had all died in Kentucky. The oldest son died soon after the father. The mother died in 1857.

The surviving son received a good education, and then learned the trade of a brick-mason. In 1861 he was in Fayette County, Virginia, working at his trade. The Civil War breaking out, and the sentiment of the community in which he lived being almost a unit in favor of secession, the young mechanic joined the ardent young men around him, and volunteered in the Confederate army. He remained in the service until the surrender of the great Southern chieftain to General Grant at Appomattox C. H., on the 9th of April, 1865, when he retraced his steps to the scenes of his early childhood, broken down in worldly wealth.

The brave young man thought it useless to lament over the result of the conflict, in which he had fought bravely, though on the losing side, and immediately began school-teaching and selling a useful and popular book, by which his finances were soon in good shape. He not only taught school and sold books, but snatched from honest mental labor and physical toil every scrap of time not thus employed, in reading medicine under the guidance of a tutor. When his bank account was sufficient to give assurance that he could dispense with the business he had taken up only as a stepping-stone to the medical profession, to which he aspired from early youth, after reading the text-books necessary to fit him to enter a medical college, he spent two full terms at one of the noted medical colleges of Cincinnati, graduating with honor. He then took a post-graduate course in clinics, and went to Hampton City, a suburb of Catlettsburg, and commenced the practice of medicine. After feeling his way carefully, he ventured down into the bustling little city, and had a suite of rooms prepared in the Opera-house building as an office. The rooms were fitted up in superb style, almost as inviting as the home of a family of fairies; and shelves, book-cases, wardrobes, and closets were supplied with every thing necessary for the outfit of the physician and surgeon.

The young bricklayer and Confederate soldier stands now among the leading physicians of his section, with good prospects ahead. He is a bachelor, yet goes much into society. He is a working member of the Methodist Episcopal Church, of which he is a steward, and has been Sunday-school superintendent. When asked by some one why he united with that Church, he said it had been his mother's Church, and how could he fail to honor her choice and memory?

He is high up in Masonry, being a Knight Templar, and is also at the top ladder of Odd Fellowship. In politics he is a strong Democrat, attending the conventions and caucuses of the party, and is early at the polls on election-day, to give his party a good start.

A son was born to the brother who settled in Pike, and about the time the great Civil War was convulsing the country he moved with his family to Catlettsburg. After the war was over, and before Marion Spurlock, John Meek, and James C. Ely had built the *Favorite,* he was owner and master of the oddly shaped Sandy steamer called the *Red Buck.* He did a thriving business with the ill-shapen craft for some time; she was the only chance. But the kind-heartedness and readiness to please both passengers and shippers made them feel kindly towards the clever steamboatman, if the accommodations were not so good as might be obtained on one of Captain Honshell's palace steamers which plowed the Ohio River. The captain prospered, and was popular, not only on the river, but with his neighbors in Hampton City, where he built a commodious dwelling.

His son, on reaching fourteen or fifteen years of age, showed signs of increasing obesity, which set in at infancy, and his parents and friends feared that it might prove troublesome; but as he neared manhood he had grown to be as solid in flesh and supple in muscle as the average young man about town, and a great deal larger in size. Like his father, he was enamored of steamboating, and turned his whole mind and attention that way. Not forgetting, however, the Scriptural injunction that "it is not good for man to be alone," he married a young lady of the highest respectability, born of one of the first families in the Lower Sandy Valley, and provided a home in the upper part of Catlettsburg, which is good enough for almost any one to live in.

By close application to business and good management, he is now among the leading steamboat owners and operators at the Mouth, and is in mercantile business besides. He is a member of the board of town trustees, and is an efficient worker in the same. He is justly regarded as one of the leading business men of Catlettsburg, and is growing in prominence. His wife is a member of the Methodist Episcopal Church, South, and it is presumable that he agrees with her. In politics he is Democratic, yet has it in a milder form than his cousin afore-named. His father, Captain Alexander Smiley (for it is needless to say that the two Sandy cousins are Dr. M. L. and Captain William Smiley) died many years ago, leaving a widow, who still likes to entertain her Upper Sandy friends in her large boarding-house in Hampton City, when they come down with their rafts on the Spring tides. The Sandy cousins are plucky fellows, and deserve the success which they enjoy.

DANIEL B. VAUGHAN,

Now living at Catlettsburg, came from Wood County, West Va., in 1843, and settled in Louisa, where he kept the "Big Hotel," and worked some at his trade, that of tailor. Daniel's grandfather Vaughan came with Daniel Vaughan from North Carolina, and finally settled at or near Falmouth, Ky. Daniel's father, Atwell Boone, learned the trade of hatter, at Augusta, Ky., under Mr. Buckner, the father of the celebrated Dr. Buckner, of Cincinnati. When a young man he went to Wood County, Va., and married a Miss Butcher. The

Butchers were a wealthy, aristocratic family, and Daniel's mother was quite well educated. Even in her extreme old age she gave evidence of refined training. Like all the Butchers and her husband's branch of the Vaughans, she was a strong Baptist. The good old lady died at her son William's, at the mouth of George's Creek, in 1886, aged eighty-nine years. The husband died at the commencement of the Civil War.

Enoch Rector Vaughan, brother of Daniel, married a daughter of William Borders, of Paintsville, connecting by the alliance the house of Vaughan with the Borders, the Mayos, and other noted families in the valley. William, the youngest son, married a daughter of David Borders, Esq., this alliance connecting him to many important families in the valley. The sisters of Daniel and brothers have all died.

Daniel Vaughan married a Miss Hanner, of Kanawha County, Va. They have two children, a son and a daughter. The son is like his father, partial to steamboating. The daughter is the wife of one of Catlettsburg's chief citizens, Judge R. B. McCall.

AS STEAMBOATMAN,

DANIEL VAUGHAN commenced life on Sandy in 1852, by running the *Tom Scott* from the Mouth to Louisa. In the same year he built, owned, and commanded for a time the *A..*, soon putting W.

Fuse Davidson on the boat as master, who had previously acted as clerk, James R. Hatcher, a Sandy young man, going into the office to succeed Davidson. He was captain of other steamers. The last one he commanded was the *Major O'Drain*, which ran on the Sandy in 1860. Captain Daniel B. Vaughan has, in his day, built five large Ohio steamers, and four smaller ones to run on Sandy. Com. W. Fuse Davidson died a Christian gentleman, and in worldly wealth a millionaire, at St. Paul, Minn., on the 26th May, 1887.

Daniel Vaughan might have been a wealthy man, like his early friend and fellow-laborer, Com. Davidson; but Davidson was always a temperate man in his habits. Captain Vaughan went into partnership with King Alcohol when not forty. The tyrannical old tyrant robbed him of wealth, health, and business capacity. But having a grain of grit left, Daniel B. Vaughan asserted his manhood, and rebelled against every thing that intoxicates in 1880, and started into business alone, asking, however, the favor of Heaven to rest upon him in his struggle with the craving old appetite for strong drink; and for six years and more not a drop of fire-water has entered his mouth to steal away his brains. At forty he was sometimes called "Dan;" at fifty he was called "Uncle Dan;" at sixty, "Old Dan Vaughan;" but now (1887) the good people tip their hats or wave their hands, and say when they pass him on the street,

"Captain Vaughan." He is almost daily adding (it is true but a little at a time) to his worldly wealth; but if he lives to be as old as did his noble mother, he will become a wealthy man. He is now sixty-eight years old. He is not only a reformed man, but is a Christian in communion with the Baptist Church.

Captain Vaughan says the best prohibitory law is the law of personal prohibition; that if he can give up his cups, every man on Sandy can do likewise. When he quit chewing tobacco recently, his wife feared that it was too much of a good thing, and that it might prostrate him. But the captain said: "Wife, God won't let me die in trying to do right. I want to part company with every filthy practice." And he did. He said he asked the Father above to help him to break away from whisky, and he did. He asked him to help him to get rid of tobacco, and he came right along to his relief. Captain Daniel B. Vaughan is a hero. Not because he drank so much fire-water, but because he quit, and sticks to it.

EUGENE CARY ELY

Was a well-known Sandy steamboat clerk; for many years running in the trade from Catlettsburg to Pike, and from Catlettsburg to Louisa. He was a young man whom every body liked, being full of sunshine and cheerfulness in his make-up, and as kind and gentle in his nature as a woman. He had his shortcomings, but they were merely the outcroppings of a too generous nature. He died with malarial fever, on his twenty-eighth birthday, December 15, 1879, at Catlettslettsburg, Ky., greatly mourned by his numerous friends and relatives.

Eugene's elder brother, William Wirt Ely, was for many years engaged in steamboating on Sandy and the Southern waters. He was a model young man in his morals, and never gave offense to any human being. By reverses in business his nervous system became impaired, and growing despondent, he raised the thin veil separating the life that now is from that which is to come, and passed away in 1882, without an enemy in the world.

These young men were both sons of the author, by his first wife.

BEN. BURK AND JOHN CRABTREE.

WHEN the Civil War broke upon the country in 1861, Ben. Burk at once declared in favor of the old flag. This sentiment was heightened by the untimely death of his son, Major Bent. Burk, a few weeks after his enlistment in the Fourteenth Kentucky Infantry, Union army. The father loved his boy with all the intensity of feeling that characterized the king of Israel for his beautiful Absalom. Mr. Burk, somehow, charged the death of his son to Southern fury, although the young man died of typhoid fever.

During the entire continuance of the struggle to set up a government in the South, Mr. Burk talked bitterly, yet never was known to do an unkind act or fail to grant a reasonable favor to any old friend, no matter how strong that friend's adherence to secession might be.

John Crabtree was an old resident near Louisa, where Mr. Burk, for many years before moving to Catlettsburg, was a prominent merchant. Some time in the Fall of 1864, Esquire John Crabtree went to Catlettsburg with a push-boat, to get a threshing of wheat exchanged at Patton's mill for flour. When ready to leave the Mouth for home, he procured a pass from the provost marshal's office on Front Street, to enable him to pass the sentinels on duty. While getting his pass, K. N. Harris, who was not only a Union man, but vindictive oftentimes in his utterances against Southern sympathizers, knowing Mr. Crabtree to be a Southern man in feeling, called him a vile name, for which the 'squire knocked him prone on the brick pavement. As soon as Mr. Harris was able to arise, with the assistance of help, he hurried away, and swore out a warrant for Crabtree's arrest; the warrant was served immediately by the author of this book, who was the acting sheriff at the time. Mr. Crabtree was told to appear on the morrow at ten o'clock before Judge C. L. McConnell, whose office at that time was the same now owned and occupied by R. C. Burns as a law office. Sharp at the hour named, judge, jury (of twelve discreet men), sheriff, prosecuting witness, and defendant were on hand, ready for the trial. Mr. Harris swore that, on the afternoon previous, John Crabtree, the defendant, committed an assault on him by hitting him and knocking him down, giving him great bodily pain. The court asked Mr. Harris if he wished to introduce witnesses to corroborate his own testimony. He said, "No, for most of the men on the jury were eye-witnesses to the assault." John Crabtree was then called forward, and asked if he had any witnesses he wished to have sworn. He replied, "No, that he admitted the offense as charged in the warrant, and that what Mr. Harris had stated was true, and all that he could ask of the jury was that they would not fine him more than they thought he deserved under the circumstances." The case then closed, when the sheriff cleared the room of judge, plaintiff, and defendant, so that the jury might make up their verdict without leaving their seats. The sheriff closed the door of the jury-room, and sat down on the step outside, to wait for the verdict. He could hear every word and movement going on within. Soon the voice of Esquire H. M. Honaker, one of the jury, rang out, urging his brother jurors to go to work and get through with the case, as he wished to return to his daily labor. After a short pause Ben. Burk, who also was on the jury, in reply to what Honaker had uttered, said that "*it would be well to get a piece of paper and write a little verdict.*" Footsteps were heard on the floor within, and a piece of paper was found and handed to a good penman, who was one of the twelve, when some one spoke up and said: "Mr. Burk, you have often been on juries, and you are the oldest man among us, and you must be the first to say what the verdict shall be." From the number of responses in favor of the suggestion, all must have assented. Mr. Burk spoke out firmly, and said: "Men, Kels Harris is as good a Union man as lives. John Crabtree gave him quite a jolt, and I feel sorry for Kels." He then paused as if framing in his mind proper words to be said, and proceded as follows: "Men, I have known John Crabtree ever since he and I were boys. I know that he is a sympathizer with the South, but he attends well to his own business. Men, a more honest man and clever man than John Crabtree does n't live on Sandy. Boys, let's not fine him any thing." And they all said, "Your verdict is ours." The verdict read as follows:

"We, the jury in the case of the Commonwealth against John Crabtree, for assault on K. N. Harris, find for the defendant.

BEN. BURK, Foreman."

Be it said, to the honor of K. N. Harris, that he never fell out with his political friend, Burk, for his action in this matter. All three of the actors are now sleeping in their graves, away from all strife and care.

REV. THOMAS COPLEY,

OF Wayne County, West Virginia, was an early inhabitant of the section where he lived so long and so honorably, and where his long and useful life ended but a few years ago. For nearly fifty years he was an able preacher in the Methodist Episcopal Church, much of the time in the itinerant ranks. He left many descendants to imitate his holy life and pure example, living in Wayne County, West Va., and Martin County, Ky. Allen Copley, a bright lawyer at Eden, is third in descent from this good and noted man of God. Many of the Copleys have come to the front in political and public life. In the great Civil War all of them were intensely loyal to the Government, and a number carried swords or muskets to defend its flag.

REV. JOHN JARRELL,

A PREACHER in the regular Baptist Church, while not so early in Wayne as Mr. Copley, was equally zealous in his labors in winning souls to Christ. This good man, for more than thirty years was a shining light to all around, as he labored, in season and out of season, to reconcile to God the people with whom he came in contact. His mother was of the house of Damron, and he married a Miss Bromley, which connected him with the Damron, Bromley, and Short families—three very prominent houses in pioneer history.

ROSTER CONTINUED.

William Shannon,	Lieutenant,	5th Virginia.
George F. Ratliff,	"	39th Kentucky.
—— Childers,	"	39th Kentucky.
William E. Frazell,	"	5th Virginia.
Eperson Fuller,		5th Virginia.
Henry C. Duncan,	"	5th Virginia.
James K. Weymer,	Major,	5th Virginia.
Jacob Ross,	Captain,	45th Kentucky.

A WAR PICTURE.

SOON after the celebrated order of General Burbridge had been promulgated, to arrest all guerrillas, bushwhackers, and other suspected persons, and ordering them to be sent to the head-quarters of the commanding general for trial, and if found guilty of the crime named, to suffer the penalty of death, inflicted by order of a court-martial, a painter, whose name is not remembered by the author, living for the time in Catlettsburg, but who a short time before had left New York City, having from that place, in the first flush of the war, enlisted in the celebrated Zouave regiment of one-year men, raised and commanded by "Billy Wilson," was arrested by the order of of the provost marshal of

Catlettsburg, a major of a Michigan regiment, with the intention of sending the man off as coming under the description of men named in the order. Before the man, or, indeed, any others suspected or accused, could be sent away for military trial, the officer in charge had to procure the assent of at least five honorable and well-known citizens, to approve of the arrest and sending away of the accused, so that they might be summoned to give testimony before the military tribunal when the case was called. The provost marshal named came to the author of this book, who was well known for his loyalty to the government, and equally well known for his fairness in discriminating between a well-founded and a trumped-up charge, although by adhering to the moral right his own side in the conflict might be injured by his refusal to act in accordance to the dictates of some prejudiced officer.

The worst that the gassy New Yorker had done to make him obnoxious to the provost marshal was in saying that "Billy Seward, of New York, would find himself mistaken, in saying that the rebellion would be put down in sixty days, for that the ex-soldier had fought three hundred and sixty-five days, and the war was going on all the same." It is supposed that the provost marshal at Catlettsburg obtained the signatures of the required number of reliable men (perhaps by false statement), for it was given out that the prisoner (for he had been already arrested) would leave under a guard of soldiers the next day for Lexington, to stand his trial for bushwhacking.

The whole affair looked so preposterous that the author wrote a letter, directed to the commanding officer at Lexington, giving a full statement of the case, and sent it by Captain Honshell's steamer, immediately leaving for Cincinnati, with the urgent request that one of the clerks of the boat would mail it as soon as the steamer arrived at Cincinnati, so that it would be sure to reach Lexington before the prisoner and his guards got there. The scheme proved successful. The letter, fortunately, on arriving at Lexington, fell into the hands of Colonel David A. Mims, of the Thirty-ninth Kentucky Infantry, who, for the time being, was holding the fort there.

Colonel Mims, while intensely loyal, and approving of the order to put down guerrilla warfare in Kentucky, not only as an act of justice, but of humanity as well, was nevertheless as fair a man as ever lived when called upon to decide the fate of a fellow-being. The statements of the letter, which were otherwise corroborated, induced him to see that the prisoner was set free. Giving him a pass, he reached Catlettsburg before his guards. This greatly chagrined the disappointed major, and he took every opportunity to heap indignities on the man who had headed him off in trying to do a mean act. The principal trouble with the New York painter was, that he talked too much, and said too little.

However, since the extreme prejudice of that day has subsided by the lapse of time, many who thought it a terrible outrage against humanity to send from their homes such men as Bill Wright, Sid. and Dave Cook, and Jim Smith, to be shot as outlaws against God and man, have changed their opinions, knowing that had Bill Wright been executed for the murders already said to have been committed by him, he would not have been able to kill George Archer, nor have caused Archer's friends all the trouble and anxiety of putting him out of the way as a common enemy of the human race; and Jim Lyons should have suffered with Bill Wright, before he had had an opportunity to corrupt his little brother, who, following the example of the elder villains in crime, graduated on the same gallows with them, at eighteen years of age.

Letting true humanity have fair play, especially if guided by Christian principles, is not so bad, after all. "Honor to whom honor is due," if it does sometimes cause us to revise our opinions.

A SANDY COUPLE'S NOBLE ACT.

In about 1850 one of the most atrocious murders ever read or heard of, was committed near Argolite, on the Little Sandy River, in Greenup County, Ky. A man by the name of Collins, with several accomplices, under the cover of a dark night, went to the house of a family by the name of Brewer, near by, and murdered in cold blood the husband and wife on the most flimsy pretense that could instigate to such a revolting deed. Several children, all small, were made orphans by the awful crime. The fiends were soon ferreted out, and brought to justice, three of them forfeiting their lives on the scaffold at Greenupsburg, and others finding a home for life in the State's prison at Frankfort. We remark, without giving details, that justice followed swiftly and surely the fiends who had so outrageously violated the law of God and man.

Great sympathy went out from the humane people to the little orphan children, and they were all taken in charge by Christian people, who were not only willing to train the little ones, but could be expected to do more, in some instances at least, for their temporal welfare, than could their natural parents, had they lived; for the Brewers were poor folks.

Elba Ulen and wife, living at Catlettsburg, and having no children, begged that they might be permitted to adopt two of the children. This favor was granted to the kind-hearted pair, who took James and Annie, brother and sister, children of the murdered pair, and reared them as tenderly as if they had been bone of their bone and flesh of their flesh. The children grew up to manhood and womanhood, the idols of the adopted father and mother, and greatly respected for the Christian graces that reflected their superior training.

The foster father and mother gave each of the young people a good scholastic education, sending James away to college to finish his course. When just stepping out on life's scene of business, he was stricken with pulmonary trouble, which soon put an end to his happy life, made so by the teachings of the Ulens. His sister Annie, not many years after, followed her brother to the Celestial City, where the wicked cease from troubling, but where no doubt she and her loving brother James will give their dearly loved foster father and mother a happy greeting on the sunlit shore.

Mr. and Mrs. Ulen still talk in a low voice when any reference is made to the death of James and Annie. The children were dearer to them than rubies.

MANY THINGS.

The most commodious stone house in the Sandy Valley is the residence of Hon. Ulysses Garred, of Lawrence.

The only stone church in the Valley is Stairs Chapel, on Pigeon, Logan County, West Va. The neatest log church in the valley is Borders Chapel, on the edge of Lawrence and Johnson.

The finest court-house in the valley is at Louisa. The largest and most costly public-school building in the valley is at Catlettsburg. The largest and most extensive private school property in the valley is the Normal at Catlettsburg. The most imposing public-school building, built of wood, is in Sandy City, a suburb of Catlettsburg.

The oldest lodge of Masons in the valley is at Prestonburg. The oldest lodge of Odd Fellows is at Catlettsburg. The Odd Fellow in the valley who has been longest a member of the order without a break, is the author of this book.

The first wedding occurring in a church in the valley came off in the Methodist Episcopal Church at Catlettsburg, July 16, 1862, the contracting parties being William Ely and Trinvilla J. Walter

The most considerable falls on any stream in the valley are the Falls of Blaine.

The largest and most wonderful gas-well south of Mason and Dixon's line is located in Martin County, Kentucky, on the Tug River, at Warfield.

The most prolific salt-well in the valley is in Martin County. More salt has been made in Floyd, on Middle Creek, than any place in the valley.

The most noted natural object in the valley is "Duty's Knob," near Pikeville, Ky.

The town in the Sandy Valley, or bordering on the same, outside of Catlettsburg, doing the largest manufacturing business, is Salyersville.

The handsomest lawyer's office in the valley is that of Walter S. Harkins, in Prestonburg.

The oldest teacher (who has taught for fifty years) is Joseph West, of Martin County.

The oldest militia officer now living in the valley is General Hager, of Johnson County.

PUBLIC LIFE OF J. M. BURNS.

HON. JOHN M. BURNS, who studied law under his brother, W. H. Burns, at West Liberty, Ky., was admitted to the bar in 1851, and formed a partnership with his preceptor in the practice of their profession, which continued near three years. W. H. Burns, at the time resided in West Liberty, and John M. in Whitesburg, Letcher County, their practice and partnership embracing Letcher, Perry, and Breathitt Counties. John M. was elected county attorney in Letcher County, and served with ability in the office until December, 1853, when he moved to Prestonburg, Floyd County, Ky. With this removal the partnership of W. H. and John M. Burns terminated.

John M. Burns then and there formed a partnership with the lamented Judge John M. Elliott, which continued for six years. They had a lucrative practice. While this partnership existed John M. Burns, in 1857, was elected to the Legislature of Kentucky from his district, then composed of Floyd and Johnson Counties. He served in that body with industry, and manifested ready powers in debate and legislative capacity. In 1860, in the begining of our *internecine* troubles, John M. Burns was nominated, and made the race, for the Senate of Kentucky in the then Thirty-third Senatorial District of the State, against Hon. Thomas S. Brown. The Senatorial District was composed of the counties of Pike, Floyd, Johnson, and Magoffin. Mr. Burns was elected by a large majority, took his seat in the Senate, and served a month there with marked ability. When it was discovered, in the apportionment of representatives for the State at a previous session of the Legislature, that the Senate had in its body too many members by one, Mr. Burns resigned his seat in that body and delivered one of the most elegant and amusing valedictories ever heard, eliciting laughter, tears, and praise from members and galleries.

Mr. Burns returned to his home, and practiced his profession from this time until actual hostilities began between the sections. His profession of the law and lecturing on education, even up to 1864, engaged most of his time in Floyd County. In 1864 he moved to Catlettsburg. He served as school commissioner of Boyd County for two terms, lecturing on education in every school district in the county, each year he held the office.

In 1867 Mr. Burns ran for the office of Commonwealth's attorney for the Sixteenth District against Judge James E. Stewart, and was defeated by a reduced political majority. In 1876 he again made the race against the same gentleman for the office of Criminal Court judge in the same district. In 1880 he made the race for the office of Circuit Court judge in the same district against Hon. G. N. Brown, a wealthy and influential man, and was again defeated. In 1886 he again ran for the office of Circuit Court judge in the same district, against Hon. George N. Brown, the same man, then incumbent of the office, and, although only in the active canvass twenty-four days, made apparently his last fight as gallantly as his first, and was triumphantly elected. At each and all of the races made by Mr. Burns, since 1864, he ran as a Republican, and was at each race, although poor, required by his party to make each canvass to his own financial detriment; yet he yielded to the wish of his party to uphold its principles. Mr. Burns's ability on the stump and in debate gave him the preference in his party, and induced his frequent candidacies, often against his judgment and to his financial embarrassment. He now holds the office of Circuit Court judge of the Sixteenth Judicial District, composed of the counties of Boyd, Carter, Lawrence, Martin, Johnson, Floyd, and Pike, and is serving the people faithfully and acceptably.

LINEAGE OF THE HOUSE OF THE AUXIERS,

Of Block-house Bottom, on Sandy.

MY father married Rebecca Phillips in 1813. They had eleven children, as follows, viz.: Nat, John B., Jemima, George W., Sarah, Joseph, Samuel, Rebecca, Martha J., Araminta, and Henry J. Then my mother died September 20, 1835, and he married Agnes Wells, his second wife. They had the following children, viz.: Margaret, Elijah B., William L., J. K. Polk, and Ann—sixteen in all—thirteen still living. Father died December 13, 1883, having lived on the same farm since 1795.

Nat. married Hester Ann Mayo; John B., Angelina Mayo, and for second wife, Mary A. Grayson; Jemima was married to John Prater; George W. to Nancy Prater; Sarah to G. W. Mayo; second, to Martin Lesley; and third, to James Denton; Joseph K., to Jane Walker; Samuel, to Rebecca Mayo; Rebecca, to Thomas Prater; Martha, to Henry Walker; Araminta, to James Nibert; Henry J., to Harriet Musick; Margaret to L. D. Chambers; Elijah B., to Margaret Richmond; William L., to Louisa Ford; J. K. P., to Emma Spradlin; and Ann, to John Richmond.

My grandmother was a Brown, the daughter of Nathaniel Brown, brother to Thomas C. Brown, who was the grandfather of W. W. Brown, now living in Paintsville. They were an English family. Grandmother died about the beginning of our late Rebellion, aged ninety-nine years.

JOHN. B. AUXIER.

WHY SO?

WE conceded the post of honor to our publisher, Rev. Z. Meek, D. D., by placing his superb likeness the first in the book as the frontispiece.

The author thought he deserved it by coming to his aid in bringing out the book.

THE AUTHOR.

THE MONTAGUES

FOR twenty-five years have been a noted family near to, or at, the Mouth of Sandy. Especially has W. W. Montague, who died at eighty-four years of age, in Catlettsburg, in 1886, been a historic character. He filled the office of constable for a period of more than thirty-five years, part in Mason County, where he lived before coming to Sandy. He was jailer for one term in Boyd County.

He was the most bitter and uncompromising partisan who ever lived on Sandy, and was equally bitter in his advocacy of the tenets of the Church of which he was a member—the Campbellite, or Christian. He often said that no matter who his party might nominate for office, he would support the nominee without question. Yet with all of his bitterness he was a man, socially, of the kindliest feelings; and while a great party worker and politician, he hated, with a perfect hatred, the whiskyseller, and pitied the poor drunkard, never advising the use of whisky in promoting his party's interest. He was an honest, fearless man.

His family of sons and daughters have all come to honor. One son, John J. Montague, is now filling his second term as county attorney of Boyd. Philip, the youngest, has for a long time been the popular conductor on the Chatterawha Railroad. Polk, the other son, is engaged in railroading. Two of the daughters married noted preachers.

The whole family, while in political matters Democrats, like their father, yet unlike him, are noted for their courtesy to those who differ from them in political opinions.

THE EASTHAM FAMILY

Is ONE of more than ordinary note in the Lower Sandy Valley. Many of them have filled official positions in the counties of Lawrence and Boyd. John H. Eastham, of Boyd, represented his county and Carter in the Legislature of the State. He has also been sheriff for two terms, and afterwards county judge. His nephew, Robert Eastham, was once sheriff of Lawrence County, and, after moving to Boyd County, was a leading timber-trader. Another nephew, John C. Eastham, filled the office of sheriff of Boyd for two terms; and still another nephew, Robert by name, was at one time sheriff of Boyd. D. D. Eastham, a son of John C. Eastham, is now serving his second term as county school superintendent of Boyd County. He is a promising lawyer of the Catlettsburg bar. John H. Eastham is a Republican in politics. The others named are all Democrats.

THE CASSADYS,

OF Martin, are a strong family in the valley. The father of Philip Cassady and brothers came to the Lower Tug country about 1837, from Tazewell County, Va. Philip Cassady has been from young manhood a live business man in the valley of Rock Castle. He has not only distinguished himself as a business man of integrity and honor, but has filled many official places in his county with credit to himself and advantage to his constituents. His brothers are also among Martin County's prominent people. The Cassadys are a well-educated people, qualifying them for foremost places in the affairs of life.

CONCLUSION.

Lack of further space admonishes us that "The Big Sandy Valley" and the history of its people must close. This work was undertaken by the author with a full realization of the fact that to collect material of sufficient importance to the public at large, to fill a volume of five hundred pages, was a work of great labor. The reader will learn by referring to the preface to the book, that it was not intended, neither was it possible, to take up the beginning of Sandy history from the time the Vancoovers, in 1789, built two forts or blockhouses on the point of land where the Levisa and Tug Rivers join, and nearly at the same time the Leslies assayed to make a settlement at the mouth of Pond Creek, on the Tug River, and in one continuous chain connect, in chronological order, each event as it took place, as each settler followed on the footsteps of his predecessor into the valley; nor, as was further stated, have we searched the records of the different counties to discover who were, at different times, elected to fill the various county, State, and national offices, for the reason that those facts are always at hand on the records of the county and other courts, or may be found among the archives at Frankfort. Rather have we, as promised, recorded the important events connected with the early settlement of the valley in the order coming to us through diligent and patient research, embracing, as the chief aim, a desire to snatch from oblivion the personal and family history of the people of the valley, while by no means ignoring the political history when the individual acts of the people might be more prominently brought forth. In every case, however, we have given dates as near as could be ascertained by the closest inquiry and research.

In preparing these pages we have met with innumerable difficulties, and have had to overcome them by increased labor and physical toil, traveling hundreds of miles, and sending out numerous appeals to those who, we thought, might be able and willing to give any information throwing light on the subject undertaken by the author, for the benefit of the people of the Big Sandy Valley. Had all of those whom we personally solicited, or to whom we sent letters of inquiry, been prompt in responding, the book would, no doubt, be more interesting than it is.

The author, however, is placed under great obligations to Colonel John Dils, Jr., of Pikeville, for the graphic article he furnished on the middle period of Big Sandy history, embracing the historical acts of quite a number of well-known men and families who have been an honor to the valley.

To Captain John B. Goff, of Big Creek, Pike County, we return thanks for favors bestowed.

Major John B. Auxier, of East Point, has contributed valuable information, connected with his own personal experience and obtained from the lips of his father, the late Samuel Auxier, of Blockhouse Bottom, and from General Daniel Hager, and the general's venerable mother, a lady of strong mind and character, possessing a retentive memory, who lived to a time remembered by many people still living in the section where she spent her long and useful life.

Allen Hatton, of Rockville, Lawrence County, added much information, as also did Rev. R. D. Callihan and Samuel P. Hager, Esq., of Ashland, Ky.

Dr. Dickson, of Johnson County, helped much in furnishing facts and dates of the early history of the valley.

Mrs. Matilda Rice, of Catlettsburg, deserves honorable mention for like favors.

K. F. Leslie, of Graham's Place, Floyd County, also has our thanks for assistance in many ways.

Hon. R. H. Weddington furnished a long and valuable paper on the early history of his house and collaterals; but unfortunately the article, unintentionally, was lost or misplaced, and was afterwards reproduced from memory, robbing it of much of its intrinsic value.

Robert A. Preston, of Richardson, has aided materially in the way of statistics.

To Rev. Z. Meek, D. D., the author is under lasting gratitude for preparing the sketch of the capture, by the Indians, of Jenny Wiley, and her escape from them to her friends at the Block-house, now Johnson County, Kentucky. The reverend gentleman having been born and having lived to manhood near the place where Mrs. Wiley resided, and being connected with her by marriage, is able, more accurately than most others, to give all the facts connected with the noted woman's awful trials.

Our labor for years in the preparation of this work, in the interim of pressing cares and prostration by almost continuous feeble health, has not been without its joys, in the hope that we were engaged in a task that would add, in some degree, to the material, intellectual, and moral advancement of the people of the Sandy Valley, the heroic deeds of whose ancestors has been the basis of all that is recorded in these pages. THE AUTHOR.

PUBLISHER'S NOTICE.

It is due to the reader that we should say some errors crept into this book, either by oversight or otherwise. To issue so large a book without errors, especially by those new to the business of bookmaking, could hardly be expected.

In referring to the counties of Johnson and Floyd, their political complexion was reversed, by the use of the word *latter*, instead of *former*.

In the article on the Hager family, *Reuben* Patrick was the name intended, but that of *Elijah* managed to get in somehow.

The article on the Hattons reads *grandfather*, in speaking of J. F. Hatton, when it should have been *father*.

Brother slipped in where it should have been *son*, in the article on the Auxier family, referring to the death of little 'Lige.

Further we need not particularize. There is some duplication of matter, caused by the author's forwarding copy to the printers direct, which was not seen by the publisher until after the articles were in type.

One other matter deserves notice. The arrangement of the book is not just as we would have had it; but it required several hundred more pages of manuscript than we calculated on to fill the space; hence, a proper classification could not be made.

We bespeak for this book a large sale, and hearty appreciation by the people.   PUBLISHER.

INDEX

This index lists all personal names in the text, including women under both maiden and married names when known. Listings in the original index have been retained.

ABBOTT, James A 324 446 Miss 62
ADAMS, A E 306 439 Alexander E 195 (portrait) 196 Captain 198 Georgie A 198 199 Green 53 Mr 197-200 Smith 397 William 396 397 447
ADKINSON, 396
AKERS, Peter 302
ALLEN, Jack 339
ALSACE-LORRAINE, 88
ANDREWS, 72 G W 21 238 239 256 257 George N 257 George W 259 260 James A 281 Mr 239 260 282 N P 238 239 256-258 260 269 360 Ralph 239 Ralph H 259 Wat 259 Watt 85 239
ARCHER, 338 340 George 479 George P 337
ARMSTRONG, 128
Army Officers of 447-476
ARTHUR, Miss 72 76
ARTRIP, William 156
ASHLAND, 315 319
ASTORS, John Jacob 196
ATKINS, Levi 324 Miss 100
ATKINSON, D M 144
Attorneys Prosecuting 438
AUCSTIER, 6
AUXIER, 6 11 20 142 322 388 494 A J 105 108 438 439 Agnes 486 Agnes 105 Angelina 486 Ann 105 486 Araminta 485 486 Daniel 106 Elijah 99 106 Elijah B 486 Emma 486 George W 485 486 Harriet 486

AUXIER (continued)
Henry J 485 486 Hester Ann 486 J B 233 J K P 486 J K Polk 486 Jane 486 Jemima 485 486 John B 103 104 107 108 448 485 486 492 Joseph 485 Joseph K 486 Louisa 486 Major 104 106 108 Margaret 105 486 Martha 486 Martha J 485 Mary A 486 Michael 106 Nancy 486 Nat 107 305 485 486 Nathaniel 108 (portrait) 108 Rebecca 485 486 Rebecca 105 Sally 104 Samuel 99 104-106 108 233 485 486 492 Sarah 485 486 Simon 104 106 William L 486
BAILEY, Wallace 24
BALLENGERS, 190
BALTIMORE, Lord 193
BANFIELD, A P 185 186 (portrait) 186 Dr 185 186 305 Mrs 186
BARBEE, Felix A 252 306 (portrait) 252 J R 252
BARNES, George O 413
BARNETT, Dr 173
BARRETT, Col 22
BARTRAM, David 227 229 Fanny 229 James 228 229 324 John A 228 229 Lindsay 229 Mrs William 137 Stephen 415 416 William 228 229 324 406 Wm 448
BEATY, Rochester 178
BEIRNE, Colonel 141 Mr 139
BELCHER, 20 48
BENTLEY, 445
BEVINS, 20 237 322 324 J M 238

BEVINS (continued)
  James 238 John 238 Joseph
  237 238 Miss 238
Big Sandy Mail 415
Big Sandy Valley 16
BIGGS, Capt 32 William 31 179
BILL (Servant), 85 86
BLACKSTONE, 57
BLAIR, Mr 348
BLENNERHASSET, Mrs 47
BLOOMER, Daniel 236 Joseph
  206 Nancy 206
BOGGS, Hugh 446 447 Nelson 299
BOLT, Major 123 402 403
  Montraville 402
BOND, H M 329
BOONE, Atwell 467 Daniel 107
  229
BOOTEN, 402 Ralph 403
BOOTON, Ralph 338
BORDER, 12 20 David 123 Jane
  120 John 24
BORDERS, 322 332 A P 134 Allen
  P 84 123 Archibald 75 77 119
  120 122 396 450 (portrait) 119
  Arthur 123 Betty 120 David 123
  468 Henry 448 Hezekiah 119
  450 Jane 75 Jane 123 Joe H
  120 332 John 119 120 123 450
  451 Joseph 120 Judge 77 123
  305 446 Julia 123 Michael 450
  Polly 120 William 84 468
BOTNER, Oliver 448
BOTTS, Aleck 461 462 Alex 419
  John Minor 461 Mrs Alex 345
BOWLER, R B 309
BOWLES, Capt 324 412 414 O C
  323 411
BRECKINRIDGE, John 27 John C
  27 411
BREWER, 20 480 Annie 480 481
  James 480 481
Bright Young Men 361
BRODERS, Mrs 84 Mrs David 205
BROMLEY, Miss 476
BROWN, 11 20 230 233 E W 144
  145 Francis Asbury 233 235 G
  N 360 484 George N 59 126 127
  231 252 276 331 438 485
  James 34 John 120 174 Joseph
  447 Judge 231 232 Katie 120
  Matilda 59 231 Mr 231 233 234

BROWN (continued)
  Mrs Thomas R 130 Nathan 233
  235 Nathaniel 233 486 Richard
  59 230 Sally 104 Thomas 233-
  235 276 401 Thomas C 233 486
  Thomas R 126 232 Thomas S
  483 Ventrees 144 W W 106
  233 486 Wallace W 233
BRUBAKER, Crate 291 Perly 291
BRUNING, Frank 460
BRUNS, Fred 235 Frederick 235
  William 235
BRYAN, John 229 Recy 230 Sarah
  White Larkin 229 Zeffie 229
  230
BUCHANAN, James 172
BUCKNER, Dr 467 Mr 467
BURBRIDGE, General 476
BURCHETT, D J 165 447
  (portrait) 224 Drew J 224 Major
  224 225 305
BURGESS, 88 225 322 448 Clara
  226 Edward 225-227 402
  George 227 239 369 George R
  226 227 238 259 Gorden 227
  John 226 Lizzie 259 Miss 97
  369 Mr 313 402 Nancy 226
  Permitta 226 Rebecca 226
  Reuben 226 Sarah 226 Strother
  226 William 226 227
BURK, Ben 34 43 281 471 473 474
  Bent 471 Bentley 447 Mr 43
  472 474
BURKS, John Creed 171 325
BURNS, 360 Elizabeth 115 116
  Harvey 58 435 James Harvey
  433 Jane H 58 Jerry 58 115 116
  433 John M 58 116-118 231
  305 438 483 (portrait) 118 La
  Fayette 116 117 Lewis 433
  Margaret 117 Milton 11 Miss
  133 Mr 115 117 484 R C 275
  331 473 R T 133 435 Robert
  115 Roland C 117 Roland T 58
  115-117 W H 116 483 William
  Harvey 438
BURR, Colonel 46
BURRISS, M T 26
BURTON, Samuel 446
BUTCHER, Daniel 468 Miss 467
BUTLER, Andrew 313 Bascom 94
  313

CALLIHAN, Dr 445 Mr 47 49 R D 24 R D 51 67 138 492 Robert D 427
CAMPBELL, A C 284 285 289 Mr 284 287 289 Nancy 216 William 168
CANTERBURY, America 95 Reuben 189
CARDWELL, Jane 216
CARLISLE, George 309 John 309 317 Mr 317
CARNAHAN, Dr 185
CARPENTER, D H 269
CARTER, G W 446
CASEBOLT, Shade 177
CASSADY, Philip 489
CASTLE, 90 G W 41 George W 90 James 90 John W 90
CATLETT, 21 159 Horatio 167 169 Miss 178 Sawney 342 Sawny 167
CATLETTSBURG, 269-310-342 Banks 281 Benefactors 280 Churches 279 Fires 269-342-351 National Bank 284 (illus.) 285 New Enterprises 349 Schools 279
CAUDILL, Colonel 54
CECIL, 20 193 C Sr 51 Cob 193 Cob Jr 194 Cob Sen 97 194 J Crittenden 154 John George 439 Kinzy B 193 231 Miss 411 Samuel 193 439 Thomas 231 William 194 411
CHADWICK, John 166 170
CHAMBERS, Elizabeth 135 L D 486 Margaret 486 Mr 135 Polly 135 Richard 135
CHAPMAN, George R 191 193 448 Lieutenant 192 Lucretia 245 Miss 184 Mr 192 William 191 192
CHAPPELL, 266 George 265 Georgia 268 Julia 268 Mr 265 Mrs 265 267 William 268
CHASE, 336
CHILDERS, 476 Abraham 76 Betty 76 William 201
CHITTY, 57
CLARK, 20 Elizabeth 178 179 Guy 407 Ira 406 John 178
CLAY, Henry 26 85 167

CLEWS, Henry 283
CLINE, Perry 444
CLINEFELTER, Mrs 181 Thomas 181 260
Close Call, A 388
CLOUD, Amelia 152 Washington 152
Coal Industries 308
Coal-oil 22
COCHRAN, Col 41
COLEMAN, 440 Rev 434
COLLEY, 48
COLLINS, 479
Conclusion 491
CONDITT, Rev 178
CONLEY, 333 Asa 333 W M 332 Wince 441
CONLY, Asa 133 Mr 133 292
COOK, Dave 479 Jay 283 John 374 379 380 381 Mr 380 Mrs 380 Sid 479 Widow 381
COPLEY, Allen 475 Mr 475 Thomas 475
COREY, Charles D 329
CORY, Mr 329
COX, 72 Leander 85
CRABTREE, John 471 472 473 474
CRITTENDEN, J J 54 55
CROMWELL, Dr 171
CROSS, 84
CRUM, 241 Adam 241 Mr 177 Nathan 241 242 William 241 242 306 (portrait) 241 William C 452
CRUTCHER, Robert 308
CULBERTSON, Congressman 275
CULVER, John 168 315
CURNUTTE, Miss 212
CUSHING, Alonzo 334 Z 335
CUSHION, Dr 182
CUTLER, Amanda 63
CYRUS, 194 Abraham 93 194 195 218 229 Abraham Sen 194 Jesse 195 Ross 93 194 195 218 Smith 194 Thomas 194 William 194 218
DAMRON, 11 400 476 James W 181 348 James w 348 Lazarus 451
DANBY, Henry 312 313 Mr 312
DANIEL, Isom 120

DANIELS, Peter 120 Polly 120
DAVENPORT, Mr 165 Mrs Garrett 164
DAVID, Bill 324
DAVIDSON, Joseph 283 Joseph M 129 251 Samuel 128 337 W Fuse 469 469
DAVIS, Betty 120 Daniel 120 Garrett 55 Harry 84 John 120 Joseph 120 Mary Jane 110 Mitch 291 Sol 448 William 120
DEAN, J R 398 James R 188 Job 187 Mrs Judge 85 Thomas 188 William H 188
DEERING, John R 190 Mollie 191 Mr 191 Richard 190 191 308 S S 190
DELONG, George 387 388 James 387 388 Samuel 387 388
DEMPSEY, Lewis 444 Mark 444
DENTON, James 486 Sarah 486
DICKSEID, George J 326
DICKSON, Dr 492
DILLON, J W 123 Julia 123
DILLS, Mrs John Jr 97
DILS, Colonel 307 Col John Jr 45 Georgie A 198 199 Henry 45 Jno Jr 51 John Jr 199 304 305 307 447 491 (portrait) 45 Residence (illus) 46 John Sr 45
DIXON, 20 George W 189 H F 188 Henry 25 188 Joseph K 189 Joyce 188
DONOHOE, Mr 226 Sarah 226
DOTSON, 445
DRAPER, Dr 182
DUNCAN, Henry C 476
DURNEY, 189
DYE, Captain 275
DYER, Nancy 134
EASTHAM, D D 184 488 John C 275 488 John H 488 Robert 488
EBA, D W 254 276 280 350 Daniel W 350 Mr 350 Mrs D W 255 Mrs W H H 255 W H H 255
Eden 295
Elk Horn Creek 412
ELLINGTON, 190 Pleasant 189
ELLIOT, John M 209
ELLIOTT, John M 234 435 437 483

ELY, Charles 420 Charley 420 Dr 138 Eugene Cary 470 471 James C 449 465 W (portrait) 5 William 482 William Wirt 471
EMERICK, Joseph J 253
ENDICOTT, Samuel 209 210
EVERETT, John 36 Talton 40
EWING, John 165 John C 169-171 Joseph 20 169 Mr 170 T J 169 448 Thomas J 171
FAIRBAIRN, Frank 459
FALKNER, James 181 John 181 423
FANNIN, Mrs 364 Philip 364
FARMERS, 188
FARROW, Kenas 140
FAULKNER, John F 37
FERGUSON, 333 387 C W 377 Capt 377 Henry 133 Lee 131 208 332 (portrait) 208 J M 403 Jemison 132 John 377 Joseph 131 Joseph M 377 Judge 133 134 Laura 378 379 382 Lucinda 152 Lynn Boyd 133 M J 131 132 219 246 305 315 321 333 340 377 381 438 (portrait) 131 Milton 376 377 378 Mr 292 333 Mrs 377 S M 152 154 182 208 447
FERRELL, Mrs 92 Richard 304 445
Fires in Catlettsburg 269-342
First Settlement of Sandy 11
FITZPATRICK, Burgess 137 Kizzie 74 Mr 129 Sarah Ann 137
FLOYD, Gov 22 27 311 328 John B 27
FORBES, Colonel 316 Mr 321 S R 321
FORD, Charles Winston 207 Glen 401 Harry 153 Henry 448 Jackson 153 James R 260 401 402 John 154 John Henry 207 275 276 Louisa 486 Moses 154 Mr 207 Mrs 207 Mrs John Henry 100 S King 154 Sally 402 Tandy Lewis 207 Thomas 442 Widow 442 William 153 448
FOSTER, James 449 William A 260 308

FRAZELL, William E 476
FREESE, F F 63 Henry 204 Milton 308
Free-will Baptists 430
FRENCH, 72 David 191 Judge 85 Mrs F R 181
FRIEND, 20 Miss 100 R S 207
FRY, Mr 168
FULKERSON, 20 Albert 94 Mrs Martin 100
FULLER, Eperson 476
GALLUP, Col 42 43 44 Fred 44 G W 42 305 447 449 (portrait) 42 George Frederick 44 George W 41 43 Lt 41 Mr 41
GAMBRELL, 446
GARDNER, Henry 207 Joseph 206 Nancy 206 Washington 206 236
GARFIELD, Colonel 300 417 James A 199
GARRARD, 20
GARRED, 322 406 David 134 135 137 138 Elders 138 Elizabeth 135 Flora 135 James 134 Jane 137 Jennie 134 137 Nancy (Dyer) 134 Polly 134 135 Ulysses 134 135 481
GARRELL, Elizabeth 151
GARRETT, Mr 165 Mrs 164 T F 434 Theodore 164
GARTRELL, H C 39 Mrs 39
GEIGER, D D 170 David D 315 325 Mrs 255 Mrs D D 255
GOBLE, George 369 370 Green 435 Greenville 123 367 369 370 371 Isaac 441 Lawyer 441 Lilian 370 M B 123 323 325 371 Montraville B 369 Mr 368 Mrs 371 Widow 369 William 441
GOFF, 20 Captain 136 137 Dixie 137 Elizabeth 135 Felix 135 Felix W 136 Hannah 137 Ira W 135 John B 135 136 306 492 (portrait) 136 John B and Daughters (portrait) 137 Maggie 137 Mary E (Small) 136 Minerva 137 Sarah 137 Sarah Ann 137
GOINGS, 49
GORDON, Miss 263-265
GRACE, David 191 Mollie 191

GRAHAM, 11 20 Jennie 134 137 John 270 355-358 Judge 218 256 Mrs James 398
GRANT, General 198 464 President 199 Ulysses S 199
GRAY, A E 445
GRAYSON, Mary A 486
GREEN, George 448
GREENE, General 104
GREER, 442
GRIM, Charles 26
GRUNDY, Felix 167
HACKNEY, Tom 410 411 412 415
HAGER, 12 20 142 400 D Milt 396 Daniel 80 104 142-145 492 (portrait) 143 Elijah Patrick 494 General 81 144-146 305 395 399 482 George 142 143 Harmon 433 Henry G 143-145 J H 433 John 142 John F 94 144 396 John J 143 144 Mary 142 Milton 144 Miss 399 Mother 104 P 492 Reuben Patrick 494 Ventrees 143 144 Violet Ventrees (Porter) 143
HAILEY, A C 260 448 Mrs Captain A C 100
HAILY, A C 162
HALE, George W 444
HALL, Mr 50 S 50
HAMILTON, 27
HAMMOND, 11
HAMMONS, 104
HAMPTON, 19 322 Amelia 176 C H 173 Elizabeth 174 Elizabeth 254 George 172 Henry 166 171 John W 173 434 Julia 176 L J 37 169 449 Levi J 166 169 173-175 177 254 325 336 Lizzie 177 Mary 176 Millard F 176 177 262 Minnie 176 Mr 423 Mrs 255 Mrs Levi J 255 Mrs William (portrait) 173 W O 173 176 418 Wade 173 Wade Jr 166 William 166 168 170-172 174 307 325 (portrait) 172
HANDLEY, Alexander 118 Elizabeth 116 118
HANEY, Elizabeth 76 Miss 77
HANFORD, Rev 275 Rev Mr 270 Thomas 358
Hanging Bill Wright & others 341

HANKS, John 12
HANNER, Miss 468
HARDWICK, Miss 236
HARGISS, John 153 Shadrach 112 Thomas 153
HARKINS, 247 Hugh 152 247 249 John 247-249 306 (portrait) 248 Mr 301 Walter S 129 152 247 249 250 301 306 307 482 (portrait) 249 Walter S Law Office (illus) 250
HARMON, 218 450 451 Matthias 451
HARRIES, Floyd 218
HARRIS, 27 Henry C 218 435 James P 218 K N 218 260 472 474 Kels 474 Mr 473 Mrs K N 205
HARRISON, General 54
HARVEY, Wm 117
HATCHER, 20 Andrew 205 Elizabeth 152 Ferdinand 205 James 205 James H 205 James R 469 Jas H 205 John L 152 Kenes F 205 Mary C 205
HATFIELD, 20 202 Alexis 202 Anderson 202 Bazell 202-204 Elias 202 Ephraim 202 Floyd 202 George 202 James 202 Johnson 202 Madison 202 Mr 204 Polly 202 Ransom 170 202-204 Wallace 202
HATTON, 214 338 340 Allen 217 492 Bascom 291 D F 187 David 216 Elijah 216 J F 291 338 400 494 Jane 216 Jonah 216-218 Joseph F 216 217 Josiah 215 Margaret 216 Mrs 93 94 338 Nancy (Campbell) 216 Philip 215 216 Rosannah 215 Sally (Purgett) 216 Samuel 214-216 Samuel K 217 Samuel Sen 216 Strother 217 Wily 217
HAWES, Allen P 75 448 Amelia 176 Asbury 75 Betty 76 Jane 75 John 75 P O 176 Polly 75 Wesley 75
HAYDEN, Minnie 176
HAYES, President 43
HAZELETT, 190
HAZLERIGGS, 297
HENDERSON, 253 Duncan 253

HENDERSON (continued) Elizabeth 174 254 John 255 448 449 Mrs 253-255 Thomas E 169 255
HEREFORD, Dr 146 182
HERRIFORD, Dr 205 Mary C 205
HINKLE, Dr 219
HOARD, C B 321 Col 321
HOFFMAN, Archibald 441
HOGAN, Andrew 271
HOLBROOK, Alonzo 204 Mrs Winfrey 398
HOLDEN, Fred 391
HOLTON, Miss 252
HONAKER, 442 374 H M 473 Hugh 260 Mr 140 Mrs Hugh 237
HONSHELL, Augustus 263 Captain 260-262 348 466 478 Gus 348 Mrs 262 Washington 177 260
HOOD, Tom 360
HOPKINS, Captain 276 Frank 129 301 John C 128 Mousie 128 130 Mrs 128 130
HOWE, Elias 379
HOWES, 200 332 Alexis 200 201 Charles J 201 434 G W 201 G Winn 434 George W 201 John 201 Wiley 201
HUFF, German 395 443
HURT, 442
HUTCHINSON, George 65 I B 65
HUTCHISON, George 427 446 I B 427 446
Indian Grave-yards, 458
Introduction, 5
IRELAND, W C 173 331
Ivy Mountain Battle, 298
JACKSON, Dr 211 General 167 J H 358 Rev Mr 270
JAMES, Dr 182
JARRELL, John 475
JAYNE, William 294 434
JEFFERSON, President 46 William 399
JEMISON, 387 Miss 131
JOHNS, 214 227 Daniel 214 366 Harvey 214 James 214 John 214 Thomas 214
JOHNSON, Andrew 24 Barney 48 Dr 182 185 Judge 335
JOLLY, Rev Mr 358

JONES, Daniel 63 164 165 225 427 John 63 Miss 225 Mrs 63 164 240 427 Widow 444
Judiciary, The, 438
Justices, The, 446
JUSTICE, 11 20 322 Fleming 445 Timothy 445 William 238
KANES, Betty 74
KASTNER, Casper 260
KAVANAUGH, Bishop 24
KEEL, Sam 324 Samuel 442
KELLY, Lindsay 263
KEYSER, Margaret 117
KIBBE, Elizabeth 178 179 Emma 179 L L 179 M L 179 Marcus L 178 Mary 179
KILGORE, Mr 100
KINCAID, Dr 183 184 260 305 J D 183 335 (portrait) 183 James W 184
KINNER, 212 270 356 357 359 Ceres 213 David 269 355 David Sen 355 Hansford H 212 213 325 Mr 214 357 S G 88 162 355 356 438 S Girard 213
KIRK, Captain 444 James 444 Joe 448
KISE, C C 137 Minerva (Goff) 137
LACKEY, 12 124 Alexander 124-126 130 256 General 126 128 Greenville M 126 James Q 61 62 Morgan 125 126 290 Mr 124
LAKIN, James 229 Sarah 229
LANDRUM, William B 23
LANGLEY, John W 222 305 439 (portrait) 223 Joseph 442 Joseph R 222 Mr 223
LANHAM, W N 275
LAWSON, Dr 409 Mont 324 Mont B 408 Montraville 409
Lawyers, The, 435
LAYNE, 12 20 400 James 142 John 147 jUDGE 309 Lieutenant 449 Lindsay 143 Lindsey 449
LEDBETTER, Mr 311
LEFFINGWELL, Dwight 448
LESLEY, Martin 486 Sarah 486
LESLIE, 11 15 20 133 322 324 333 491 J K 332 K F 492 Mr 154 Pharmer 210 211 Robert 210 William 210 211

LEWIS, Charles 70 Judge 330 Lucy 70 329 Nelums 329
LINCOLN, Abraham 53 418 President 335 336 Secretary 275
LINDSAY, Marcus 23
LITTERAL, Austin 397
LOAR, Harman 357 Mr 357 Peter 156
LOCKWOOD, 242 Abraham 243 Isaac 243 Jacob 243 244 John 244 307 John residence (illus) 244 Sarah 243
LOOMAN, Job 147
LYCANS, Goodwin 24
LYONS, Jim 339 341 479 John 339 341
McBRAYER, Sol 392 394 Solomon 390
McCALL, R B 236 260 448 468 Robert B 28 237
McCLELLAN, 38 GEORGE B 418
McCLINTOCK, Rev Mr 232
McCLURE, 245 443 Mr 41 264 Mrs 265 William 191
McCONNELL, 435 C L 376 472 Charles L 66 Charles Lewis 71 James H 61 66 John M 57 64 66 69 85 Mr 58 65 70
McCOY, James 180 260
McDOWELL, 20
McDYER, John 65
McGEE, D H 448
McGINNIS, Elizabeth 216
McGRANAHAN, 226 Permitta 226
McGUIRE, Nicholas 404 405
McHENRY, 309
McKENZIE, 270 355 358 359 Colonel 275 James 269 353
McKINSTER, 448
McSORLEY, James 26 John 28
McSORLY, James 236 John 236
MAGANN, Mr 370
MAGOFFIN, 394 Governor 54
MAGUIRE, 20
Many Things, 481
MARCEUMS, 11
MARCUM, 20 Captain 101 103 306 Josiah 101 T D 101 332 448 449 (portrait) 101 Thomas D 101 438
MARR, 12 81 James 82 Mrs 148

501

MARR (continued)
 150 Mrs Thomas 150 Thomas 81 82
MARSHALL, General 299 417
MARTIN, Alexander L 127 232 Dr 144 145 J P 126 John P 12o 127 435 437 O W 117
Martinsburg, 295
MASON, Salena 172
MAUPIN, Mrs 93
MAY, A J 83 298 David 83 Mahala 183 Malinda 159 Miss 82 Mr 437 Thomas 82 Tom 109
MAYNARD, 48 Dr 444 John B 444
MAYO, 12 20 207 322 324 442 468 A I 49 Angelina 486 Cynthia 96 Dick 401 G W 486 H B 49 Harry B 83 141 Hester Ann 486 Jacob 83 Lewis 26 83 84 96 123 Mr 51 Rebecca 86 Sara 486 Wilson 83
MEAD, 20 322 Abraham 74 Katie 151 Susan 74
MEAN, Rhoads 152
MEANS, Archie 448
MEDLEY, J F 165 239 340 Mr 240 Mrs 165
MEEK, Green 416 Hessie 114 John 325 465 Lafayette 113 Mary Jane 110 Mr 113 114 Rev Mr 276 Z 107 120 122 155 306 329 388 399 433 486 493 Zephaniah 110 (portrait) 1
MELLEN, Mr 310-312 William B 309
MENIFEE, 72 Colonel 54 Richard 85
Methodist E Church 426
Methodist E Church South 426
Middle Creek Battle 299
MILES, Mr 308
MILLARD, 20 A J 15 Charles 15 16 Emla 15
MILLER, James J 328 Miss 73 Mr 328 329 Nancy 74 Pricie 73
MIMS, D A 447 David A 100 478 John 100 John D 99 100 177 Lon 100 Martin 140 Mr 100 Robert 100 Theodore 100
MITCHELL, Joseph 321 Mr 321
MONROE, James 191
MONTAGUE, John J 487 Philip

MONTAGUE (continued)
 487 Polk 488 W W 487
MOORE, 72 87 142 Billy 36 Col 38 39 41 F 138 Frances 30 Fred 41 305 Frederick 21 28 34 41 168 231 245 292 303 (portrait) 29 Frederick Jr 35 L T 35 41 167 Laban T 37 168 275 366 438 447 Mr 29 30 32-36 139 Mrs 31 32 33 35 138 Mrs Frederick 251 Mrs Tip Frederick 164 Mrs Tip Frederick Jr 164 Mrs W F 164 Rebecca 41 Sarah 30 31 39 W F 35 William 36
MORGAN, 11 20 Daniel 124 David 124 256 337
MORIARITY, Patrick 357
MORRELL, Mrs Frank 205
MORRIS, Dr 335 Jonathan 335
MORSE, A F 280 Arthur F 350 Mr 351
MOTT, Frank 448
MUNDUS, 264 Mrs 264 265
MURPHY, 263 Anna 179 180 265-268 Dixie (Goff) 137 Floyd W 137 James K 263 268 Julia 179 180 265-268 Misses 180 Mr 179 264 265 Mrs 266 268 William 26 268
MURRAY, Sally 455 Samuel 455
MURRY, 49
MUSIC, Alexis 202 Polly 202
MUSICK, Harriet 486
National Bank, A, 284
NEAL, Chris 313 John 300
NELSON, Capt 254 Christine 455 Mrs 255 Willian 298
NEWMAN, Joseph 190 Peter 190 Peyton 190 Widow 189
NIBERT, Araminta 486 James 457 486
NICHOLS, Frances 30 40 Mr 40 Mrs 40 W T 40 168 William T 30
NICKELS, William 258
NORTHUP, Colonel 275 320 J H (portrait) 320 Jay H 306 315 320 323 359 370 Jay N 274 Miss 370
Navigation, 19
Newspapers of Sandy, 328

OBRIAN, Byron 164 Hannah 164 James 164
Office-holders, 437
Officers of the Army, 447-476
Ohio River Flood in 1883, 272 in 1884 273
Old-time Incidents, 440
ORMSTED, Ralph 448
OSBURN, 20 Ed 337 Jerry 412 413 414 John 86 Judge 414 Mr 414 Walter 123 124 443
OWEN, 48
OWENS, Dad 67 152 John 152 Thomas 303
Paintsville, 293
PARSLEY, 443 Jesse 444 Moses 444
PARSONS, C M 332
PATRICK, 395 Captain 145 Dr 335 Elijah 144 395 494 Reuben 145 395 494 Wiley 395 448
PATTON, 88 221 George B 221 326 448 449 James 221 John S 218 305 (portrait) 219 Joseph 67 222 Mr 219 220 Rebecca 276 W A 221 239 259 W M 67 William M 221 222
Peach Orchard, 309
Peach Orchard Coal, 318
PECK, 443 George 442
PEERY, David 74 79 Miss 205 Nancy 79 Sarah 74
PELPHREY, James 24 256
PETERS, Jacob 406 James 228 406
PHELPS, Col 46
PHERGO, Mr 154
PHERIGO, Mr 332
PHILLIPS, Rebecca 105 485
PICKELSIMER, Dr 441
Pictorial Embellishments, 305
PIKE, 434 Samuel 330
Pikeville, 303
Pioneer, Clothing 12 Preachers 23
PINSON, 11 48
POAGE, 68 Dora 251 George Bernard 251 John 39 Miss 61 231 Mrs 39 Sarah 30 39 William 61 231 251 252
POE, Edgar A 360
Political Convention, 364
POLK, President 51

POLLARD, Mrs William 93
PORTER, 20 Benjamin P 24 Catherine 152 Henry 401 James 402 James A 152 John 143 401 Logan 402 Samuel 146 152 400 401 402 Violet Ventrees 143 Walker 401
POTTER, 413
Potter's Clay, 22
POWELL, Mrs 93
POWERS, 395 John 116 396
PRATER, 395 Jemima 486 John 486 Nancy 486 Rebecca 486 Thomas 486
Preachers, The Early 432
Preface, 3
PRESTON, 322 324 448 Arthur 74 76 79 220 306 (portrait) 220 Betty (Kanes) 74 Captain 145 Coby 76 78-80 121 Colonel 297 Elizabeth (Haney) 76 Frank 80 144 307 Frank Residence (illus) 80 Henry 74 Isaac 73 220 James 81 Jane 120 121 123 John 74 Kizzie (Fitzpatrick) 74 Linda 75 M C D 293 Martin 81 McDonald 74 Milton T 73 Moses 72 73 75 76 79-81 Moses (Coby) 305 Moses (portrait) 77 Moses 1st 120 Moses Sen 220 Mr 77-80 Mrs Arthur 205 Mrs Bird 400 Mrs Coby 205 Nancy (Miller) 74 Nancy 79 Polly 75 Polly 73 75 Pricie (Miller) 73 Robert A 492 Robert M 73 Sarah 74 South G 152 Stephen 73 Susan 74
Prestonburg, 297
PRICE, A J 75 Edmund 236 George W 24 Jesse 75 Linda 75 Washington 75
PRICHARD, 87 A J 239 Allen 187 Amelia 374 375 Columbus 163 284 285 290 G W 186 Henry 376 J Lewis 285 291 James 185 364 K F 186 Keen F 375 Kenas F 374 Lewis 185 Millie 374 Miss 239 Mr 290 291 375 384 Mrs 383 384 Mrs K F 376 Robert H 285 289 291 325 Robert J 177 Wily 186

Prominent Physicians, 182
Publisher's Notice, 494
PURGETT, Sally 216
QUEEN, Rosannah 215
RAISONS, 206
RAMY, 446
RANDLE, Mahala (May) 183
  Malinda 159 Mrs 183 P S 159
  182 P S Jr 183
RANDOLPH, Wm N 26
RANSOM, (Negro) 47
RATCLIFF, 322
RATLIFF, 97 Ann 51 Butler 324
  Garred 324 General 67 97
  George F 476 Harold 138 Harve
  137 James 97 Jane (Garred)
  137 Miss 181 Thos 67 W O B
  97 William 137 157 228 Wm
  51 194
REILY, James W 360
REYNOLDS, 442
RICE, 72 435 446 Amanda 63 Ida
  66 Jacob 60 Jake 60 61 James
  M 55 56 59 62-64 66 85 116
  231 438 John M 65 115 252 315
  438 John McConnell 61 Judge
  59 62 63 65 66 85 116 423 Martin 66 Master 85 Matilda 60
  492 Mr 57 58
RICHARDSON, 87 293 George S
  306 313 317 (portrait) 314 J N
  52 Jno N 51 John 203 John C
  170 John N 67 97 289 Meriba
  68 Mr 313 314 316 317 Mrs 276
  William 68
RICHMOND, Ann 486 James 99
  John 99 430 486 Margaret 486
RIGG, R B 179
RIGGLESTON, Louis 226 TON
  Rebecca (Burgess) 226
ROBBINS, Silas W 140
ROBERTS, St Clair 36
ROBINSON, 20 442 James 54
ROGERS, 404 Miss 404
ROLAND, Elizabeth 115 116 118
ROSS, Jacob 476 John D 123 124
ROUSE, James 362 Margaret 362
  Samuel 362
RULE, Andrew 99 Miss 395
RUNYON, 20 Aaron 98 Asa 170
  Asa H 98 Floyd 263 John 98
  John C 98 Matilda 98 McCoy

RUNYON (continued)
  98 Mitchell 98 410 Thomas 98
  Wm A 98
RUSSELL, John 284 285 288
  Thomas 448
RUST, Henry M 299
RUTHERFORD, Dr 409
Salt Springs and Wells, 26
SALYERS, 397 Ben F 398 John
  398
Salyersville, 296
SAMUELS, 206
SANDS, William 360
Sandy, Couple's Noble Act 479
  Timber Trade 322 Valley
  Progress 430 Wash-out 270
SAVAGE, Alfred 40 Frances 40
  Frank 40 Judge 420 427
  Pleasant 39 420 S S 39 Samuel
  39 Sarah 30 39 427
SCHAEFER, Mary 142
SCHAUER, Peter Paul 269 343
SCHMUCKER, Mr 129
SCOTT, 91 A J 152 Henderson 92
  John 92 Nannie 152 William
  91 92
SCOVILL, Mary 176 Matthew 176
SEATON, James 449
SEE, Flora (Garred) 135 Garred
  135 Miss 406
SELLARDS, Jenny 450
SEWARD, Billy 477
SHANNON, 443 William 476
SHARP, Captain 254 Mrs 255
SHEARER, Aunt 375 376 Mrs 382
  386 Rev Mr 383 Walter 382
SHERITT, C W 239
SHERMAN, 42
SHERRITT, C W 259
SHORT, 476 Samuel 63
SHORTRIDGE, 19 Colonel 170
  171 Eli 165 George 165 John
  165 166 Melinda 166
SICK, 442 George 400
SLATER, 410
SLOAN, Mrs 230 Polly 73
SMALL, Mary E 136
Small-pox in Floyd, 300
SMILEY, Alexander 467 Dr 354 M
  L 467 Thomas 67 William 467
SMITH, 328 442 Edmund M 93
  166 195 Jacob 409 Jim 479

SMITH (continued)
   John 93 94 195 409 Kirby 54
   Lindsay 93 Lindsey T 195 Mr
   94
SOVAIN, 377 Henry 371 372 Mary
   Jane 372 373 380 Millie 373
   380 Mrs 372 373
SOWARDS, Lewis 51
SPARKS, 446
SPEARS, Samuel 457
SPENCER, E T 276
SPERRY, 448 Benjamin 156 157
SPRADLIN, Emma 486
SPRADLING, Benjamin 90
SPURLOCK, 226 Burwell 24
   Marion 465 Stephen 24 25
STAFFORD, 20 John 92 134 William 144 145
STAIRS, James 407 Jimmy 408
STAMBAUGH, 397
STANDISH, Miles 174
STANTON, R H 219
STEEL, D W 448 Dr 182 185 445
   John 445 Samuel 445
STEIN, Albin 88 89 (portrait) 89
   Charles 88 Mr 88
STEPHENSON, James 47
STEPP, Judge 91
STEWART, 301 A H 300 Amelia
   374 America (Canterbury) 95
   Colonel 95 Cynthia (Mayo) 96
   Did 374 Henry R 374 376 J
   Frew 305 449 (portrait) 87
   James 95 James E 84 95 96
   438 484 John 97 John Frew 86
   Judge 88 Mary 373 374 Mary
   Jane 377 Millie 374 Mitchell
   374 376 Mr 96 Mrs 376 377
   Ralph 95 97 226
Store Dress, The, 14
STRATTON, 20
STRINGFELLOW, 174
STRONG, Dr 182 184 Mrs Dr 205
   W Mate 360
STROTHER, Joseph 25 Philip 25
STUMPS, 20
STURGILL, John 399
SULLIVAN, C M 41 John T 252
   Mrs 41
SWAP, George 330
SWEATNAM, Mr 72 123 Neri 71
   123 395

SWEATNUM, Claiborne 85 Dr 85
   385 Elza 85 H S 445 J M 86
   382 386 John 85 Mildred Cross
   386 Mr 85 86 Mrs Dr 385
   Nellie 384 385 386 Neri 84 85
   188 398 Neri Sen 85 Zephaniah
   85
TAYLOR, Green 410
Teachers of Early Days, 25
Tell-tale Coat 337
THAYER, Eli 391
Then and Now, 415
THOMAS, Benjamin 62 Colonel
   330 R M 164 447 Rees M 330
THORNSBERRY, Martin 448
THORNTON, 146 Adie 330 Bascom 163 E C 146 161 328 330
   Ezra 164 Ezra C 161 Mr 328
   Mrs E C 163
Thrilling Adventure 15
TIPTON, Miss 152
TOLER, 56
TOMLINSON, A A 422 447
TRIMBLE, James 127 128 285
   290 Malcolm 127 128 Mousie
   128 Mr 127
TURMAN, James 362 363 Margaret 362 364 Mr 364 365 366
   Mrs 366 Samuel 364 Margaret
   362
TURNER, Dr 81 144 145 301 397
   James 397 Sud 397
Two, Churches 426 Historic
   Sisters 371 New Churches 429
   Sandy Cousins 463
ULEN, C S 254 276 Charles S 159
   160 Dr 160 Elba 160 480 Mr
   481 Mrs 255 481 Ulba 159
UNCLE JIM, 34
United, Baptists 430 States
   Government Officers 439
VANCOOVER, 490 Charles 12
VAN HOOSE, Felty 120 Jemima
   120
VAN HORN, John 29 165 231 245
   251 399 Miss 29 32 231 399
   Mrs 143
VANNATA, John 423
VAUGHAN, 442 Captain 469 470
   Daniel 467 468 469 Daniel B
   467 469 470 Enoch Rector 468
   Patrick Henry 293 William 468

VERMILLION, 197 D l 195
VINSON, James 156 157 Richard 183 Richard F 11 S S 305 (portrait) 158 Sam'l S 325 Samuel S 158 159 William 37 135 157 159 366 Z C 159
WADE, 336
WALDRON, Dr 406
WALKER, 11 20 122 Henry 486 Jane 486 Martha 486 Robert 70 435
WALLACE, Frank 41 Margaret 216 Mrs 40 Thomas 40 41
WALTER, Calvin 398 399 E L 398 M M 398 Mr 72 Robert 1 86 188 398 399 Trinvilla J 482
WALTON, 147 148 L D 84 146 260 Mr 147 Mrs 148
War Meeting, 334
War Picture, 476
WARD, 388 Big Foot 155 Bit Nose 155 Hawkum 155 James 155 Jim 155 Jim's Jim 155 Jimper 155 Joseph 155 Little Jim 155 Nine Toes 155 Solomon 155 White Head 155 William Jefferson 155
WARREN, Charles H 94
WASHINGTON, George 28 296
WEDDINGTON, 11 20 322 Amelia 152 C C 152 Catherine 152 Elizabeth 151 152 Harry 152 Henry 151 Jack 152 Jacob 151 153 James 151-153 Katie 151 Lucinda 152 Marion 152 Martin 152 Miss Tipton 152 Nannie 152 R H 492 R M 154 306 332 (portrait) 153 Rhoads 152 Robert M 151 153 William 151-154
WEISE, D K 335
WELLMAN, Bennett 246 Calvin 381 Ceres 213 Fred 247 James 247 275 381 Jerry 163 213 246 247 Judge 381 Maguffey 370 Morris 163 Mr 381 382 Noah 162 381 Samuel 132 246 247 381
WELLS, Aaron 459 Agnes 105 486 George 459 John P 459 M L K 107 459 William 460 William A 459

WESLEY, John 163
WEST, Joseph 25 482
West Liberty, 297
WEYMER, James K 476
WHALEY, Cal 334 Kellean Verplanck 334 335 Mr 335 336
What the People Eat, 13
WHEELER, Daniel 309 399 400 430 Samuel 399
WHITE, David 19 20 166 243 Samuel 229 Sarah 229 243
WHITTEN, James 448
Why So?, 486
WILEY, Adam 455 Adam P 455 Christine 455 Hezekiah 455 Jane 455 Jenny 294 450 454 456 457 458 493 Mr 451 456 Mrs 451 452 453 Sally 455 Thomas 450 Vard 456 William 455
WILLIAMS, 21 Jno S 52 M L 461 Mordecai M 325 Mr 226 325 Nancy 226 Thomas 430 Wallace J 324 Wiley 430
WILLIAMSON, 12 20 322 Adelbert 156 Ben 305 (portrait) 149 Benjamin 82 148-150 Floyd 149 Hibbard 149 Jane 455 John 148 John I 156 Mrs 148 R F 263 Richard 455 W J 150 Wallace J 148 149 181 285 290
Williamson & Hampton, 326
WILSON, Billy 476 Charles 137 Daniel 281 Hannah (Goff) 137 Mr 282 Polly 134
Wilson & Andrew's Bank 281
WINFIELD, Clara 226 Edward 226
WITMAN, Henry J 176 Julia 176
WITTEN, G M 283 Green M 129 130 283 Thomas 130
Witten & Davidson's Bank 283
WOLF, Alberto 259 Lizzie 259
WOOD, Watt 448 Wm 399
WORTHINGTON, W J 185
WRIGHT, Bill 339 341 479 Joe H 94 Joseph 189
YATES, Dr 182 184
YORK, 445 Joshua 446
YOST, Christian 455 Sally 455
YOUNG, David 137 Sarah (Goff) 137 W T 100

ZEIGLER, J L 447 John L 421 426

www.ingramcontent.com/pod-product-compliance
Lightning Source LLC
Chambersburg PA
CBHW051333230426
43668CB00010B/1245